The **SIGHTS** and **SOUNDS** of **BLACK POWER**
1965-1975

PAT THOMAS

LISTEN, WHITEY!

FANTAGRAPHICS BOOKS

In 1972, while I was still in college, I had one of the greatest jobs of my life: I worked mornings at Will's Record Store on 125th Street in Harlem. A 45 rpm single record cost a dollar; an album could be had for four bucks. Will's idea of marketing was to set an old beat-up speaker out on the street and blast music all day long. Usually, Will would instruct the staff to play Top 40 tunes. But sometimes, when he went out, we'd dig deeper into the stacks of vinyl and cardboard and play something a little more obscure: Gil Scott Heron, maybe, or the Last Poets.

That was the music that spoke to me at a time when I was trying to figure out who and what I wanted to be, just when the whole world seemed to be shifting on its axis. Blasting Gil Scott from the sidewalk in front of Will's, rather than the latest hit from the Temptations or the Four Tops, felt meaningful. It even felt a little subversive.

A lot of great music was created during the years from 1965 to 1975. But what makes this period unique is that so much of its content was revolutionary. This was music with a purpose, a magnificent purpose that went far beyond getting people up on the dance floor, and certainly beyond selling records. Surely the artists wanted the music to inspire listeners to do all of these things, it was fundamentally the music of change. The music was the product of a time when the idea of revolutionary change was legitimate, and revolution itself, to young people, seemed to be

around the corner. The culture change was right on the surface of popular media. But as Pat Thomas makes clear in this book, there was an even more overt call for revolutionary change in recordings that were not heard on the radio, though they were in many cases easily accessible. These recordings were not only of music, but poetry, speeches, and interviews.

I got the job at Will's Record Store as the Black Power Movement was in full swing in New York and across the country. After the dignified reserve of the Civil Rights Movement, the Black Power Movement was in-your-face impatience. Where the fulcrum of the Civil Rights Movement was the rural South and black preachers, the Black Power Movement was urban, young, and angry. Rather than pushing for integration, these new leaders and activists prized self-determination, self-sufficiency and independence. Promoting that philosophy required the use of

STANLEY NELSON

all means available, including the recording industry. Because African Americans had no access to Hollywood movies or to production of TV shows, writing and recording were the best ways to reach an audience. And Black Americans listened to music, and bought records – a lot. But as Pat Thomas makes clear, revolutionary music was more than an underground recording phenomenon. Mainstream executives and labels picked up on the political current in African American culture and pushed it to a broader audience.

What Pat Thomas has done in this magnificent volume is extraordinary. He has resurrected the sounds of those years, and through words and pictures, made us hear them. Whether we are discovering those recordings for the first time or being reminded of tunes long forgotten, it is exhilarating to be in their presence.

If I have one small quibble with Thomas, it is with the title of the book – *Listen, Whitey*. I think that most of these were not directed at the white community at all. In fact I believe one thing that makes this period unique is that these recordings were directed solely at the black community. They were bugle calls meant to rouse the troops, to get the minds and the feet of the black community moving in a different direction. If that's the case, then a more apt title might be, *Listen, Brother*. But it is easy to see why *Listen, Whitey* is a better title – if I was in a bookstore, I'd pick up *Listen, Whitey* before I even thought about *Listen, Brother* myself. So it's a small, small quibble.

As I sit writing this, I'm listening to some of the music cited in this volume. I fact, I find it impossible to read more than a few

pages without downloading a couple of songs. I've built a great "Black Power Playlist." See if you can get through this volume without doing the same thing. It's as if the music leaps off the page and demands to be heard again.

In the twenty-first century, ubiquitous mp3 players and access to the Internet and social networks have made recording and listening to music exponentially more accessible than was the case in the late '60s and early '70s. Music and spoken word can be recorded cheaply and distributed instantly. Will's Record Store is long gone.

But the future of the content of that music is still being written. As I write this, groups of (mostly) young people are starting a movement of their own. What began as "Occupy Wall Street" has grown from its New York City beginnings and spread across the United States and overseas. And because of these young activists, for the first time in my lifetime, income inequality in the United States has become an open topic for discussion. Will it amount to real change? Who knows. But if it continues, and we listen hard enough, we may hear a new song rumbling up from the streets, music that speaks to the urgent needs of this generation and moves the whole culture forward.

Read Pat Thomas's book, and keep listening.

Stanley Nelson is the director and producer of documentary films including *Freedom Riders*, *Wounded Knee*, *The Murder of Emmett Till*, *Marcus Garvey: Look for Me in the Whirlwind*, and *Sweet Honey in the Rock: Raise Your Voice*

FANTAGRAPHICS BOOKS
7563 Lake City Way NE
Seattle, Washington 98115

Designed by Jacob Covey
Edited by Kristy Valenti and Mitch Myers
Editorial Assistance by Conrad Groth, Ben Horak,
Kara Krewer, Janice Lee, and Jennifer Williams

Associate Editor and Visual Consultant: Kathy Wolf
Associate Publisher: Eric Reynolds
Publishers: Gary Groth and Kim Thompson

To receive a free full-color catalog of comics, graphic novels, prose novels, artist
monographs, and other fine works of artistry, call 1-800-657-1100, or visit
www.fantagraphics.com. You may order books at our web site or by phone.

Distributed in the U.S. by W.W. Norton and Company, Inc. (800-233-4830)
Distributed in Canada by Canadian Manda Group (800-452-6642 x862)
Distributed in the U.K. by Turnaround Distribution (44 (0)20 8829-3002)
Distributed to comic stores by Diamond Comics Distributors (800-452-6642 x215)

ISBN: 978-1-60699-507-5
First Fantagraphics Books printing: February, 2012
Printed in China

TABLE OF CONTENTS

FOLKWAYS RECORDS FD 5402

HUEY!

BLACK PANTHER PLATFORM WITH SEALE, CLEAVER, RAP BROWN

LISTEN, WHITEY!

BLACK COMMUNITIES REACTION TO THE ASSASSINATION OF DR. MARTIN LUTHER KING, JR.

MUSICIANS AS REVOLUTIONARIES,

REVOLUTIONARIES AS POP CULTURE ICONS

I

In the 21st century, the word "revolution" has lost its edge. Advertisements tout a "revolution" in hair care or describe a "revolutionary" new automobile. During the late 1960s and early 1970s, when young whites spoke of revolution, they wanted to take "the establishment" down and stop the Vietnam War. For African-Americans, "revolution" meant the Black Panther Party or Black Nationalism. There were a number of revolutions taking place, and none of them was going to make your hair smell terrific or provide a more comfortable driving experience.

This book is about how Black Power influenced folk, rock, soul and jazz between 1965 and 1975, when musicians were viewed as revolutionaries and revolutionaries were considered pop culture icons. However, this book is not just about John Lennon hanging out with Bobby Seale and Mick Jagger recording a song about Angela Davis; it is *a definitive catalog of Black Power-related recordings* that I uncovered during five years of intensive research — a diverse collection of albums and singles, stray cassettes and reel-to-reel tapes and a handful of films that have been suppressed for decades. *Music is the primary focus*, but there are also speeches, interviews, poetry and even militant

religious sermons. Huey Newton, Eldridge Cleaver, Bobby Seale, H. Rap Brown, Stokely Carmichael and Angela Davis all released albums of narration. The primary characters in this narrative are African-Americans reflecting the rhetoric of the Black Power movement through recordings — the majority of which haven't

OPPOSITE: Here's Stokely Carmichael at the lectern, speaking at the "Free Huey Rally" at the Oakland Auditorium on Feb. 17, 1968. Carmichael's name does not appear on the cover, nor in the detailed liner notes contained within, but listening to the recording, coupled with this photograph, documents his participation, as does the *Free Huey* LP released on the Black Forum label.

been reissued and aren't available on iTunes. Even the most ardent crate-diggers will discover records that they haven't heard before.

For example, there are numerous books about Motown, but none has delved deep into Motown's early 1970s subsidiary label, Black Forum. An extensive section focuses on those groundbreaking — but largely forgotten — albums. Black Forum's discography includes a spectrum of recordings reflecting the movement: from a collection of political songs written and sung by Black Panther Elaine Brown to a provocative lecture on racism by Stokely Carmichael; poetry from Langston Hughes and rapping from Amiri Baraka; and interviews with African-American GIs fighting in Vietnam.

As a whole, the Black Power movement was not just political, but about humanity: about a way to live. The phrase "Black Militant" gets thrown around, and yes, there are period photographs of beret-wearing, shotgun-carrying African-Americans. Often, however, "militant" was a label put on a group of people who simply wanted their equal rights. In 1991, Nina Simone summarized it as such: "Black Power was a lot more than black men with guns — it was a way of returning the black man's pride." She aptly pointed out:

When you mention Black Power, people automatically think of the Black Panthers, but although the Panthers evolved out of these ideas,

they were only part of the overall philosophy. A good part, though. I thanked God for them, because they showed young blacks who thought the only means of protest was passive nonviolence, that there was another way, that they didn't have to take all the mental and physical cruelty inflicted on them by whites. With the arrival of the Panthers, black kids realized there were black heroes who would fight and die if necessary to get what they wanted. I thought that was wonderful. They scared the hell out of white folks too, and we needed that, we needed to show that our goodwill could not be taken for granted any more.

Yet more people used a pencil, a book of poetry, a typewriter or a musical instrument to evoke change. But those images don't make for good press. Emerging artists like the Art Ensemble of Chicago altered the face of jazz, while established musicians, such as Max Roach, headed in a new direction reflective of the events around them. Albums by female poets Nikki Giovanni, Jayne Cortez, Maya Angelou and Sarah Webster Fabio shed new light on black consciousness. Comedian Dick Gregory released entertaining records as hard-hitting as the Black Panther Party newspaper. Religious leaders jumped into the fray as well. The Rev. Jesse Jackson's album included photos of him with Amiri Baraka and Fred Hampton. Aretha Franklin's father C.L. Franklin put a sermon to wax titled "The Meaning of Black Power." The movement also responded regionally, with 45 rpm singles of protest music cropping up on small labels in Austin, Milwaukee, Chicago and Birmingham. Meanwhile, the Watts Prophets and Last Poets laid the groundwork for the emergence of rap a decade later.

The Black Panthers are often interchangeable in many people's minds with Black Power: although the most important and influential, the Panthers were just one of many Black Power groups. It's important to recognize key differences separating the Panthers from Black Nationalists. Black Nationalists were prone to wearing dashikis and taking African names. The Panthers did not. While the Panthers and the Black Nationalists shared a desire of independence from white society, the Panthers always remained multicultural, encouraging the alliance of all non-whites (in fact, some of their financial support came from Bert Schneider, executive producer of one of the highest-grossing

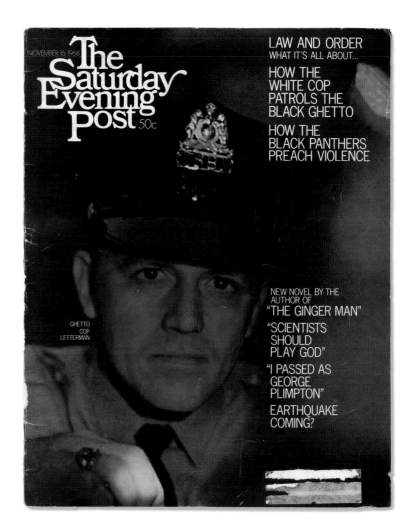

OPPOSITE: *Rolling Stone* featured Huey Newton on the cover of its Aug. 3, 1972 issue, during the period in which the magazine was considered a Bible for the white hippie counterculture. Now Black Panthers were able to tell their stories alongside gonzo critics engaging rock 'n' roll icons.

ABOVE: Known for its homey, cozy Norman Rockwell cover paintings, *The Saturday Evening Post* was the vanguard publication for traditional American values for over a century. It featured increasingly reactive cultural critique by conservative commentators like William F. Buckley. The implicit establishment-friendly messages about "Law and Order" ("What's It All About?") and "How The White Cop Patrols The Black Ghetto" are splayed above the concerned face of a police officer, the shining badge on his hat next to the bold assertion "How The Black Panthers Preach Violence."

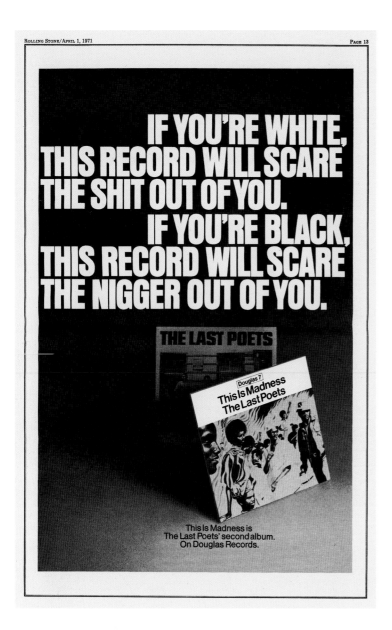

IF YOU'RE WHITE, THIS RECORD WILL SCARE THE SHIT OUT OF YOU. IF YOU'RE BLACK, THIS RECORD WILL SCARE THE NIGGER OUT OF YOU.

THE LAST POETS

Douglas 7
This Is Madness
The Last Poets

This Is Madness is
The Last Poets' second album.
On Douglas Records.

films of the 1960s, the hippie classic *Easy Rider*). The Black Nationalists focused on a strong African identity, maintaining a cultural connection to their native origins. Black Panther Huey Newton loved the music of Bob Dylan, while Black Nationalist Amiri Baraka debated if certain blues and jazz music was "black" enough to listen to.

This book is more than just a list of righteous vinyl; it takes its inspiration from my experiences as a record company A&R man, reissuing Black Power-era recordings by The Watts Prophets, Gene McDaniels, Les McCann, Eddie Gale and Elaine Brown. In the course of doing so, I got to hear firsthand their memories and grievances about one of the most pivotal movements in American history. I was honored to befriend David Hilliard and Elaine Brown, as well as to meet Bobby Seale, Ericka Huggins and other former Black Panthers living in Oakland, Calif. — all of whom inspired me. I rarely conducted formal interviews, but at times I've folded in bits and pieces of our discussions (from memory) with a focus on their facts rather than my opinions.

I've tried to frame these recordings within the context of the Black Panther Party, SNCC (Student Nonviolent Coordinating Committee) US and other organizations essential to the movement. I decided not to address contemporary rap and hip-hop nor delve into the climate of African-American society today. Those topics are the focus of other books, written by people whose views I respect more than my own. Whenever possible, I give facts rather than opinions, but like all humans I'm not only subject to error but to bias. As Bob Dylan sang, "something's happening here and you don't know what it is." While I can't claim to know what happened, much less what it felt like to participate, it's my hope that readers will find the personalities and the music as inspiring as I did. Dig deep; the blood is thicker than the mud.

— *Pat Thomas, November 2011*

LEFT: Arguably the word "nigger" has been used so often in rap songs in the past two decades that it's lost all its provocation. Yet, in today's politically correct world, would a record company dare run an ad like this one, and would *Rolling Stone* agree to publish it (as they did in 1971)? I think not. Meanwhile, the author would love to see the term "honkies" brought back into the public vernacular.

Is It Too Late For You To Be Pals with a Black Panther?

ICONIC IMAGES:

The Black Power Salute, Berets and a Wicker Chair

1

Between 1965 and 1975, Black Power grew from a social-political underground movement into a significant force in American pop culture. Several iconic images are associated with this decade-long strange trip. On Oct. 16, 1968 at the Olympics in Mexico City, Tommie Smith and John Carlos (two of the world's fastest sprinters at that time) won the gold and bronze medals in the 200-meter race. After receiving their awards, they stepped onto a multi-tiered podium on the grounds of the Olympic stadium. As the American national anthem began to play,

Smith and Carlos bowed their heads and then, with each of them wearing one black glove (Smith on his right hand, Carlos on his left), they raised their fists high in the air, giving the entire Olympic stadium and an estimated television audience of four hundred million people the clenched-fist Black Power Salute. A renowned photograph of that moment has been reproduced countless times in the decades since as an indelible statement of Black Power — including the Oct. 26, 1968 issue of the Black Panther Party newspaper, published just ten days after the event. Such was the growing popularity of the Black Power clenched fist that the August 1969 issue of *Liberator* (a political magazine)

featured an advertisement from TCB Products selling, for $4.50, a 6-inch high "Power Symbol" fist hand-carved in mahogany. For $5.75 you could purchase a 9-inch version (add 50¢ for postage and handling).

OPPOSITE: Amongst the "pals with a Black Panther" in this satirical *Esquire* magazine photo shoot are Roberta Flack, Les McCann and Oscar Brown Jr.; McCann and Brown are discussed elsewhere in this book as part of the movement. Flack also recorded a version of the seminal "Compared to What," but in recent years has shed all ties to her artistic past. She would not be amused to see this photo now.

Another classic image of Black Power is the 1967 photo of Huey P. Newton sitting in an oversized wicker chair, wearing the Panther uniform of a beret and leather jacket, holding a shotgun in one hand and a large African spear in the other. Thousands of these posters were distributed by the Black Panthers to fuel the "Free Huey" campaign following Newton's arrest for the October 1967 shooting of two Oakland police officers. As a result of the shooting incident, Newton was convicted of manslaughter and, after a lengthy and much publicized legal battle, was acquitted and released in August 1970. The iconic image of Newton sitting in the wicker chair has been reproduced numerous times as a poster and in various publications. It is without a doubt the single most famous photograph of any Black Panther member.

For African-Americans, just wearing a black beret became a symbol of unity, even among non-Panthers. For example, Tommie Smith and John Carlos were not the only members of the 1968 U.S. Olympic team to show their solidarity for the movement during the Mexico City games. Several other runners who won the 400-meter relay donned berets during their medal acceptance ceremony.

By 1970 — probably to the chagrin of Huey P. Newton — the black beret entered the pantheon of mainstream American pop culture, the weekly television sitcom, via the white-bread musical comedy show *The Partridge Family*. In an episode entitled "Soul Club," broadcast on Jan. 29, 1971, the lovable all-American Partridge Family find themselves in a ghetto of inner-city Detroit to perform in a club run by down-and-out blacks, played by

comedian Richard Pryor and actor Lou Gossett Jr.

Keith Partridge (David Cassidy) writes a new "Afro-styled" pop tune in celebration of the family's newfound surroundings, but the song requires a horn section and conga drums. Freckle-faced youngster Danny Partridge (Danny Bonaduce) convinces the local chapter of the "Afro-American Cultural Society" (aka the Black Panther Party) to come to the rescue with members who play horns and drums. The Partridge Family and the Panthers perform Keith's song together as part of a ghetto street fair. As the episode comes to a close and the family is boarding their bus in search of more fun and games, one of the "Afro-American Cultural Society" leaders arrives at the last minute to present Danny with a black beret, and announces that Danny is now an honorary member. Danny suggests that he open a local chapter when he gets back home and everyone laughs. The only thing more bizarre than this sitcom storyline is the fact that in 1997, *TV Guide* picked this episode as #78 in the list of the 100 Greatest TV episodes of All Time. *TV Guide* wrote, "This may be the most outlandish episode on our list; it's certainly one of the best-intentioned." Say what!?!

Even the corporate side of the music business was eager to jump onto the Black Power bandwagon. During the EMP music conference at UCLA in February 2011, Charles L. Hughes brought to my attention a *Billboard* magazine article from April 1969: "the era of Black Nationalism and awareness has created a positive feeling among young blacks to be associated with music of their heritage." The *Billboard* article focused on Capitol Records' desire to "foster the growth of black culture." Hughes' research suggests that the Los Angeles-based company that had made millions of dollars from selling Beatles records to whites were now employing black regional sales managers and marketing directors in a sincere attempt to connect with the African-American community through artists such as saxophonist Cannonball Adderley and singer Lou Rawls.

ABOVE: "Red hot young Negroes plan a ghetto war" is the subtitle of the article "Plot To Get 'Whitey'" above the pale, fear-stricken face of Elizabeth Taylor in this June 10, 1969 issue of *LIFE* Magazine. The cover shot is from Taylor's role in *Who's Afraid of Virginia Woolf?*, but the magazine "accidentally" infused the image with a not-so-subtle undercurrent of racial terror.

'ONE OF THE NEGRO BOOK CLUB BEST SELLERS'
—New York Times Book Review, February 16, 1969

THE BLACK POWER REVOLT

Published
April 22, 1968

Black essays trace black power from the past to the present

$5.95 cloth, $2.95 paper
288 pp.

Floyd B. Barbour, Editor

- 4th Major Printing
- Required Reading In Over 750 Schools & Universities
- Italian & Spanish Translations
- Serialized By Minneapolis Star
- Negro Book Club Of The Month Selection

- Praised By Publishers' Weekly, Look, Booklist, Ebony, Washington Post, Saturday Review Syndicate
- Selected For The Libraries Of The Eastern Regional System Reading List

'Significant compilation of historical sources (from 18th to 20th century) and contemporary statements on the development of awareness of power among U.S. Negroes. Good bibliography.'

—School & Society

RECOMMENDED BY:
Tom Wicker, Jonathan Kozol, Julius Lester, Nat Hentoff, Howard Zinn

At leading bookstores or direct from:
PORTER SARGENT PUBLISHER
11 Beacon Street   Boston. Mass. 02108

CARMICHAEL'S "BLACK POWER" RALLY
AND POWELL'S "KEEP THE FAITH, BABY!" MESSAGE

While it's impossible to determine who originally coined the phrase "Black Power," the one thing generally agreed on is who popularized the term and when: SNCC (Student Nonviolent Coordinating Committee) chairman Stokely Carmichael, with his Black Power speech in the hot Southeastern summer of 1966. SNCC was one of the primary organizations of the Civil Rights movement. When Stokely Carmichael became chairman in May 1966, he took over from John Lewis, who'd led the SNCC since

June 1963. Carmichael had big shoes to fill — Lewis had been a noted speaker at Martin Luther King Jr.'s historic March on Washington Aug. 28, 1963. When Lewis left SNCC, Carmichael wasted no time making himself a name. On June 5, 1966, James Meredith began a solitary "March Against Fear" from Memphis to Jackson to protest racism. During the march, a sniper wounded him. Martin Luther King Jr. and Carmichael decided to continue the march in Meredith's name.

Later in June, as they descended upon Greenwood, Miss., several hundred gathered for a rally. In Carmichael's words, "The march was gathering momentum. I could see it was going to be our largest rally." In his autobiography, published posthumously in 2003, Carmichael wrote, "The [black] school board had given

ABOVE: In the years before DVD and videotape sales and rentals, key historic moments were captured on audio and would be brought into the home as a keepsake on vinyl. The other way to remember an event was by postcards such as this one, with a photo composition that included the Washington Monument in the background: a classic souvenir of the event.

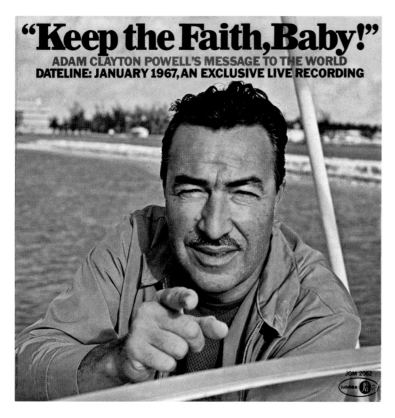

"Keep the Faith, Baby!"
ADAM CLAYTON POWELL'S MESSAGE TO THE WORLD
DATELINE: JANUARY 1967, AN EXCLUSIVE LIVE RECORDING

ABOVE: Adam Clayton Powell strikes a pose similar to the famous Uncle Sam recruiting poster: "I Want You for US Army." Recorded under duress — as Powell was under investigation by his fellow congressmen in the House of Representatives — Powell urged his supporters to "Keep the Faith, Baby!" As a result of the investigation, Powell retreated to Florida to regroup; hence the cover photo of him on the waterfront.

us permission and stood their ground. It was their school so it was an issue of community control, black power if you will. I told the workers to put up the tent unless the local community leaders stopped them. Words were exchanged and I was dragged off to jail. But the tent went up."

Carmichael continued: "By the time I got out of jail, I was in no mood to compromise with racist arrogance. The rally had started. It was huge […] I raised the call for Black Power again. It was nothing new — we'd been talking about nothing else in the Delta for years. The only difference was that this time the national media was there. And most of them had never experienced the passion and fervor of a mass meeting before. That was the only difference. As I passed Mukasa [Willie Ricks, the speaker preceding Carmichael], he said, "'Drop it now. The people are ready. Drop it now.'"

SNNC member Willie Ricks (later known as Mukasa Dada) had reported to Carmichael that he'd tested the waters at other gatherings and gotten tremendous response when calling out for "Black Power." In fact, the slogan had been used just a month earlier on May 29, 1966, when Congressman Adam Clayton Powell Jr. addressed a Howard University audience in Washington, D.C. and said, "To demand these God-given rights is to seek Black Power."

Powell Jr. was a progressive leader, whose popularity amongst black Americans was solidified through speeches, walking picket lines, church sermons and his effort to push sixty major bills through Congress as chairman of the Education & Labor Committee. In 1967, Jubilee Records released *"Keep the Faith, Baby!" — Adam Clayton Powell's Message To The World. "Keep the Faith, Baby!"* featured six speeches recorded in January of that year. One was titled "Burn, Baby, Burn," in which Powell delivers a ten-minute diatribe on the Watts Riots. He expounded on how the inhabitants of Watts burned down their own homes, destroyed their neighborhood stores — reducing their poor quality of life even further. He understands that "Burn, Baby, Burn" is the cry of last resort for ghetto residents who have nowhere to go. However, Powell suggests alternatives. He suggests changing "Burn, Baby, Burn" to "Learn, Baby, Learn," replacing violence with education, so that you can "Earn, Baby, Earn." As he poignantly says (with cheering from the audience), "Black Power doesn't mean anything without Green Power — the only thing the white man respects are two things — your vote and your dollar!"

By Carmichael's account, Ricks encouraged him to seize the moment on June 16, 1966 as Carmichael took the stage in Greenwood.

SNCC member Cleveland Sellers was there, capturing the moment in detail.

Stokely, who'd been released from jail just moments before the rally began, was the last speaker. He was preceded by Floyd McKissik [of the Congress of Racial Equality/CORE], Dr. King, and Willie Ricks. Like the rest of us, they were angry about Stokely's unnecessary arrest. Their speeches were particularly militant. When Stokely moved forward to speak, the crowd greeted him with a huge roar. He acknowledged his reception with a raised arm and clenched fist. Realizing that he was in his element, with his people, Carmichael let it all hang out. "This is the twenty-seventh time I have been arrested — and I ain't going to jail no more!" The crowd exploded into cheers and clapping. "The only way we gonna stop them white men from whuppin' us is to take over. We been saying freedom for six years and we ain't got nothin'. What we gonna start saying now is Black Power!"

The crowd was right with him. They picked up his thoughts immediately.

"BLACK POWER!" they roared in unison.

Willie Ricks, who is as good at orchestrating the emotions of a crowd as anyone I have ever seen, sprang into action. Jumping to the platform with Stokely, he yelled to the crowd, "What do you want?"

"BLACK POWER!"

"What do you want?"

"BLACK POWER!"

"What do you want?"

"BLACK POWER!! BLACK POWER!!! BLACK POWER!!!!'

Everything that happened afterward was a response to that moment.

In the following days, the media had a conniption fit over Carmichael's Black Power speech, while he remained nonplussed. Cleveland Sellers wrote in *The River Of No Return: The Autobiography of a Black Militant and the Life and Death of SNCC*, "The nation's news media, who latched on to the slogan and embellished it with warnings of an imminent racial cataclysm, smugly waited for the predictably chaotic response. Dr. King's assistants were among the first to react. [King had also spoken at the event.] They rushed in and demanded that he dissociate himself from Black Power, no matter what its meaning. They insisted on a 'change of emphasis' for the march. They demanded more whites be brought in and that we stop using Black Power for the duration of the march." Carmichael commented that the slogan had been tossed around the South

for years, and it was merely the first time the national media had been around to witness it.

Following that historic moment, the SNNC staff was instructed that "Black Power" was to be their battle cry for the remainder of the "March Against Fear." When the march concluded in Jackson, Miss., on June 26, 1966, Carmichael raised the ante. He told the crowd of eleven thousand that blacks should institute a base of power that "will bring whites to their knees every time they mess with us." After his speech, feeling empowered, Carmichael approached a white member of Dr. King Jr.'s SCLC (Southern Christian Leadership Conference) organization and blasted him between the eyes with a water pistol. The first shots of the Black Power movement had been symbolically fired.

THE BIRTH OF THE BLACK PANTHER PARTY
AND "BALLAD OF A THIN MAN"

Meanwhile, on the other side of the country, in Oakland, Calif., some amazing shit was about to go down: the formation of the Black Panther Party and the composition of a new declaration that for African-Americans had more relevance than the Declaration of Independence. Thomas Jefferson had declared that all men are created equal (unless you happened to be one of Jefferson's slaves)! It was time for revision.

For the general population, then and now, the terms Black Power and Black Panther Party are interchangeable. No other organization of the Black Power era enjoyed such a high profile. No other group provocatively captured the media's attention. This meant that by default, much of black and white America had some idea who the Panthers were. Even today, as I mention this book to friends and family, I get a range of reactions from those who lived through that era.

In 1962, Huey P. Newton and Bobby Seale met while attending Merritt College in Oakland. By 1966, through both academic and independent study, Newton, at the tender age of 24, had the wisdom of an old sage. He'd soaked up everything from black radical ideologies (Malcolm X and Robert F. Williams were influences), to Chairman Mao's *Little Red Book*, to the emerging "free love" crusade in neighboring San Francisco.

Smart as a whip, Newton had memorized much of California's legal and penal codes, which would come in handy for dealing with "The Pigs."

Bobby Seale was 30 years old, having served a painful stint in the Air Force before making his way to Oakland. The highlight of Seale's military career was the opportunity to buy a drum set and develop his chops as a jazz drummer, jamming with others stationed at the base. Seale shared Newton's interest in political consciousness and scouted out relevant events happening around the Merritt College campus.

They observed various coalitions such as the Afro-American Association (AAA), the Revolutionary Action Movement (RAM) and the Soul Students Advisory Council (SSAC). In 1966, as summer rolled into fall, they shifted from inspiration to disillusionment. Newton and Seale concluded that they had to form their own organization, which they established by composing the Black Panther Party for Self Defense "Ten Point Program" on Oct. 15, 1966.

The bold statement above their ten points read "What We Want, What We Believe," and below the individual points was a paragraph explaining the meaning behind each. Point One stated: "We want freedom. We want power to determine the destiny of our Black Community." Other highlights included Point Three, "We want an end to the robbery by the white man of our Black Community," and Point Seven — "We want an immediate end to POLICE BRUTALITY and MURDER of black people." Most electrifying was Point Ten: "We want land, bread, housing, education, clothing, justice, and peace. And as our major political objective, a United Nations supervised plebiscite to be held throughout the black colony in which only black colonial subjects will be allowed to participate, for the purpose of determining the will of black people as to their national destiny."

Newton was headstrong and defiant and it didn't take long for word to spread amongst the East Bay black community that a serious plan of action was in place. On April 1, 1967, the sheriff in Richmond, Calif. (a city neighboring Oakland) shot a 22-year-old, unarmed black named Denzil Dowell. Dowell's family contacted the Panthers for support, and thus *The Black Panther Community News Service* was born. The April 25, 1967 debut issue of the Panther newspaper was four pages long and centered on Dowell's murder. The paper quickly expanded, changing its name to *The Black Panther Intercommunal News*, with circulation eventually growing to one hundred thousand copies weekly. The paper continued on throughout the 1960s and '70s, ending around September 1980.

Despite wide circulation, few copies of the newspaper exist today. Originally sold on the street for a quarter, surviving editions currently trade for collector's prices. In 2007, David Hilliard (Panther Chief of Staff during the exhilarating years that Newton and Seale were at the helm), compiled a facsimile collection of key articles into a book: *The Black Panther Intercommunal News Service 1967-1980*.

Hilliard mentions in his 2006 *Huey, Spirit of the Panther* book that in the early days, the paper was assembled by Newton, Hilliard and others to the sounds of Bob Dylan's album *Highway 61 Revisited*, and that Newton particularly liked the song "Ballad of a Thin Man." Seale's 1970 book *Seize The Time* also recalls Panther members laying out the paper while listening to "Ballad of a Thin Man." Seale's account includes a fascinating interpretation of Dylan's song by Newton and why it had a unique appeal for the Panthers. Newton explained to Seale the racial and social class messages hidden within "Ballad of a Thin Man." He saw Dylan's character Mr. Jones as an upper class white man who indulged in black ghetto exploration on Sunday afternoons to check out the prostitutes and inhabitants of the decaying black community. Mr. Jones saw these people as geeks; in other words, the white man got off on watching the black freak show.

The lyrics, about a man who enjoys watching circus geek shows, struck a chord with Newton. According to Newton, The circus freaks mentioned — the sword swallower and the one-eyed midget — represent the disadvantaged ghetto residents who aren't interested in entertaining Mr. Jones. They demand payment for a trick or some food or drink, otherwise they'd like Mr. Jones to shove off and go home. According to Seale, "Huey says that whites looked at blacks as geeks, as freaks. But what is so symbolic about it is that when the revolution starts, they'll call us geeks because we eat raw meat. But the geek turns around and hands Mr. Jones a naked bone and says 'How do you like being a freak?' And Mr. Jones says 'Oh my God, what the hell's goin' on?' And Bobby Dylan says, 'you don't know what is happening, do you Mr. Jones?'"

Not long after the Panther newspaper was born, Newton and Seale orchestrated an event that would capture the media's attention, bringing the Panthers into households nationwide via TV and newspaper coverage. In 1966, when the Panthers were initially gaining power in their local communities, it was legal to openly carry a gun while walking down the street or driving a car. Since their formation, the Panthers had been on patrol, following policemen on foot or in vehicles as the cops made their rounds in the black community. They were able to observe police conduct and, when necessary, step into the situation with force. Most of the policemen were white, and weren't about to do anything too disrespectful to a black citizen while surrounded by several armed Panthers observing the proceedings. There are numerous accounts of how effective this was. Stories abound of Newton's cleverness in defusing potential powder kegs by persuading the police to chill out and move on.

By the spring of 1967, an assemblyman (clearly inspired by the gun-toting Panthers) was preparing to pass legislation prohibiting the public display of weapons. On May 2, 1967, Seale led a group of armed Panthers to the State Capitol building in Sacramento, Calif. They marched into the Capitol Building, defiantly carrying their firearms, wearing the Panther uniform of berets and leather jackets. Seale read a proclamation protesting this attempt to keep the black community disarmed and powerless.

As predicted, newspapers throughout the world, including *The New York Times* and the *Guardian* in London, reproduced photographs of Seale and his comrades brandishing their weapons. The headlines were as impressive as the photos, with taglines such as "Armed Negroes Enter California Assembly" and "Armed Gang Invades State Capitol." The Panthers had stepped onto the world stage. ◉

RIGHT: As discussed elsewhere, the media grabbed hold of the Black Panthers' image and ran with it (sometimes reverently, occasionally in satire) or often twisted it to fit their own political agenda. But one thing is certain: the image of young, strong, defiant black men dressed smartly in turtlenecks and leather jackets was too striking for a photo editor to pass up. Inside, according to *Newsweek*, "They were the Bad Niggers of white America's nightmares come chillingly to life… They were, they announced, the Black Panthers, and the name alone suggested menace."

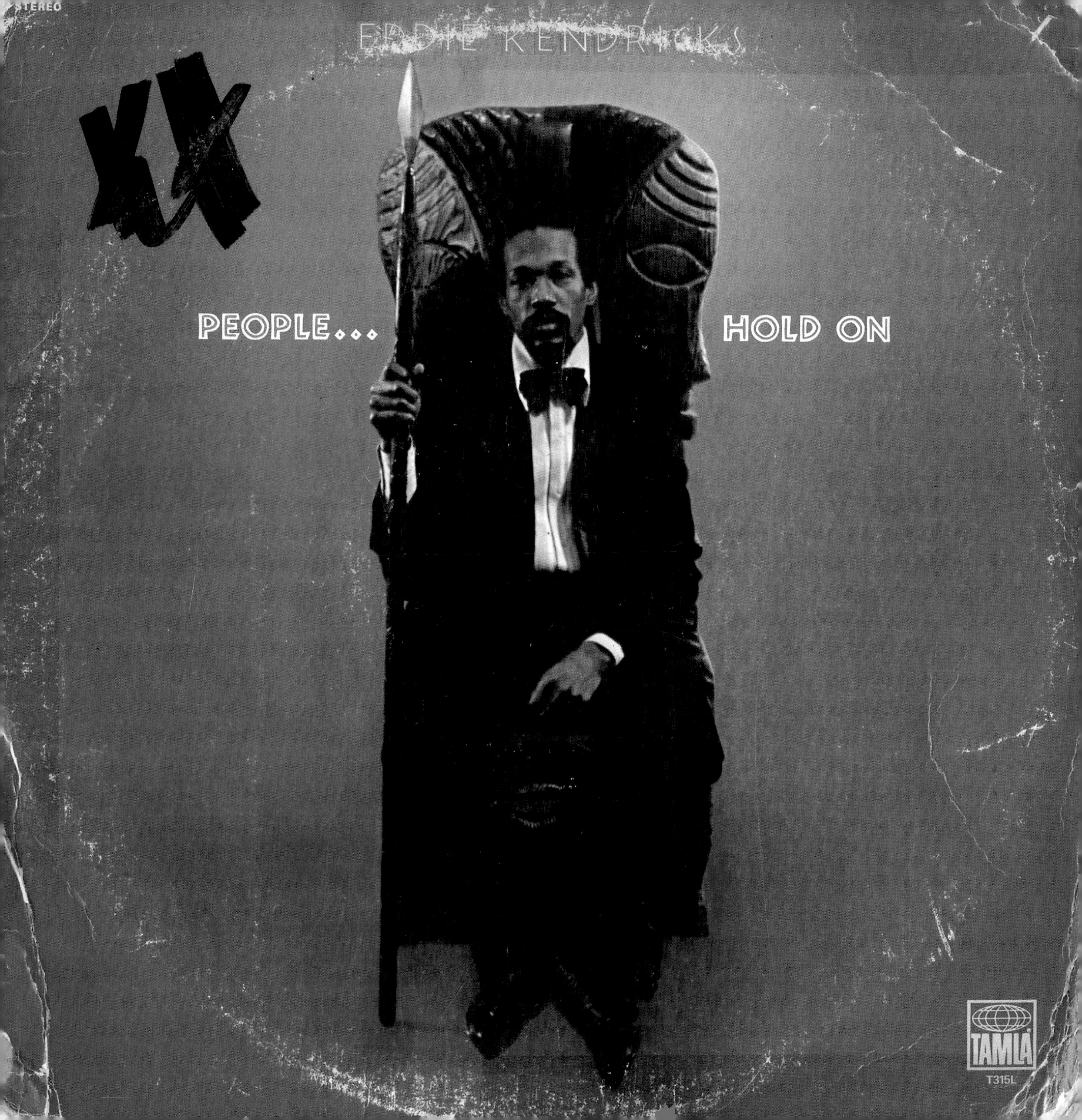
STEREO
EDDIE KENDRICKS
PEOPLE...
HOLD ON
TAMLA
T315L

THE MOVEMENT, MOTOWN AND POPULAR MUSIC

2

As the Black Power movement expanded, it influenced established artists such as Marvin Gaye, James Brown and the Isley Brothers. The movement would shape the voice of emerging songwriters like Sly Stone and Gil Scott-Heron, both of whom were embraced by fans because of their politicized lyrics. It would force Jimi Hendrix, an icon to white hippie audiences, to reconsider his apolitical stance. There would be rank-and-file Black Panther members like Nile Rodgers of Chic and Chaka Khan of Rufus who would go on to pop music fame in the 1970s.

Popular music and black power merged in *Ebony* magazine when a summer 1967 issue declared it the year of "'Retha, Rap, and Revolt." For a mainstream publication like *Ebony* to link the Queen of Soul, militant SNCC leader H. Rap Brown and the wave of ghetto riots that were sweeping across the nation in one succinct headline signaled a major paradigm shift in black America.

Aretha Franklin's version of the Otis Redding song "Respect" was a #1 single in 1967 — her revamped lyrics demanded respect for black women, certainly the first hit song ever to do so. In 1972, Franklin reflected on the Black Power movement, "I believe that the black revolution certainly forced me and the majority of black people to begin taking a second look at ourselves. It wasn't that we are all ashamed of ourselves, we merely started appreciating our natural selves — sort of, you know, falling in love with ourselves just as we are. We found that we had far more to be proud of. So I suppose the revolution influenced me a great

OPPOSITE: Eddie Kendricks' 1972 solo album *People...Hold On* featured Kendricks sitting in an oversized wooden African chair, holding a large spear, in tribute to the iconic 1967 Huey P. Newton photograph.

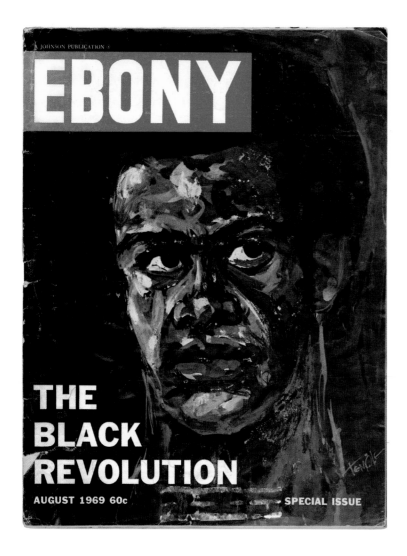

EBONY

A JOHNSON PUBLICATION

THE BLACK REVOLUTION

AUGUST 1969 60c   SPECIAL ISSUE

stories he'd told of senseless civilian killings and the racial injustices toward black soldiers he'd witnessed firsthand in Vietnam. Marvin Gaye was ripe for artistic change, and it came in the form of a song given to him by Renaldo Benson of the Four Tops. Benson had written an epic tale of anti-war and social protest, coupled with the need for love and understanding. Never a prolific songwriter (his strong suit was his baritone singing), Benson became inspired during a Four Tops tour that, while passing through the San Francisco Bay Area, coincided with the violent protests happening in Berkeley at People's Park. The vacant city lot became a battle ground during the spring of 1969 between local residents (led by Yippie Stew Albert) who wanted the space as a public park, and the police, acting on behalf of the University of Berkeley, who wanted it for an athletic field.

The police beating the innocent longhaired kids gathered at the park enraged Benson; he imagined those same kids shipped off to Vietnam against their will. With the help of his next-door neighbor Al Cleveland (who occasionally wrote lyrics with Smokey Robinson), Benson put together a rough sketch of what was on his mind. The Four Tops refused the song for being too political. Soon after, the Tops performed in England, where Benson ran into folk singer-political activist Joan Baez backstage on a TV show. He played his work in progress and she was interested (like Benson, Baez wasn't a prolific songwriter, often performing songs written by others). That brief moment passed, as the two quickly lost touch — and the rest, as they say, is history.

Gaye played around with the lyrics, adjusted the melody and "What's Going On" was born — exactly the statement that Gaye yearned to make. On June 1, 1970, Gaye and Motown session musicians recorded the basic tracks. Gaye was in charge: playing piano, producing and directing the proceedings. A month later, Gaye recorded his vocals. In September, strings were added and the song was ready to be released. Motown chief Berry Gordy refused, claiming it was too political and too eccentric. According to Gaye's brother Frankie's account, Gordy said, "Nobody will buy this garbage."

A standoff occurred between Gaye and Gordy, with Gaye refusing to record more music for Motown until "What's Going On" was released. Gaye eventually won out, and the song was released in January 1971, hitting #2 on the Pop charts and #1 on the Soul charts. Gaye was further vindicated when the song

deal, but I must say that mine was a very personal evolution — an evolution of the me in myself."

Marvin Gaye was a megastar via his love-themed hits "How Sweet It Is (To Be Loved By You)," "I Heard It Through The Grapevine" and his duet with Tammi Terrell, "Ain't No Mountain High Enough." When Terrell died tragically of a brain tumor in March 1970, Marvin was already in an introspective mood, sparked by his brother Frankie's return from the war and the

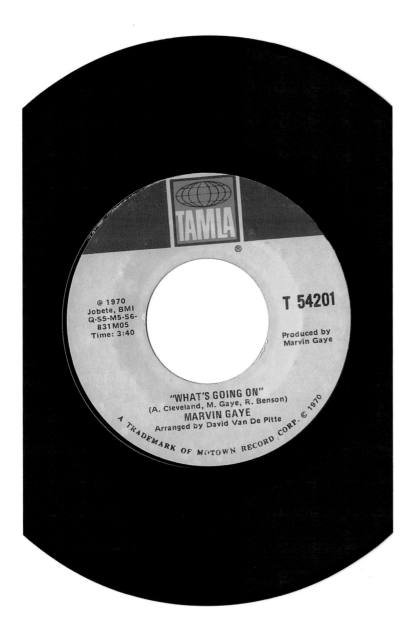

as the first Motown release to list the musicians, finally acknowledging the Funk Brothers.

While working on the *What's Going On* project, Gaye took a break to do some interviews in Chicago, where, according to Frankie Gaye's memoir, "[Marvin] made highly publicized remarks in support of the Black Panthers and the Black Power movement. Marvin loved the Panthers even though he never completely agreed with their policies. "What I like, I really like," he admitted. "The brothers need waking up because so many of us are being killed and hurt. There's no need for the beatings and shootings that go on in the inner city. And too many of our people are homeless and going hungry. The Panthers go door-to-door for donations of food or money to help the poor. I support that." According to Ben Edmonds' 2001 book on Marvin Gaye, it wasn't uncommon for Gaye to turn up at interviews carrying well-read copies of books by Malcolm X and the Peruvian shaman Carlos Castaneda.

Gaye's milestone recordings weren't Motown's first explorations into the social-political arena, nor would it be its last. The 1969 Temptations album *Puzzle People* included a standout Norman Whitfield/Barrett Strong composition, "Message from a Black Man," which was as provocative as anything Gaye had done. "Message from a Black Man" starts off with a funky psychedelic groove (think Sly Stone) featuring a distorted guitar sound (think Hendrix). The deep bass of Melvin Franklin speaks: "Yes, my skin is black, but that's no reason to hold me back." The high falsetto of Eddie Kendricks sings, "I have wants and desires just like you, so move aside, because I'm coming through." All The Temptations join in and sing, "No matter how hard you try, you can't stop me now." Franklin's spoken part returns, with "Yes your skin is white. Does that make you right?" It's a long way from "The Way You Do The Things You Do," but like the juxtaposition between Gaye's earlier hits and "What's Going On," The Temptations maneuvered their way from love songs to political material with ease: such was the genius of Motown.

In 1970, Stevie Wonder recorded the socially charged "Heaven Help Us All" written by Ron Miller and on the 1973 *Innervisions*, Wonder penned a sublime anthem of determination, "Living for the City." As far back as 1964, Motown was plugged into political consciousness; Martha and the Vandellas' "Dancing in the Street" foreshadowed the rebellions that would rock the streets

stayed in the charts longer than his classic "Heard It Through The Grapevine." By then Gordy had seen the light (and has gone on record in the decades since acknowledging his mistake), and wanted a full album with "What's Going On" as its centerpiece.

During the second half of March 1971, the groundbreaking album was recorded, released on Motown's Tamla label on May 21, 1971. Not only was the LP monumentally successful, it was the first Motown LP to have the lyrics printed on the jacket as well of Watts in '65 and Detroit in '67. One could arguably fold their 1965 hit "Nowhere to Run" into the same prophesying niche. During the funeral of Panther Fred Hampton, assassinated by the police in December 1969, The Supremes' "Someday We'll Be Together" blared outside on loudspeakers as mourners at the Rayner Funeral Home on Chicago's South Side passed by his casket to pay their final respects.

Eddie Kendricks' 1972 solo album *People…Hold On* featured Kendricks sitting in an oversized wooden African chair, holding a large spear in tribute to the iconic 1967 Huey P. Newton photograph. *People…Hold On*, although not as successful as *What's Going On*, was a sincere concept album dedicated to black America. The Anita Poree/Leonard Caston-penned title track, "My People…Hold On," was a particular highlight.

Motown would also start a subsidiary label, Black Forum, which released eight politically charged albums between 1970 and 1973 — Including an LP of speeches by Stokely Carmichael and an album of songs by Black Panther spokesperson Elaine Brown.

Motown artists weren't the only popular acts to become politically engaged. The Chi-Lites, a Chicago-based quartet that recorded for Brunswick Records, are fondly remembered for their 1971 ballad "Have You Seen Her" and their equally memorable 1972 follow-up, "Oh Girl." What has been sadly forgotten are their political-message songs of that era. The Chi-Lites released a single and album entitled *(For God's Sake) Give More Power To The People*. Forsaking the smooth soul of their hits, the band turns up the heat with a heavy funk beat in which the band's four vocalists demand "Power To The People" — a slogan popularized by the Black Panthers. The lyrics and cutting-edge

production are equal to anything Norman Whitfield did when he gave The Temptations a psychedelicized-militant makeover in '69. The B-side of "(For God's Sake) Give More Power To The People" was "Trouble's A' Comin." Chi-Lites lead singer Eugene Record penned both songs. Record's lyrics (pitted against a friendly upbeat melody) told listeners that "trouble is coming in more ways than one…so get it together."

James Brown started funking it up in 1956 with "Please, Please, Please." For the next five decades he'd continue to write and record countless funky soul landmarks until his death in 2006. Brown's influence on music and African-American culture are far too broad to detail here, but I'd be remiss if I didn't mention his archetypal song, "Say it Loud (I'm Black and I'm Proud)." Brown's 1968 patriotic single, "America Is My Home," coupled with his friendship with Vice President/Democratic presidential candidate Hubert Humphrey, had alienated many of his followers. Brown was feeling the pressure to make another dynamic social statement as he'd done with "Don't Be A Drop Out."

On Aug. 7, 1968, Brown and his band, including saxophonist and co-writer "Pee Wee" Ellis, entered the studio to record "Say It Loud (I'm Black and I'm Proud)." It immediately struck a chord with the community. Just months earlier Martin Luther King Jr. had been assassinated, and the resentment surrounding that tragedy was still fresh. Brown's anthem provided a much-needed shot of black pride across the nation.

Only nine days later, on Aug. 16, the record was sent to radio stations and became available in stores in September — quickly becoming #1 on the R&B charts for six weeks and #10 on the pop charts. The resonance of that song on the airwaves that summer can't be underestimated. For an introduction to "Say It Loud (I'm Black and I'm Proud)," as well as a snapshot of Brown's legendary stage act, one could do no better than to seek out the album *James Brown Say It Live and Loud: Live in Dallas 08.26.68*. Recorded just ten days after the song had first received airplay, the live recording sat in the vaults for thirty years. The CD's cover reflects the summer of '68 — an image of James Brown superimposed over a drawing (based on the famous photo) of athletes giving the Black Power Salute at the Mexico City Olympics.

Before performing "Say It Loud," Brown tells the audience, "You know, one way of solving a lot of problems that we've got in this country is letting a person feel that they're important, feel

that they're somebody. And a man can't get himself together until he knows who he is and be proud of what and who he is and where he comes from." He then mentions the song by name — "Say It Loud (I'm Black and I'm Proud)" — upon which the crowd lets out a loud cheer.

Amazingly, with just two weeks of airplay and before the record hit the stores, people already know the song. Brown encourages his black audience to sing along to the phrase "I'm black," and says that everyone (including whites) should chime in with "I'm proud." The audience erupts into a roar, as Brown's slogan was already becoming part of the African-American vernacular. In the CD liner notes, Chuck D writes that in 1968, he was an elementary school second-grader and that "'Say It Loud — I'm Black And I'm Proud' was a phrase that prepared me for the third grade, 1969, and the rest of my life." The impact of "Say It Loud (I'm Black And I'm Proud)" was immense. It helped usher in "black" as the favored term for African-Americans, pushing "negro" out the door. It blazed a path for The Temptations' "Message From a Black Man" and Sly Stone's "Don't Call Me Nigger, Whitey," released the following year.

Despite their short-lived ascendancy, Sly and the Family Stone achieved a monumental status that nearly matches James Brown's influence, despite having a career that lasted only a

fraction as long. Their popular reign started with the Top 10 "Dance to the Music" in 1968, and ended with the release of their last great album, *Fresh*, in 1973. In between, Sly and the Family Stone released five masterful albums and a couple of non-LP singles, including 1969's "Hot Fun In The Summertime" and 1970's "Thank You (Falettinme Be Mice Elf Agin)."

In May 1971, Marvin Gaye's LP asked *What's Going On*. In November of that year, Sly and the Family Stone responded to that question with *There's A Riot Going On*. *Riot* was a dark conceptual album that declared the end of 1960s: the assassinations of Malcolm X, King Jr. and Fred Hampton; the riots in Watts and Detroit; the decline of the Civil Rights movement; and the emergence of the Black Power movement. *There's A Riot Going* On is the soundtrack to the African-American apocalypse.

The years between 1968 and 1973 were filled with landmarks, not the least of which was Stone's multi-racial and multi-gender band, which included three black men, two black women and two white guys. No other popular act of the era had that cross section of color and gender. Sly and the Family Stone were one of only three black-fronted acts to play at Woodstock (the others being Richie Havens and Jimi Hendrix). A year before their renowned Woodstock performance, the Santana Blues Band (as they were known then), played a bandwagon parade on Fairfax Avenue in Los Angeles in December 1968 to raise awareness for The Peace & Freedom Party (PFP), a new organization that got off to an illustrious start by nominating Black Panther Eldridge Cleaver as president for the '68 national election.

THE LAST POETS PROCLAIM:
"WAKE UP, NIGGERS!"

It seems so commonplace now with the absorption of rap music into the mainstream, but Sly and the Family Stone's 1969 *Stand!* was the first major label album to use "nigger" in a song title: "Don't Call Me Nigger, Whitey." Stone's record was released on Epic, which was part of Columbia Records, a multinational, multi-million dollar company, i.e. "a major label."

The Last Poets soon followed in Stone's footsteps. Their eponymous 1970 debut contained several songs with "nigger" in the title. Although released on an independent label, Douglas

meter, changing the inflection as they go. The word "nigger" is theirs — they own the word. From their mouths it's a noun, a verb, a sense of pride, a statement and a feeling of empowerment. There's no self-conscious hang-up with the Last Poets using the word "nigger" as an art form.

As Last Poet Umar Bin Hassan told the London newspaper the *Guardian* in September 2010, "The Last Poets out-niggered everybody [....] Our thing was not to use that word as casually as kids

Records, one of their songs, "Wake Up, Niggers," was also included on the 1970 soundtrack to the movie *Performance* starring Mick Jagger: both the film and soundtrack album were released by Warner Brothers, another major corporation.

Although the New York-based Last Poets are often described as the first proto-rappers, it's worth noting that a Los Angeles group, The Watt Prophets, beat the Poets to the punch. The Prophets released their debut in 1969 with several songs incorporating the word "nigger" in the title. Sadly, they didn't benefit from any major label connections and remained the unsung heroes of rap until the 1990s, when their albums were reissued on compact disc.

The Last Poets are revered as the "godfathers of rap," and when listening to their early recordings it's easy to hear why. They sing and rap about more than just the word "nigger." Their words encompass revolution, sex, death, drugs and Black Power, but their creative use of the word "nigger" is captivating. They riff on it; they repeat it over and over, changing the tempo, changing the

today. You got young kids who think it's OK to be a nigger. Nah, it ain't OK. We were trying to get rid of the nigger in our community and in ourselves. The difference between us and hip-hop is that we had direction, we had a movement, we had people who kept our eyes on the prize. We weren't just bullshitting and jiving."

Although the legacy is strong, the Last Poets, like other pioneers, have gone in and out of fashion throughout the ensuing decades. Their recordings have been out of print many times as one record company dissolved and another one sprang up to take over. (It doesn't help that the Last Poets' lineups have changed often through the years with ex-members forming their own "original" Last Poets, forcing different groups using the Last Poets moniker to challenge each other like heavyweight boxers battling for the crown.) Their legacy is undisputed amongst those who would know best, as noted by Last Poet Hassan in the *Guardian* article. Black Panther chief of staff David Hilliard told him a few years ago, "People listened to the [Last Poets]. [They] made people want to be Panthers and join the Nation of Islam. You were as important as anyone because you made people think."

Despite their underground status at the time, the Last Poets' debut did manage to get at least two significant aboveground reviews in 1970. The May 31 issue of *The New York Times* featured a six-paragraph album review by Peter Bailey, an editor of *Ebony* magazine. Bailey compared their poems "Niggers are scared of

ABOVE: The streets of Harlem, the inner city of trashcans and fire hydrants: The clothing of the band members combines both traditional dashikis and contemporary fashion. The Last Poets were progressive artists that bridged Harlem and West Africa, while the presence of a drum cements tribal rhythms with the "hip-hop" beats the band invented a decade before the term existed.

DOUGLAS RECORDS RADIO STATION SERVICE ■ NOT FOR RESALE Z 30583

SIDE 1 SUGGESTED CUTS	LENGTH OF CUT		SIDE 2 SUGGESTED CUTS	LENGTH OF CUT
TRUE BLUES—ALAFIA PUDIM	2:00		WHITE MAN'S GOT A GOD COMPLEX ALAFIA PUDIM	3:35
RELATED TO WHAT CHANT NILIJA, PUDIM, BEN HASSEN	1:08		OPPOSITES—ALAFIA PUDIM	1:43
RELATED TO WHAT—OMAR BEN HASSEN	3:09		BLACK PEOPLE WHAT Y'ALL GON' DO CHANT NILIJA, PUDIM, BEN HASSEN	:46
BLACK IS CHANT—NILIJA, PUDIM, BEN HASSEN	:56		BLACK PEOPLE WHAT Y'ALL GON' DO OMAR BEN HASSEN	3:20
BLACK IS—OMAR BEN HASSEN	2:29		O.D.—ALAFIA PUDIM	3:06
TIME—OMAR BEN HASSEN	1:39		THIS IS MADNESS CHANT NILIJA, PUDIM, BEN HASSEN	1:04
MEAN MACHINE CHANT NILIJA, PUDIM, BEN HASSEN	1:22		THIS IS MADNESS—OMAR BEN HASSEN	4:50
MEAN MACHINE—ALAFIA PUDIM	4:03			

Editions Douglas Mus., A Div. of Douglas Mus. Corp. (BMI)   Editions Douglas Mus., A Div. of Douglas Mus. Corp. (BMI)

Dear Broadcaster:

You hold in your hands the most totally expressive material ever recorded.

THE LAST POETS have broken every theory in the recording business. Their first album sold nearly a half a million pieces without ever being played on commercial radio and without being hyped.

I must caution you to carefully audition any material before broadcasting same. Much of the material on this lp might be objectionable for commercial radio, as it is done in a totally honest and hard-hitting manner.

Whether you agree or disagree with, like or dislike this album, you will surely learn and expand your awareness of our society by listening to it.

Regards,

Mike

Mike Kagan
Director, National Promotion
Epic and Columbia Custom Labels

Revolution" and "Wake up, Niggers" to childhood taunts. He wrote, "When I was a child and my buddies would try to shame me into a desired action by taunting me: 'You a chicken. You a scary cat.' This seems to be what The Last Poets are trying to do, only they are pushing for much larger stakes. They want to shame and taunt Black people into getting themselves together so they can take care of business."

In the Sept. 3 issue of *Rolling Stone*, the Last Poets were the subject of a feature in which Jonathon Cott drew some interesting parallels. His opening sentence: "Like Noah or Daniel, we're feeling the Last Days eerily approaching us again." He mentions John Lennon's "Instant Karma," The Stones' "Gimme Shelter" and Dennis Hopper's *The Last Movie* in the same context with the Last Poets and their apocalyptic chant: "Time is running out on bullshit changes." Cott writes that in May 1970, the Last Poets played to an enthusiastic audience at the Apollo Theatre — sharing the bill with Carolyn Franklin (Aretha's sister) and Jerry Butler of The Impressions. No surprise that he adds: "although the Apollo's manager and a few others got squeamish about The Poets' language."

Record producer Alan Douglas had already released speeches by Malcolm X, poetry by Allen Ginsberg and a spoken word/musical jam session with Timothy Leary, Jimi Hendrix and Buddy Miles on his Douglas Records imprint when he stumbled upon the Last Poets in action on a Manhattan TV station in 1970. As Douglas explained to journalist Michael Davis in August 1995:

I heard a snatch of material on television one night, and it stopped me short. It was on PBS, so I called the station, and I got an address and a telephone number. I called the next day and got a very hostile voice on the phone. I told them who I was and that I had heard a little bit of their material on television the night before, and I would like to talk to them about

LEFT: For those wondering if the Last Poets received airplay, this radio station promo copy at least shows that Douglas Records tried. The painting by Mati Klarwein depicts an image of fire; this is not the fire of Dante's Hell, but a cleansing fire, a redemptive fire, as in James Baldwin's *The Fire Next Time*. Fans of Miles Davis will recognize the woman's face on the left side of the cover; similar artwork by Klarwein appears on *Bitches Brew* and *Live Evil*.

making records. So he said, "Well, if you want to hear it, man, you gotta come up here, and you have to be alone."

Real hostile shit! So I said, "Where's up here?" and he made a date with me at 137th Street and Lennox Avenue. So, I went up there, and it was a schoolyard with two old, funky basketball courts with rims and no nets. I looked over at one of the courts, and there was a whole bunch of black guys — must have been 25 of them — standing there. I got out of the car and walked over, thinking, "This is either suicide or a great sign." As I got there, the crowd kind of separated, and these four guys were left. There were three rappers and a conga player standing underneath a basket.

They pointed at the foul line and said, "You stand there," and they did the material that ended up on the first album with me.

So I said, "Come to the studio with me right now, and we'll record this. If you like the tape, we'll do a deal; if you don't like it, you take the tape with you." They thought that was reasonable. They all jumped in my car, and we went down to a friend of mine's studio on 66th Street, and we recorded the whole thing in one afternoon. They liked it. I got whatever money together I could — $1,000 or something — and we did a deal. I put the record out, and the rest is history.

According to a full-page ad in the music trade publication *Billboard*, the debut album *The Last Poets* sold over three hundred thousand copies. While it isn't surprising that the album sold well given the political climate, it *is* astonishing that it sold well given the fact that it had no airplay and a nonexistent marketing budget. With song titles like "Run, Nigger," "Niggers Are Scared Of Revolution"

March, 1971

THE LAST POETS: THIS IS MADNESS   DOUGLAS #7

When the Last Poets' first album was released last year we had to stomp our feet into the ground and hold fast against indignant distributors, skeptical editors and confused retailers --- all of whom were thrown back by the unusual musical form and its accompanying language.

The only thing on our side was the fact that everyone who looked past the shadow of the album's heavy-but-justified language recognized the album as among the most significant and communicative recordings ever made.

As it were, after the initial brunt, channels opened up and the album quickly shot up the charts (where it stood for over nine months) thanks to excited word-of-mouth on the street level, honest references in print, and a little help from friends (like Mick Jagger, who included 'Wake Up Niggers' in 'Performance,' and Jimi Hendrix, who wrote and recorded the radio spots).

Because of the language most of the cuts couldn't get airplay; the total number of spins were few.

THIS IS MADNESS is the Poets' second album. It is also Douglas' first release through Columbia Records' distribution. Most of the cuts on this release can be played; the first album by the Poets dealt exclusively with Black situations -- it was a record by Black poets for Black people -- on this second LP the Poets focus their insights into America-at-large.

We believe that 'This Is Madness' is a particularly positive album, and an important one. It makes people think. It confronts. It challanges. And it uses the record medium like it should once-in-a-while be used.

                          ---KBS

145 WEST FIFTY-FIFTH STREET, NEW YORK, NEW YORK 10019 / (212) 581-2212

and "Wake Up Niggers," and lacking the sales force of a major label, one has to wonder how people heard about it at all. The explanation, according to the *Billboard* ad, is that they sold three hundred thousand copies by "word of mouth." Additional ad copy implies that everyone who bought the LP played it for someone else, who bought it and played it for someone else, and so on.

One person who'd certainly checked out the Last Poets was poet/songwriter Gil Scott-Heron, on the cusp of becoming a legend himself. Scott-Heron attended Lincoln University in Pennsylvania, mainly because his hero, writer Langston Hughes, had enrolled there in the 1920s. In 1969, the Last Poets performed at Lincoln University, making an impression on Scott-Heron. In the Aug. 9, 2010 issue of *The New Yorker*,

Last Poet Abiodun Oyewole told Alec Wilkinson: "After the gig, he came backstage and said, 'Listen, can I start a group like you guys?'"

GIL SCOTT-HERON
AND THE REVOLUTION

By 1970, Scott-Heron had left Lincoln to focus on writing. *Small Talk at 125th and Lenox: A Collection of Black Poems by Gil Scott-Heron* was published by the World Publishing imprint, while an LP (with the same *Small Talk* title) followed on Flying Dutchman. With the exception of three songs that featured Scott-Heron

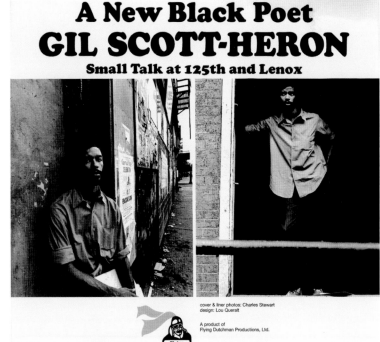

ABOVE: Gil Scott-Heron's 1970 recording debut exemplifies a new era of poets making the crossover from books to albums; in fact, he released a book of poems with the same title as this LP beforehand. It is of note that he's holding his poetry notebook in his hands as he leans against the wall, near 125th and Lenox.

on piano, just like the Last Poets, his debut was mainly spoken word raps accompanied by conga drums. As he recalled in the December 2003 issue of *Mojo*, "I'd seen them. It was very exciting. The interplay between them and the drummers, and each other, was very theatrical."

For anyone who has heard Scott-Heron's seminal "The Revolution Will Not Be Televised" from his second album, 1971's *Pieces Of A Man*, it will be surprising to hear his earlier version. Unlike the better-known (and reworked) full-band arrangement, on the *Small Talk at 125th and Lenox* original, Scott-Heron recites the piece accompanied only by drums. The stark, bare bones nature of the recording reinforces the urgency of the lyrics.

The words are a bit different between Heron's 1970 and 1971 recordings due to the contemporary nature of the piece, which referenced key social, political and cultura issues. Timothy Leary's slogan "Turn on, tune in, and drop out" was converted to "Plug in, turn on, and cop out." Name-dropped are: Richard Nixon and Attorney General John Mitchell, actors Natalie Wood and Steve McQueen, and television sitcoms *Green Acres* and *The Beverly Hillbillies*, amongst dozens of pop culture references. It would make sense that, a year later, Scott-Heron was still fine-tuning the names and references.

The Last Poets' "When The Revolution Comes" is a treat for those familiar with either version of "The Revolution Will Not Be Televised." Predating Gil Scott-Heron's recordings, presumably the Last Poets' song served as a template for "The Revolution Will Not Be Televised." In *On A Mission*, an autobiography written by two of the three Last Poets, Abiodun Oyewole and Umar Bin Hassan, that appears on their debut album, Oyewole, author of "When The Revolution Comes," set down:

> *The truth was, many of us still saw ourselves as "niggers" and slaves. This was a mindset that had to change if there was ever to be Black Power. The major problem in the Black community was lack of unity. The fact is, we probably had just as many Black people working diligently for the system, as those fighting tooth and nail against it. So there I was, on the front lines of this great would-be revolution. I wondered, how can I say something that hasn't been said before? One of the most common expressions was,*

"When the Revolution comes." You'd hear it when you saw a brother with a big afro, dashiki, beads, and white girl on his arm. Somebody would yell out: "You gonna have to get rid of Miss Ann, when the revolution comes, brother." Folks would break out in laughter. These moments inspired "When the Revolution Comes."

Gil Scott-Heron's stark, original recording of "The Revolution Will Not Be Televised" also begins with a conga beat. While the rhythm of the words is different, the lyrical concept is similar to "When The Revolution Comes." At various points, Scott-Heron drops in the slogan "The revolution will not be televised" while taking the development of the verses a bit further, riffing on dozens of contemporary references. But the conceptual statement of Scott-Heron's anthem is very close in spirit to the Poets' song, as a cross section of the lyrics reveal "The revolution will not be televised...there will be no pictures of pigs shooting down brothers in the instant replay...the theme song will be not be sung by…Glen Campbell, Tom Jones, Johnny Cash…the revolution will not be televised."

"When the Revolution Comes" may have infused Scott-Heron's classic, but its enjoyed a long life on its own merits — with tributes from Public Enemy, Prince and The Disposable Heroes of Hiphoprisy as well as Elvis Costello and Steve Earle. Some readers may (sadly) only know it from the 1990s Nike TV commercial in which the tune was re-recorded by rapper KRS-One, with lyrics reconfigured to focus on a basketball game. The less said about that, the better.

VOODOO CHILD:
JIM HENDRIX' MACHINE GUN

Many years ago I read a statement by a friend of Jimi Hendrix' along the lines of, "Jimi was not hung up on being black, Jimi was just into being Jimi." Most of what has been written about Hendrix along racial lines is just speculation. There are stories of the Panthers pressuring Hendrix to take a public stand supporting Black Power. There are accounts of the Panthers wanting Hendrix to have an all-black band, hence the Band of Gypsys. Portions of these tales just don't make sense. First of all, by the time of his appearance at Woodstock, Hendrix wanted to get away from his management's stranglehold on his career and was eager to move away from the Jimi Hendrix Experience with Mitch Mitchell and Noel Redding (regardless of the fact that they were white). Hendrix was already in the throes of a change in musical direction and band-mates no matter what.

The all-black Band of Gypsys trio, Hendrix, Billy Cox and Buddy Miles, came together in the final months of 1969 because Hendrix *wanted* it to happen. He was tired of his management, who'd recently made him cancel a benefit concert for the Young Lords organization so that he could appear on the *Dick Cavett Show*. According to David Henderson's *Jimi Hendrix: Voodoo Child of the Aquarian Age*, "[Hendrix'] management was all in an uproar over his alleged 'Black Power' turn of mind, as if it were unnatural for him to have concern about his people in a political way."

Hendrix played an outdoor street fair in Harlem in September 1969 hosted by WWRL (a popular black radio station). Using the same expanded lineup that he'd had at Woodstock, Hendrix delighted in playing for a black audience. But he wanted to remain neutral when it came to making a political stand. According to Henderson, "Walking back the equipment truck after the set [at the Harlem street fair], a Black Nationalist type came up to Jimi and said 'Hey, brother, you better come home.' Jimi quickly replied, 'You gotta do what you gotta do and I gotta do what I got to do *now*.'"

While the Panthers would have surely wanted Hendrix' public or financial support, they were not Black Nationalists; they wouldn't be telling him not to perform with whites. Anyone who has studied the writings of Huey P. Newton should know that. Unlike the US organization formed by Black Nationalist Ron Karenga, the Panthers mingled with white militants such as Jerry Rubin and Hollywood types like Candice Bergen and Marlon Brando.

One thing is certain: they did meet with Hendrix backstage at some concerts, as Noel Redding remembers being barred from the Experience's dressing room by a Panther during one such gathering. Despite whatever interactions took place, Hendrix would not make a public endorsement. In an interview with the *Los Angeles Free Press*, Hendrix answered the following questions:

LAFP: But you do feel the Black Panthers are necessary, though?

Jimi: Yeah, only to the word necessary. You know, in the back of their minds they should be working toward their own thing. They should be a symbol only to the establishment's eyes. It should only be a legendary thing.

LAFP: Is it necessary as a step on the road to liberation and freedom?

Jimi: It all depends on what freedom means. Some people don't even know the meaning.

LAFP: How about for each individual that's involved in the Black Panthers?

Jimi: No, see, most of that comes from any kind of aggressive group like that. It's good when you start adding up universal thoughts, and it's good for that second. The rest of it should probably be in a legendary figure. In a, what do you call it, a symbol, or whatever. So what they are doing now is fighting among their individual selves. There's nothing we can explain to them. Most of it is from bitterness. There's no color part now. There's no black and white. It's very small. It's just like animals fighting among each other — then the big animals will come and take it all away.

Ultimately, any statements Hendrix wanted to make were made musically. In his most overtly political song he mainly used his guitar, not his voice, to make a stand. "Machine Gun" was recorded live at the Fillmore East on Jan. 1, 1970 and released in April on the album. Hendrix' spoken introduction makes it clear what the song is about: "Happy New Year first of all. I hope we'll have a million or two million more of them … if we can get over this summer. Right, I'd like to dedicate this one to the dragging scene that's going on: all the soldiers that are fighting in Chicago, Milwaukee and New York … Oh yes, and all the solders fighting in Vietnam. Like to do a thing called 'Machine Gun.'"

His guitar emulates the sounds of a battlefield. Over the course of twelve minutes, Hendrix uses his ingenuity to make the guitar screech and howl, creating a wholly expressive view of the urban unrest of American's inner cities and the Vietnam War. The few lyrics are ambiguous as to whether they reference the war on the home front, the war overseas, or both… "Don't you shoot him down, he's about to leave here, don't you shoot him down, he's got to stay here, he ain't going nowhere."

Also during the January 1st Fillmore show, Hendrix introduces "Voodoo Child (Slight Return)" by saying, "We're gonna do the moratorium, the Black Panthers National Anthem." On May 30, 1970, at the Berkeley Community Theatre, during the

shows that comprised the *Jimi Plays Berkeley* movie, after a performance of "Purple Haze" and just before launching into another searing version of "Voodoo Child (Slight Return)," he tells the audience, "Now we're gonna play *our* American Anthem…this is especially dedicated to the People's Park and especially the Black Panthers."

Hendrix rambles on that he hopes the audience has some kind of feeling about the next thing he's about to play, that it's nothing but determination and knowing that you're gonna get it together. For those looking for more reciprocity between Hendrix and Black Power, it's been suggested that Hendrix setting a guitar on fire at the 1967 Monterey Pop Festival was his artistic interpretation of the slogan "Burn, Baby, Burn."

TWIST AND SHOUT: THE ISLEY BROTHERS ENGAGE SOCIAL PROTEST

Before Hendrix was an international icon, he was a guitar player for hire, a sideman to King Curtis, Little Richard and The Isley Brothers. In 1962, The Isleys were the first to have a hit with "Twist And Shout," which The Beatles covered soon after. Perhaps inspired by Sam Cooke, who'd done it in 1959 with SAR Records, the Isleys declared their artistic and financial independence in 1964 by starting T-Neck Records. It was unique at the time for any musicians, black or white, to own their own label.

Like many popular artists, the Isleys tended to sing about love, but by the end of the 1960s the group had turned on and tuned in to social protest. Their 1971 T-Neck album *Givin' It Back* contained an energized medley of Crosby, Stills, Nash & Young's

"Ohio" and Hendrix' "Machine Gun." The song is a cross-cultural blend of hippie rock ("Ohio" is an account of the May 1970 shootings of four Kent State University students during a campus anti-Vietnam War protest) and Afro-psychedelic blues (the anti-war and urban unrest of "Machine Gun"). Coupled with the Isleys' gospel-tinged vocals (one of them starts testifying from the Bible asking forgiveness for the killers as "Ohio" segues into "Machine Gun") and underlined by the acid-rock tone of Ernest Isley's guitar channeling both Hendrix and Neil Young — the end result is wild! For those who need more of Ernest Isley's wicked playing, check out the thirteen-minute version of "Ohio/Machine Gun" on the 1973 *The Isleys Live*.

IF THERE'S A HELL BELOW, WE'RE ALL GOING TO GO:
CURTIS MAYFIELD TESTIFIES

Curtis Mayfield made endless artistic contributions to black culture and Civil Rights. Mayfield wrote classics that transcended genres, sang elegantly and was a masterful guitar player and producer. Subtlety was the key to Mayfield's special talents — his songs flawlessly captured the cultural progress of the times, yet his voice never shrieked in anger and he never played a long-winded, ego-driven guitar solo. Like the Isley Brothers, Mayfield started his own record company, Windy C, in 1966. Although Windy C was short-lived, he came back in force two years later with his landmark Curtom Records, which released not only Mayfield's own music, but recorded Baby Huey, Donny Hathaway, Major Lance and other Chicago-based musicians.

Mayfield was a member of the vocal group The Impressions for whom he penned several hits, including 1964's anthem "Keep On Pushing," which encouraged blacks to rise above a life of segregation and discrimination. A year later "People Get Ready" became a standard covered by Aretha Franklin, the Chambers Brothers and others — including Bob Dylan, who recorded it no less than three times: the 1967 *Basement Tape* sessions, in 1975 for his *Renaldo and Clara* movie soundtrack and again in 1988 for the film *Flashback*. The Impressions single "Choice Of Colors" was especially poignant: "If you had a choice of color, which one would you choose, my brothers. If there was no day or night,

which would you prefer to be right?" The song contained all the Mayfield trademarks — poetic lyrics, a compelling melody and a grand, but not overproduced, sound, all of which drove the song to the #1 spot on the R&B charts during the summer of '69.

In September 1970, Mayfield stepped forward with his first solo album: *Curtis*. The record opens with the prodigious "(Don't Worry) If There's A Hell Below We're All Going To Go," a narrative on the social cataclysm of black America. The song begins with a fuzzed-out bass guitar riff (think Larry Graham with the Family Stone), overlaid with a woman's voice suggesting that if people read the Book of Revelations, they can avert the coming apocalypse. Curtis proclaims, "Sisters! Niggers! Whiteys! Jews! Crackers! Don't worry, if there's hell below ... we're all ... gonna go!" The whole band and a string section kick into a devastatingly funky groove while Curtis preaches that the corruption of society, especially the lies of judges and politicians, will eventually bring everyone down. Blacks, whites, police, junkies, et al., will all ride together on an expressway to hell.

Mayfield's "We The People Who Are Darker Than Blue" takes the message of "Choice Of Colors" to a deeper level. "We people who are darker than blue, are we gonna stand around this town, and let what others say come true? We're just good for nothing they all figure." The song has that distinctive Mayfield vibe: earnest vocals accompanied by a hearty horn and string section. But at the two-minute mark, Mayfield steers it in a new direction as the song mutates into a tribal percussion breakdown, all the vocals and other instruments drop out, then slowly come back one at a time with an uplifting Latin-rock rhythm, like a groove from the first Santana album.

Mayfield speaks: "Get yourself together, learn to know your side, shall we commit our own genocide, before you check out your mind?" It's psychedelic *and* sincere, much like The Temptations' "Message From A Black Man" on *Puzzle People*. Motown producer Norman Whitfield would be proud. The song continues to bubble and brew, eventually using a stringed harp to fold back into the original rhythm of the song's beginning. "We The People Who Are Darker Than Blue" is six minutes of psychedelia, classical, funk, pop and Afro-Latin music channeled through Mayfield's inspirational mind — astonishing work from one of the patriarchs of soul.

YOUNG, GIFTED AND BLACK:
THE PASSION OF NINA SIMONE

Last, but certainly not least, amongst an overview of popular black artists that incorporated politics into their music is Nina Simone. She was the embodiment of genius, infamous for her mercurial nature — but famous for her distinctively expressive voice, her repertoire of self-penned classics and her discriminating taste in performing songs written by Dylan, George Harrison and Sandy Denny, amongst others.

Nina Simone was a badass from the beginning. When she signed to Colpix Records (owned by mega-giant corporation Columbia Pictures) in the 1950s, she demanded and received complete creative control over her work. This included her choice of which songs she would record. In a pre-Beatles music industry, especially for a black female recording artist, this was unheard of. Simone's songwriting eloquently echoed the Civil

Rights struggle. After the murder of Medgar Evers in Jackson, Miss. (followed by the Sunday morning bombing of a Baptist Church in Birmingham) Simone wrote "Mississippi Goddam" for her 1964 *Nina Simone in Concert*.

Recorded at Carnegie Hall, Simone introduces the song as "a show tune, but the show hasn't been written for it yet." The lyrics reveal her disgust. "Alabama's got me so upset, Tennessee's made me lose my rest, and everybody knows about Mississippi Goddam." Simone then rages against those who suggest the Civil Rights movement should slow down. "Keep on saying 'go slow' — to do things gradually would bring more tragedy. Why don't you see it? Why don't you feel it? I don't know, I don't know. You don't have to live next to me, just give me my equality!" Years later, Simone reflected, "After the murder of Medgar Evers, the Alabama bombing and 'Mississippi Goddam,' the entire direction of my life shifted, and for the next seven years I was driven by Civil Rights and the hope of black revolution."

On the 1969 *Nina Simone Sings The Blues*, Simone set the poem "Backlash Blues," written by her friend Langston Hughes, to music. "Mr. Backlash, just who do you think I am? You give me second-class houses and second-class schools, do you think all colored folks are just second-class fools?"

Although Simone respected King Jr.'s efforts, she really embraced SNCC, especially under Stokely Carmichael and H. Rap Brown's leadership, as well as the Black Panther Party and the philosophy that violence may be the only way to bring about change. Carmichael was a close friend who declared Simone "the true singer of the Civil Rights movement."

In her own words, she was "through with the turning the other cheek, through with loving her enemies. It was time for some Old Testament justice." Nevertheless, like everyone else, she was devastated when King Jr. was assassinated. Three days after he was shot, Simone played the Westbury Music Fair in New York State — where she dedicated the entire set to his memory and performed a new song, "Why? (The King Of Love Is Dead)," written by her bass player Gene Taylor immediately after they'd received the news that King Jr. was dead. "Why?" along with other selections from the Westbury concert, was included on Simone's 1968 *Nuff Said*.

Simone's most significant contribution to the canon of songs that spoke to the movement was undoubtedly "To Be

Young, Gifted and Black." Playwright Lorraine Hansberry had been working on a play entitled *To Be Young, Gifted and Black* when she died of cancer in 1965. The unfinished manuscript was completed posthumously by adapting other Hansberry writings into the work and was performed off-Broadway in 1968.

Meanwhile, Simone, who'd been a close friend of Hansberry, was aware of the unfinished draft. Simone decided to honor her deceased friend by borrowing the title and writing a song around it, in collaboration with organist Weldon Irvine. In her autobiography, Simone credits Hansberry with educating her on how Civil Rights was part of a wider racial and class struggle.

In August 1969, Simon recorded "To Be Young, Gifted and Black" for RCA Records, who released it as a single to widespread acclaim. Two months later, she performed a version at New York Philharmonic Hall, released on the 1970 *Black Gold* album. Here, Simone introduces it with a passionate tribute to Hansberry, including a mention of the play (then being staged in Manhattan) and noting the song had just been released as a 45. She wraps up her intro by stating, "Now it is not addressed primarily to white people, though it does not put you down in any way, it simply ignores you. For my people need all the inspiration and love that they can get. So, since this house is full and there are 22 million blacks in this country, I only want one million to buy this record, you understand."

The phrase "Young, Gifted and Black" quickly became a slogan akin to "I'm Black and I'm Proud." The Congress of Racial Equality (CORE) declared the song the "National Anthem of Black America," with a version by Aretha Franklin becoming the title song of her 1972 album.

LEFT: Not nearly as shocking as the Last Poets' "Nigger" ad that ran in *Rolling Stone* in 1971, this one for Nina Simone ran a year earlier. Would a mainstream white publication in today's marketplace run an ad like this? "Listen to what you miss out on by not being black." Any ad selling an African-American singer/songwriter wouldn't present this kind of racial statement: "If all of us had the same sense of togetherness as America's black people, America would be a much better place to live." In 2012, nearly everyone is afraid to compare one race to another. However, there are times when being "correct" is better than being "politically correct."

The Black Forum Label

Even among diehard collectors of Motown's considerable output, Motown's subsidiary Black Forum label remains obscure. It is overlooked in most Motown biographies, and no Black Forum recordings have ever been included in any Motown label anthology.

Even the thirty-song, double CD released by Motown in 2007 *Power To The People: Civil Rights Anthems and Political Soul 1968-1975* includes no Black Forum artists, or even a mention of the label in the booklet's overview of Motown during the Black Power era. And yet, the cover features a clenched fist salute as its main artwork and a photograph of Huey Newton and Bobby Seale is inside the jewel case. There's also a sticker announcing that this CD includes "30 Militant Soul Anthems." OK then, where are selections from Elaine Brown of the Black Panther Party or poet/activist Amiri Baraka? Each had released albums of songs (rather than speeches) on Black Forum during the period covered on the compilation.

The label released eight albums between 1970 and 1973. The albums were: a speech denouncing the Vietnam War by Martin Luther King Jr.; a very heated address on race relations by Stokely Carmichael; and interviews with black soldiers fighting in Vietnam conducted by a *Time* magazine correspondent. There was also a narrative by writers Langston Hughes and Margaret Danner, an LP of poetry including Amiri Baraka, members of the Last Poets, and Stanley Crouch, as well as an album of songs featuring Amiri Baraka as a vocalist backed by free jazz musicians. The final two releases were Ossie Davis and Bill Cosby speaking in front of the first Congressional Black Caucus, and the aforementioned singer-songwriter LP by renowned Black Panther Elaine Brown.

When I realized that Motown boss Gordy had authorized the Black Forum label and allowed The Temptations (amongst others) to release political songs well before Marvin Gaye's *What's Going On*, I wondered: why the double standard? In June 2008, I posed the question to Miller London — an employee of Motown for three decades, beginning in the '60s. London felt that Gordy was afraid of damaging Gaye's incredible mass following; he didn't want to mess with a winning formula. OK, fair enough, but why did Gordy initiate Black Forum in the first place, and who ran it for him? Miller cited the Civil Rights movement in general as inspiration to implement the label, and named Ewart Abner as one of the in-house forces behind it. However, Abner had passed away in 1998, so I couldn't ask him.

In his 2002 book *Motown: Music, Money, Sex, and Power*, Gerald Posner suggests several factors that may have led to the start of Black Forum. During the late 1960s, black radio disc jockeys around Detroit that had always been supportive of the label began to feel that Gordy was more interested in courting favor with white DJs, as Motown's singles increasingly gained attention outside the African-American community with each passing year, which eventually led to a temporary boycott of Motown releases by Detroit-area black DJs.

Meanwhile, internationally successful acts like The Supremes were getting asked questions about their stand on the Vietnam War and the Black Power movement while touring England, and the artists didn't how to respond. There were letters from African-American fans sent to Motown suggesting that The Supremes wear their hair natural (afro-style), which Gordy

resisted, worried it could make the popular female trio look too radical for white America. While Gordy himself had remained non-political throughout much of the 1960s, he had released an album of speeches by Martin Luther King Jr. titled *Free At Last* on the Gordy imprint in June 1968. He also supported the NAACP, one of the oldest Civil Rights organizations, founded in 1909 by W.E.B. Du Bois. But times were changing with new, more outspoken black rights coalitions gaining in popularity, while some young blacks began to criticize Motown for sounding too white.

The assassination of Martin Luther King Jr. on April 4, 1968, was the wake-up call that Gordy had to make accommodations and embrace the Black Power movement. Some time after that tragic event, Gordy brought together three employees — Ewart Abner, Junius Griffin and George Schiffer — to organize the Black Forum label and oversee its output.

Before coming to work for Motown in the spring of 1967, Abner had been one of the partners in the Vee-Jay label, best known as the first American company to release records by The Beatles before Capitol Records stepped in. It's important to note that through Vee-Jay, Abner released The Impressions' first nationally distributed single, "For Your Precious Love," in the summer of 1958. In 1975, Abner became the manager of Stevie Wonder, an arrangement that lasted a decade. During his long career, Abner was passionate about black pride as an advocate of minority education, a founding member of the Black Music Association, a member of the NAACP and the Urban League, as well as organizing two Civil Rights-era marches on Washington. Abner helped infuse Motown with his beliefs, and was the logical choice to be a driving force behind Black Forum.

ABOVE: King Jr. is dead, so he is now "free at last." This contains his immortal last public address, "I've been to the mountaintop" — the children pictured represent future generations who will not only go to the mountaintop, and not only see the promised land, but actually reach the promised land.

Also joining Motown in 1967 was Junius Griffin, who'd been the first African-American reporter for the New York desk of the Associated Press during the early 1960s. In 1965, the Southern Christian Leadership Conference asked him to write speeches for Martin Luther King Jr., which he did until joining Motown's publicity department two years later. He remained at Motown until the early 1980s, and at end of that decade was public relations advisor to the Martin Luther King, Jr. Center for Nonviolent Social Change in Atlanta. According to an interview in the Feb. 12, 2004 issue of the *Los Angeles Times* with actor Max Julien, who starred in the 1973 Blaxploitation movie *The Mack*, Griffin is credited with coining the term "Blaxploitation" in 1972, when he complained in *Variety* about negative images of African-Americans in the just-released film *Superfly*. Griffin's comments about the emerging cinematic genre apparently didn't stop there; in an op-ed piece published in *The New York Times* on Dec. 17, 1972, Griffin wrote, "these films are taking our money while feeding us a forced diet of violence, murder, drugs and rape. Such films are the cancer of 'Blaxploitation' gnawing away at the moral fiber of our community."

The third person behind Black Forum was George Schiffer, a white liberal who'd been Gordy's copyright lawyer since the early days of Motown. He worked for Motown from 1959 to 1975, as well as serving as lead attorney for the Congress of Racial Equality (CORE) in New York City during the 1960s. Although CORE is usually mentioned in context with the Civil Rights era and the Deep South, it originated in Chicago during 1942, inspired by Gandhi's theories on organizing people through nonviolent protest. The Freedom Rides began May 1961, guided by CORE director James Farmer. As the 1960s progressed, the organization debated internally on which direction to take. Farmer resigned in 1966 in support of nonviolence and was replaced by Floyd McKissick, who led CORE in a Black Nationalist direction.

The first three Black Forum albums included the following mission statement on the back cover:

> *Black Forum is a medium for the presentation of ideas and voices of the worldwide struggle of Black people to create a new era. Black Forum also serves to provide authentic materials for use in schools and colleges and for the home study of Black history and culture. Black Forum is a permanent record of the sound of struggle and the sound of the new era.*

THE BLACK FORUM LABEL DISCOGRAPHY

DR. MARTIN LUTHER KING JR.
WHY I OPPOSE THE WAR IN VIETNAM (LP)

In October 1970, Martin Luther King Jr.'s *Why I Oppose the War in Vietnam* became Black Forum's debut release, giving the label an auspicious start. As the *Philadelphia Tribune* reported in their April 3, 1971 edition, "In its very first venture into the spoken word recording category, Motown Records has won the coveted Grammy award for its Black Forum album, 'Why I Oppose The War In Vietnam,' a speech by the late Dr. Martin Luther King Jr."

Black Forum co-founder Junius Griffin accepted the award at the 1971 Grammy ceremonies. He said, "You have honored two Kings tonight, B.B. King, for the best performance by a Rhythm and Blues artist, and Dr. King, voicing his conviction against the war in Vietnam. With 'Bridge Over Troubled Water' as the year's best song, Dr. King's selection seems doubly appropriate, for so many times in his life, he himself bridged troubled waters in the cause of peace and racial brotherhood."

King Jr. began speaking out against the war in 1965, after a number of the reforms that he'd fought for were passed into law by President Lyndon B. Johnson via the July 1964 Civil Rights Act. King Jr. then focused on other issues, including Vietnam. By April 1967, King Jr. had turned up the heat on the subject of the war, giving at least two well-known sermons that month on the subject. Besides the sermon on this album, previously, on April 4 (exactly one year before his death), King Jr. delivered an equally passionate diatribe at Riverside Church in Manhattan, in which he orated, in part:

> *After the French were defeated, it looked as if independence and land reform would come again through the Geneva Agreement. But instead there came the United States, determined that Ho should not unify the temporarily divided nation, and the peasants watched again as we supported one of the most vicious modern dictators, our chosen man,*

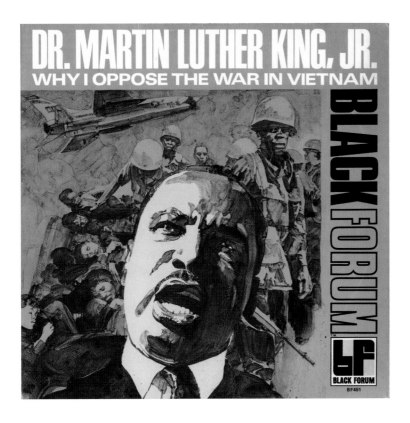

it also provides a concise history of post-World War II Vietnam, documenting America's continued stranglehold on the Southeast Asian country, even after our French allies were defeated by the Vietnamese in 1954.

King Jr. is not as dynamic as he is on the famous "I Have A Dream" and "I've Been To The Mountain" speeches from '63 and '68. It's because he's speaking not only from the heart, but also from the mind as he tries gallantly to convince Americans not to submit to the Military-Industrial Complex: "A nation that continues year after year to spend more money on military defense than on programs of social uplift is approaching spiritual death."

King Jr. sets the tone:

The sermon which I am preaching this morning in a sense is not the usual kind of sermon, but it is a sermon and an important subject, nevertheless, because the issue that I will be discussing today is one of the most controversial issues confronting our nation. I'm using as a subject from which to preach, "Why I Am Opposed to the War in Vietnam."

Now, let me make it clear in the beginning that I see this war as an unjust, evil, and futile war. I preach to you today on the war in Vietnam because my conscience leaves me with no other choice. The time has come for America to hear the truth about this tragic war. In international conflicts, the truth is hard to come by because most nations are deceived about themselves. Rationalizations and the incessant search for scapegoats are the psychological cataracts that blind us to our sins. But the day has passed for superficial patriotism. He who lives with untruth lives in spiritual slavery. Freedom is still the bonus we receive for knowing the truth. "Ye shall know the truth," says Jesus, "and the truth shall set you free." Now, I've chosen to preach about the war in Vietnam because I agree with Dante, that the hottest

Premier Diem. The peasants watched and cringed as Diem ruthlessly rooted out all opposition, supported their extortionist landlords, and refused even to discuss reunification with the North.

The peasants watched as all of this was presided over by United States influence and then by increasing numbers of United States troops who came to help quell the insurgency that Diem's methods had aroused. When Diem was overthrown they may have been happy, but the long line of military dictators seemed to offer no real change, especially in terms of their need for land and peace. The only change came from America as we increased our troop commitments in support of governments which were singularly corrupt, inept, and without popular support.

Taken from a sermon delivered on April 16, 1967, at the Ebenezer Baptist Church in Atlanta, King Jr.'s address, spread across the two sides of *Why I Oppose the War in Vietnam,* not only gives his personal and theological reasons against the war, but

ABOVE: King Jr.'s image is intertwined with soldiers and Vietnamese citizens who have been killed. One of the soldiers is trying to help those that have been wounded; the airplane represents long-distance, anonymous killing, as many bomber pilots said if they'd seen the "enemy" they would not have been able to do what they did … Meanwhile, black soldiers understand that the real shit that goes on is not in the air, but on the ground.

places in hell are reserved for those who in a period of moral crisis maintain their neutrality. There comes a time when silence becomes betrayal.

Thirteen minutes into Side One, King Jr. focuses on a nation at war with itself inside America's cities:

> *My third reason moves to an even deeper level of aware-ness, for it grows out of my experience in the ghettos of the North over the last three years — especially the last three summers. As I have walked among the desperate, rejected, and angry young men, I have told them that Molotov cock-tails and rifles would not solve their problems. I have tried to offer them my deepest compassion while maintaining my conviction that social change comes most meaningfully through non-violent action; for they ask and write me, "So what about Vietnam?" They ask if our nation wasn't using massive doses of violence to solve its problems to bring about the changes it wanted. Their questions hit home, and I knew that I could never again raise my voice against the violence of the oppressed in the ghettos without first having spoken clearly to the greatest purveyor of violence in the world today: my own government.*

I've long felt the reason King Jr. was assassinated was his criticism of the Vietnam War. If the federal government was less than pleased to see him become the spokesman for an entire racial movement, they were extremely unhappy to see King Jr. use his influence to sway public opinion against the increasingly controversial war. Political commentator Tavis Smiley also thinks so, as theorized on HBO's *Real Time with Bill Maher* on March 24, 2008, during a discussion surrounding the 40th anniversary of King Jr.'s death.

Now, some forty-plus years after King Jr.'s speeches, the world is still at war and more often than not, America is at the

root of it. Imagine a time when a presidential candidate rep-resenting one of our two major parties paraphrases King Jr.'s anti-war speeches during his or her campaign. Now that would be something to get excited about.

STOKELY CARMICHAEL
FREE HUEY (LP)

Also released in October 1970 was Stokely Carmichael's *Free Huey*, recorded at the "Free Huey Rally" at the Oakland Auditorium on Feb. 17, 1968. The Free Huey Rally was a landmark event with five

OPPSOSITE: To call for the release of Huey Newton is to call for the release of all African-Americans and other races from historical imprisonments. Carmichael's expressive face in mid-speech is as much an iconic image of the movement as the seminal photo of Newton sitting in the wicker chair.

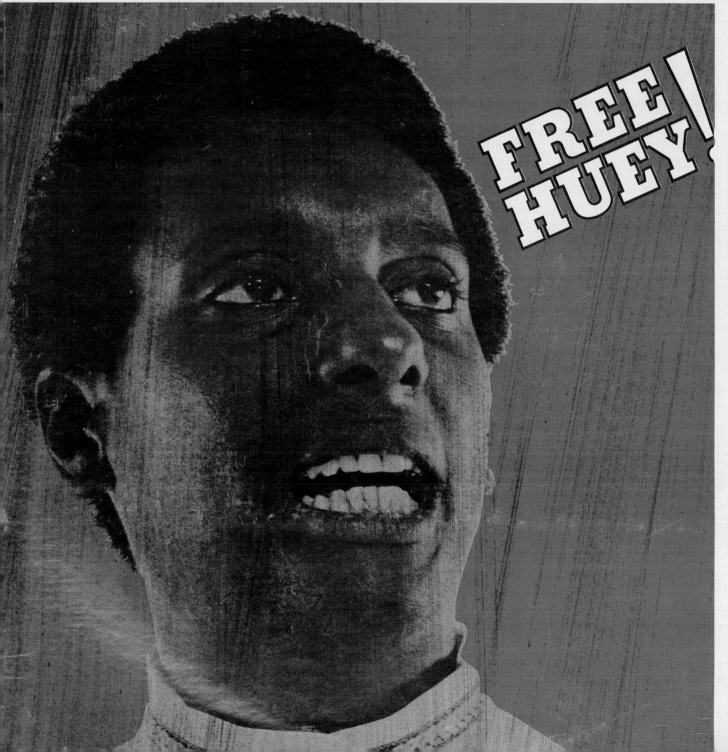

thousand attendees, and a Black Panther/SNCC coalition was announced that evening. The 17th was also Huey's birth date, so the event was co-billed as "Huey Newton's birthday party," with an appearance by Huey's mom! Speakers at the rally included fellow SNCC leaders James Forman and H. Rap Brown. Eldridge Cleaver and Bobby Seale represented the Panthers. Also speaking that night was Bob Avakian of the Peace and Freedom Party and Berkeley Councilman Ron Dellums (later a congressman and mayor of Oakland).

One day short of a year later, on Feb. 16, 1969, Hollywood High Auditorium in Los Angeles was the site of another birthday celebration in Newton's honor. The event included speeches from Kathleen Cleaver and writer James Baldwin (author of the influential 1963 race-relations classic *The Fire Next Time*) and a taped greeting from Netwon, recorded in his prison cell. Berkeley legends Country Joe & the Fish performed, along with the L.A. blues band Pacific Gas & Electric. PG&E was a multiracial band and while touring through Raleigh, N.C. during that period, the Southern audience couldn't handle seeing black and white musicians together on stage, which led to minor rioting and gunfire.

Carmichael was controversial in a movement overflowing with controversial figures. Over time, Carmichael's political mantra became as focused on being anti-white (including shunning and denouncing the white liberals who supported SNCC and the Black Panthers) as it was about being pro-black. By the time his February 1968 speech in support of Huey Newton was released as an album in October 1970, the two men were no longer speaking to each other, and Carmichael had moved to Africa.

Here is a timeline of key events in the relationship among Carmichael, Newton and the Black Panther Party:

Oct. 28, 1967. Huey Newton is involved in an altercation involving the death of Oakland police officer John Frey and the wounding of another police officer Herbert Haines. Newton is also seriously wounded.

Nov. 13, 1967. An Oakland grand jury indicts Newton on charges of first-degree murder and attempted murder.

Feb. 17, 1968 Huey Newton Birthday Rally. Speech by Carmichael as well as others detailed above. During the rally, Eldridge Cleaver

announced that SNNC's James Forman was now Black Panther Party Minister of Foreign Affairs, H. Rap Brown was Minister of Justice, and that Stokely Carmichael was Prime Minister of the party, joining existing Black Panther leaders Chairman Bobby Seale, Minister of Information Eldridge Cleaver, Chief of Staff David Hilliard and Minister of Defense Huey Newton.

June/July, 1968. David Hilliard travels from Oakland to New York to meet with James Forman to merge the two organizations. Forman accuses the Panthers of trying to take over the SNCC. Hilliard counters the accusation by pointing out that the Panthers want SNCC leaders to spearhead the consortium. After much discussion, it's apparent that SNCC no longer wants to move forward with the Panthers.

July 15, 1968. Newton's trial begins at Alameda County Courthouse in Oakland. More than six thousand protesters are outside in support of Newton.

July 27, 1968. At a New York press conference, SNCC leader Phil Hutchings announces that Carmichael has been expelled from SNCC. Among the reasons listed was that SNNC and Carmichael "were moving in different directions." SNCC also accused Carmichael of "engaging in a power struggle" with Forman which "threatened the existence of the organization." This was most likely a reference to the recent clash between Forman and Hilliard over the SNCC/Panthers alliance. Carmichael wanted to continue his relationship with the Panthers.

However, Newton was beginning to have his doubts about Carmichael. As Newton recalled later in his 1973 autobiography *Revolutionary Suicide*, "a lot of [Carmichael's] ideas had changed in a short time. The only thing that would get me out of jail, he said, was armed rebellion, culminating in a race war... Stokely warned that whites would destroy the movement, alienate Black people, and lessen our effectiveness in the community... I did not believe him when he was running these things down to me. We were not into a racist bag, I told him."

Sept. 28, 1968. Newton is sentenced to two to fifteen years on a manslaughter conviction. David Hilliard takes interim command of the Party.

BLACK FORUM

"Black Forum is a medium for the presentation of ideas and voices of the worldwide struggle of Black people to create a new era. Black Forum also serves to provide authentic materials for use in schools and colleges and for the home study of Black history and culture. Black Forum is a permanent record of the sound of struggle and the sound of the new era."

June/July 1969. In an open letter, Carmichael announces his resignation from the Black Panthers and condemns the alliance that exists between the Black Panthers and white radicals.

Earlier, in the spring of 1969, Carmichael had married popular South African vocalist Miriam Makeba and moved to Ghana, Africa. Reportedly, Makeba traveled to America in the summer of '69 to deliver Carmichael's Black Panther Party resignation, making sure a copy was given to the Party's Central Committee in Oakland.

Aug. 5, 1970. Newton wins an appeal and is released from prison. By the time of the October 1970 release of Carmichael's *Free Huey* album, Carmichael and Newton had mutually ended their association and Newton was out of prison, although to be fair, given the album's October release, it was probably well into the production stage by early August. Still, one wonders at what point did Carmichael give his blessing to the album, and why?

Regardless, I am glad this recorded document exists. Carmichael, no matter what one think of his radical views, was a compelling orator. The first several minutes of his speech put the genocidal acts of the white man against other races into a perspective that I've never heard so cogently summarized. Carmichael's forty-five-minute dissertation is packed with decisive moments, so it's hard to excerpt just a few lines, but these are representative:

Tonight we have to talk about several things. We're here to celebrate brother Huey P. Newton's birthday. We're not here to celebrate it as Huey Newton the individual, but as Huey Newton part and parcel of black people wherever we are on the world today...today. [Applause.] And so, in talking about brother Huey Newton tonight, we have to talk about the struggle of black people, not only in the United States, but in the world today, and how he becomes part and parcel of that struggle, how we move on so that our people will survive America.

We are talking about the survival of a race of people — that is all that is at stake. We are talking about the survival of black people — nothing else...nothing else...nothing else. [Applause.] And you must understand that. Now why is it necessary for us to talk about the survival of our people?

Many of us feel...many of our generation feel that they're getting ready to commit genocide against us. Now, many people say that's a horrible thing to say about anybody. But if it is a horrible thing to say, then we should do as brother Malcolm [X] says: we should examine history. The birth of this nation was conceived in the genocide of the red man ... [applause]...genocide of the red man...of the red man. In order for this country to come about, the honky had to completely exterminate the red man, and he did it! And he did it! He did it! [Applause.] And he did it where he does not even feel sorry, but he romanticizes it by putting it on television with Cowboy and Indians ... Cowboy and Indians.

Then the question we must ask ourselves is, if he's capable of doing it to the red man, can he also do it to us? Let us examine history some more. People say it is a horrible thing to say that white people would really think about committing genocide against black people. Let us check our history out. It is a fact that we built this country — nobody else. I'll explain that to you. When this country started, economically it was an agricultural country. The cash crop on the world market was cotton. We picked the cotton! [Applause.] We picked the cotton! We did. So it is we who built this country. It is we who have fought in the wars of this country. This country is becoming more and more technological, so that the need for black people is vastly disappearing. When the need for black people disappears, so will we, and he will consciously wipe us out. He will consciously wipe us out. Let us check World War II. He will not do it unto his own. Notice who he dropped an atomic bomb on: some helpless yellow people in Hiroshima. Some helpless yellow people in Hiroshima... [Applause]...in Hiroshima. If you do not think he's capable of committing genocide against us, check out what he's doing to our brothers in Vietnam! Check out what he's doing in Vietnam! [Applause.] We have to understand that we're talking about our survival and nothing else. Whether or not this beautiful race of people is going to survive on the earth, that's what we're talking about — nothing else [Applause]... nothing else. If you do not think he's capable of wiping us out, check out the white race: wherever they have gone, they have ruled, conquered, murdered, and plagued.

As Carmichael begins his closing thoughts, he focuses on the same ideologies that Newton had mentioned in *Revolutionary Suicide* as off-putting.

Now then finally before I sit down, let me say two things. I want to read a statement that brother Huey P. Newton wrote yesterday when I saw him in jail. You have to understand this statement. He says: "As the racist police escalate the war in our communities against black people, we reserve the right to self-defense and maximum retaliation." [Applause.] All of the things we spoke about tonight centered around brother Huey P. Newton, because all of the things we spoke about tonight exemplifies what he was trying to do. Now, we have to understand something. It is no need for us to go to jail today for what we say. They did that to brother Malcolm X: they just offed him for what he was saying. We have to progress as a race. Brother Huey may or may not have wiped out that

honky, but at least it shows a progression. At least we're not getting offed for it, we're trying to get offed for what we do. Understand this concept! [Applause.] Understand this concept! When they offed brother Malcolm, we did nothing. If they off brother Huey, we got to retaliate!...[Applause.]...we got to retaliate!...we got to retaliate!...we got to retaliate!...got to retaliate! Do you think that any other race of people will let them off somebody, and the rest of them sit down? Where, in God's name, would you find a race of people like that?...All we say: brother Huey will be set free, or else. [Applause.]

LANGSTON HUGHES AND MARGARET DANNER
WRITERS OF THE REVOLUTION (LP)

Langston Hughes and Margaret Danner's *Writers Of The Revolution* was the third Black Forum LP, released in October 1970 in conjunction with the Martin Luther King Jr. and Stokely Carmichael albums. Hughes was a legendary poet, novelist and playwright from the 1920s until his death in 1967. His work is particularly known for its astute and colorful portrayals of black life in America. Hughes was also engaged with jazz and the influence it had on his writing. His signature poem was 1921's "The Negro Speaks Of Rivers," but he was equally renowned for his novels, including *Not Without Laughter* (1930) and the 1934 short story collection, *The Ways Of White Folks.*

By some accounts, Hughes' literary reputation received a mixed response during the 1960s as younger black writers felt his earlier writings of black pride were out of date. Reportedly, Hughes understood the message of Black Power, but he believed some of the up-and-coming writers caught up in the movement expressed too much anger in their work.

Well worth investigation is *Weary Blues,* the 1958 collaboration between Hughes, who reads his "bittersweet poems of protest and joy" over the "surging cadence of jazz" by Charles Mingus and Leonard Feather. Mingus composed and played on half the performances, while Feather wrote and conducted the other half. Initially released on MGM Records and reissued later on Verve Records, Feather blurbs on the back of the Verve edition, "Some of Hughes' poems evoke the *zeitgeist* of another age, but many are as timely today as when other poems from this album were used at a Los Angeles poetry jazz recital by Jayne Cortez (Mrs. Ornette Coleman). She had selected them with no knowledge of this record." Decades later, Amiri Baraka explained that Langston Hughes was the first person he'd seen reading poetry set to music and it inspired him to do the same.

Margaret Danner's poems often focused on the vivid imagery of Africa. Her first collection, *Impressions of African Art Forms*, was published in 1960. In 1966, she traveled to Africa and, upon her return, she produced more volumes, including *Iron Lace* in 1968. She is best remembered for providing an artistic voice for those wanting to find purpose in the connection between Africa and black America. In 1976, she published her last major collection, *The Down Of A Thistle*, in which African culture continued to be a major theme; it included several poems paying homage to Hughes.

Although the album notes don't reference a date, it was apparently recorded in 1964. I've been unable to ascertain the events surrounding its origins — whether it was produced by Motown or if, like the King Jr. and Carmichael LPs, it was recorded by a third party and then licensed by Motown afterwards. Unlike those two albums, it's not recorded live in front of an audience. The forty-five-minute discourse has the air of a PBS radio broadcast: serious and occasionally playfully entertaining.

Hughes and Danner read their poems to each other and converse about them, offering personal and cultural insights

TOP: Langston Hughes spoke of different kinds of revolution: cultural as well as political, mental as well as physical. It seems appropriate that his face is superimposed on an image that could be an archeological dig or a scene from the war-torn Middle East. While Motown was best known for uplifting pop-soul music, having Langston Hughes on the label's roster signaled a change was in the air — this ain't Diana Ross, baby.

BOTTOM: This LP is better known (and easier to find) with its cover art of steel "chains" featured on the Verve Records reissue edition — here is the rare and original cover (issued by MGM Records) that features a weathered door that no longer opens, as it's partially boarded over; it suggests an abandoned house in Harlem. So many different colors and types of boards have been scavenged that, at a glance, they look like the spines of books, paying tribute to Langston Hughes rich literary legacy: "a dream montage" of various colors.

B 454L

GUESS WHO'S COMING HOME

Black Fighting Men Recorded Live in Vietnam

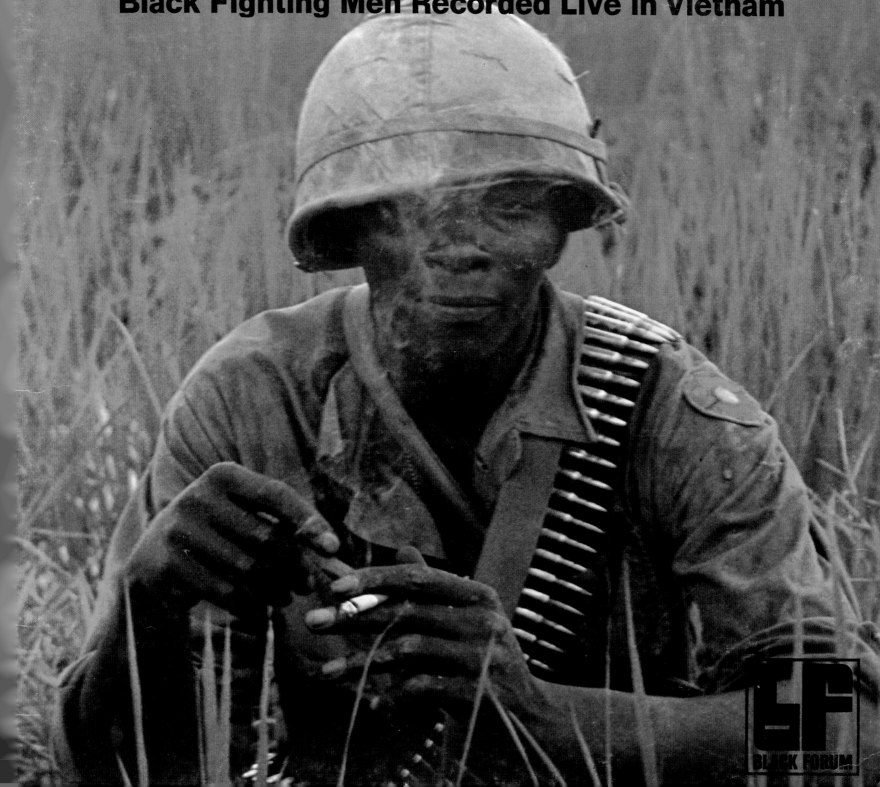

BLACK FORUM

along the way. The poems address slavery, African art and music, modern African-American culture, jazz and daily life in Harlem — Hughes, a long-time resident, notes that the only white people he sees in Harlem at night are policemen. Most of the poetry is gentle and reflective, so I was struck by a more aggressive piece Hughes read about junkies, heroin and atomic bombs — it reminded me of writings by Beat Generation icon Allen Ginsberg.

BLACK FIGHTING MEN
RECORDED LIVE IN VIETNAM
GUESS WHO'S COMING HOME (LP)

After releasing three albums in October 1970, Black Forum didn't release its fourth album until February 1972. One of the most exhilarating albums ever released by any label, *Guess Who's Coming Home* documented fifty minutes of anonymous interviews with black soldiers recorded on location in Vietnam. The GIs speak candidly with fellow African-American Wallace Terry, a *Time* magazine war correspondent who curated the album.

After a stint writing for the *Washington Post*, Terry went to Vietnam in 1967 where he became the deputy bureau chief for *Time* in Saigon and the first black war correspondent on permanent duty. Terry's 1967 cover story for *Time*, "The Negro in Vietnam," was acclaimed and he promised that he would one day write a book about the sacrifices of black Americans fighting in Vietnam.

The LP's notes mention a corresponding book, *The Bloods*, to be published by Viking Press in spring 1972, delayed until 1984 when Random House finally issued it under the title *Bloods: An Oral History of the Vietnam War by Black Veterans*. Obviously, the Viking deal had fallen through. As Terry's wife and collaborator Janice recalled, "getting his book published became an obsession, a shadowy thing that was like another heartbeat in our household… After thirteen years, we had sent the manuscript to a hundred publishers and received a hundred rejections." His tenacity paid off: it became a best-seller and was nominated for a Pulitzer. In 1986, Terry appeared in *The Bloods of 'Nam*, a PBS TV special in which he talked with black veterans about their experiences in the midst of the war and their often-disillusioning return home.

Describing the intensity of this album is difficult, but Julian Bond, a founding member of SNCC and its communications director from 1961 to 1966, does an able job with his liner notes:

> *I doubt that you will ever listen to a more remarkable and important record than this. It is the first recorded history of black fighting men in any war. And they rap about everything. Lyndon Johnson. Richard Nixon. Ho Chi Minh. Black Power. The Bloods (themselves). The Beasts (white folks). Black women. White women. Coming home. And going to the moon. These raps are so good and their message so heavy that this record may shatter your sensibilities. It may make you angry. It may frighten you. It may make you cry. It will make you laugh. And you will discover the war within the war. White against black on the battlefield. Racial slurs. Confederate flags. Cross burnings. Knifings. Fraggings.*

Less than a minute into the album, a brother mentions "Lazarus, Come Forth," a chapter from Eldridge Cleaver's *Soul On Ice*, and then says, "Come home bro, wake up, open up your motherfucking eyes and bleed, motherfucker, bleed." Terry then begins his narration: "Listen to the black soldiers in Vietnam… They are fed up with dying in a war they believe is the white man's war. They are coming home determined to get their share, even if it means turning to violence…" All of the interviewees are anonymous, allowing the soldiers to speak freely. Terry asks, "Has anybody messed with you for using the Black Power sign?"

> *Three brothers was walking up out of the mess hall and I gave 'em the sign. And so the sergeant, he was my sergeant of the first platoon, he was a beast, a thin motherfucker with a big head, he said, "What are you doing?"*
> *I said, "Well, I gave my brothers the sign."*

OPPOSITE: This black soldier is chilling with a cigarette, his ammo belt and a blissfully stoned look of calm on his face; but one should keep in mind he'll be coming home armed and ready. Many of the soldiers interviewed on this LP express their admiration for the Black Panther Party and how they were fighting for a freedom in Vietnam that they didn't have in the United States.

He said, "The next time I catch you doing that I'm gonna take you right up to CID's office with me."

I said, "For what?"

He said, "You know what it means?"

I said, "What?"

He said, "Black Power."

I said, "No shit."

He said, "I'll run you straight up to CID."

I said, "Well, I'll go up there with you right now motherfucker because that's the way I greet my brothers every goddamn day, just like you big head motherfuckers put up that peace sign."

Almost as if they'd heard Stokely Carmichael's *Free Huey* album, many soldiers on the record echo Carmichael's comments that the white man won't destroy his own race, only other races — referencing how the atomic bomb was dropped on Japan and not Germany. Other soldiers ask why they are fighting on behalf of Americans, when in America the black man doesn't have the same freedom as whites. The Black Panthers are mentioned several times, always in a positive and supportive light, with many soldiers saying that they look forward to hooking up: "[the Black Panthers are] the best thing the Negro got going for them, I'm gonna join 'em by the time I get back…"

Another soldier:

To me the Black Panthers is what we need as an equalizer, the beast has got his KKK, plus he's got his good points too, as far as the Black Panthers is concerned it gives them something to fear, just like they've given us something to fear all these many years. When the Panthers first started from what I understand it was to keep the beast from fucking over the people when they demonstrate and the honkies made the Panthers as violent as they are and I figure anytime you got the fucking KKK who been kicking our people's asses and burning crosses, fucking over our people, then you start fighting force with force and then motherfuckers start hollering, they got to be coming back this inspired and a whole bunch of shit like that. I think the Panthers, I would join them and I'd help kill all these honky motherfuckers. Because do onto him before he do onto you.

OSSIE DAVIS AND BILL COSBY
ADDRESS THE CONGRESSIONAL BLACK CAUCUS (LP)

Just two months after releasing *Guess Who's Coming Home*, Black Forum quickly followed up with three more albums. Their fifth title featured actor Ossie Davis and comedian Bill Cosby addressing the inaugural banquet of the Congressional Black Caucus on June 18, 1971, at the Sheraton Park Hotel. The Caucus was founded in February of that year by black members of the House of Representatives, and was helmed by Shirley Chisholm of New York, Louis Stokes of Ohio and William L. Clay of Missouri.

Chisholm has an illustrious history. She became the first black woman elected to Congress in 1968 and on Jan. 23, 1972, she became the first major party African-American candidate for President of the United States. She won twenty-eight delegates during the primaries and gained many more at the '72 Democratic National Convention, in which she received one hundred and fifty-two first-ballot votes.

Louis Stokes was a Democrat who served in the House from 1968 to 1999; his brother Carl B. Stokes was the first black mayor of a major city, overseeing Cleveland from 1968 to 1971. During his mayoral term, Carl B. Stokes recorded an album of poetry and music that I'll be discussing later. (As a nod to offbeat trivia, I must mention that funk superstar Rick James was a cousin to the Stokes brothers.)

William L. Clay served in the House for thirty-two years, representing the St. Louis area from 1968 to 2000. Clay made news in 2007, when, as co-founder of the Congressional Black Caucus, he sent a memo to current members stating it was "absolutely critical" that membership remain "exclusively African-American" when white congressman Steve Cohen from Tennessee attempted to join. Although the Caucus bylaws do not mention race as part of membership, since its inception in

OPPOSITE: This image of the flag superimposed with a child's face brings together themes of political action and the future of America's youth. A pair of aged hands rests on the child's shoulders to suggest the responsibility of the black community in raising and supporting its own.

1971, all members have been black. Clay also issued the following statement to the public:

> *Quite simply, Representative Cohen will have to accept what the rest of the country will have to accept, there has been an unofficial Congressional White Caucus for over 200 years, and now it's our turn to say who can join "the club." He does not, and cannot, meet the membership criteria, unless he can change his skin color. Primarily, we are concerned with the needs and concerns of the black population, and we will not allow white America to infringe on those objectives.*

Since its beginning in 1971, the Caucus has grown from thirteen to forty-three members as of 2011. More than half of the forty-five-minute album is devoted to Ossie Davis' motivational address discussing the African-American gathering in historical terms:

> *We might remind ourselves that we are at a spot where the Irish were some 100 years ago. The Irish of course had the distinction of being the niggers of their day. And they responded rather angrily, and violently to that classification. I don't know if you were around in 1863, but in July of that year, the Irish pitched a dinger in New York, which cost the lives of one thousand people.*
>
> *Now LIFE Magazine has given us the credit of having created the biggest riot in the United States. But they forgot that in 1863, there was a riot in New York where over one thousand people died. At that time in the minds of Virginia, the Irish were so embittered by the treatment they received, that they blackened their faces and put on women's clothes and they went into the mines and they blew them up and they shot people and they hung people, they did all kinds of bad things.*
>
> *The Molly Maguires wrote a quite considerable chapter in our history and not all of it was nonviolent. But the Irish had to learn an additional factor, before they were able to walk into the promised land and that factor was that it wasn't enough just to be violent. The Irish had to have a plan. And they had their plan and they got it together in a little town called Boston.*

> *They got their thing together, they planned it out and they said to themselves, now look there's a lot of us Irish men here in Boston. A whole lot of us. And we've been petitioning the white Anglo-Saxon protestants for years about better schools and better houses and jobs and the drug problem and the drinking problem and what we are gonna do for the future? And we don't get no response from them. So why don't we Irishmen get together and put our votes in one place and see what we can do if we take power at city hall and do you know that's exactly what they did? They put their votes together according to the plan and came up with one man, the first Irish catholic mayor of Boston whose name was John Fitzgerald. And you can see where I'm heading 'cause that's the first two names of the first Irish Catholic president, who was his grandson, John Fitzgerald Kennedy. Now if it happened to the Irish, who certainly don't represent 25 million people, why can't it happen to us?*

The reminder of the second side is given over to Bill Cosby, who uses racial humor to make a point:

> *[…] it's like church, because I feel while you're here you'll say "right on" and two hours later after you're outside it will be "right off," so I say "Good evening niggers" because that's what a lot of you are gonna be when you leave this room. And I mean the white people sitting there too. Niggers come in all colors. If you think I'm lying ask Martha Mitchell tomorrow morning.* [The room roars with applause and laughter, at the thought of the wife of Nixon's Attorney General, John Mitchell].

Cosby continues to provoke the audience:

> *Ray Charles can't make the money he used to make because Joe Cocker's doing it. Can't blame white people. It's because who are you looking at? Who are you paying your money to support and see? So when you leave here, depends on just how long it's gonna take you before you go back to being a nigger. I'll be here next year, I'll be here for every caucus that ever exists, even if they only have one.*

BLACK SPIRITS: FESTIVAL OF NEW BLACK POETS IN AMERICA (LP)

The next LP in the Black Forum series was a collection of poets recorded live at Harlem's Apollo Theatre during a three-day festival. Although no dates can be found, it's safe to assume the gathering took place during 1971, given the April 1972 release date.

Amiri Baraka gets top billing on the LP cover, introduces the event at the beginning of the album and performs a poem of his own at the end. The Original Last Poets (not to be confused with the Last Poets — more on that later) get second billing, with the remaining poets listed randomly at the bottom of the album jacket: Johari Amini, Clarence Major, Norman Jordan, Kali, Jackie Earley, Aski Mohammad Touré, David Henderson, Stanley Crouch, Larry Neal and Amus Moore. *Black Spirits* was produced by Woodie King, whose résumé includes productions of Amiri Baraka's, Ed Bullins' and J.E. Franklin's plays, a cameo in the Al Pacino movie *Serpico*, and a stint as a writer for the 1970s TV sitcom *Sanford and Son*. He also co-produced the 1971 film *Right On!*, featuring The Original Last Poets.

Many of the writers featured on *Black Spirits* were instrumental in establishing the Black Arts Movement (BAM), which revolutionized African-American literature during the 1960s and 1970s. Poet and playwright Larry Neal was one of the Black Arts Movement's most influential participants and, in a 1968 essay, he aptly declared BAM the "aesthetic and spiritual sister of the Black Power concept."

BLACK SPIRITS CONTRIBUTORS

AMIRI BARAKA: Amiri Baraka has been inspiring and pissing off blacks and whites from the 1950s to the present day. His work as a poet, novelist, journalist, teacher and political activist (amongst other things) has made him a pivotal figure in

ABOVE: A chained, ready-to-lash pose (you can see the strains of the black man's back) with a beacon of light where his hands are tied together. "The history of America is written on the backs of blacks," in the scars of the whip and in the work they did across the nation on plantations, in factories and railroads.

several different eras of social, cultural and artistic movements. He first ventured into the literary world using his birth name LeRoi Jones (he changed it to Amiri Baraka in 1968). As Jones, he founded Totem Press in 1958, giving Beat Generation writers Jack Kerouac and Allen Ginsberg some of their first exposure.

In 1963, he wrote *Blues People: Negro Music In White America*, still revered today as an indispensable assessment of the then-burgeoning Free Jazz movement. Centered on the omnipresent conflicts between blacks and whites, his 1964 play *Dutchman* remains a polarizing classic. *The New York Times* wrote, "*Dutchman* is designed to shock, its basic idea, its language and its murderous rage." Publicly critical and disparaging of the white race, Jones/Baraka is often accused of the hate mongering that he despises in the characters portrayed in the *Dutchman* script. After the assassination of Malcolm X in February 1965, he distanced himself from the group with which he'd gotten his start: the (mostly) white Beat Generation of writers. Eventually he left his white wife, Hettie Jones, and moved to Harlem to fully immerse himself in black culture — though initially dazzled by the Black Panthers, he fell under the influence of Ron Karenga (and would eventually become guilty-by-association in some Panthers' eyes), considering himself a Black Nationalist. The name change to Amiri Baraka was to follow.

THE ORIGINAL LAST POETS: The Original Last Poets consisted of Gylan Kain, Felipe Luciano and David Nelson. While none appear on the 1970 eponymous *Last Poets* album, all three are key to the Last Poets' legacy. Kain and Nelson were certainly "original" Last Poets, as they were founding members, along with Abiodun Oyewole (who does appear on the 1970 album).

Besides early membership in the Last Poets, Felipe Luciano was a co-founder of the New York City chapter of The Young Lords. Although founded in Chicago in the late '60s, The Young Lords quickly spread to New York and other major American cities, becoming a symbol of Puerto Rican ascendancy similar to that of the Panthers in the urban black communities. At one point before his appalling murder in 1970, Fred Hampton, head of the Chicago Panthers, formed an alliance with the Puerto Rican Young Lords and the Patriot Party (consisting of impoverished Chicago whites). Hampton announced this multi-racial banding

as "a Rainbow Coalition," years before Jesse Jackson co-opted the term for his own political means.

Somewhere between the birth of the Last Poets and the recording of their debut album, Kain, Luciano and Nelson left the group, probably around January 1969. About a month later, Umar Bin Hassin arrived in New York from Ohio to join the ever-changing outfit and was informed of their exit by the remaining members. The departing Kain, Luciano and Nelson teamed up with producer Willie King and, billed as The Original Last Poets, released a movie and soundtrack recording titled *Right On!* in 1971.

Although much less heralded than the Last Poets' debut LP, the "original" Last Poets' *Right On!* on Juggernaut Records is an equally inspiring opus. The album's cover appears much like any soundtrack, with producer and director movie credits, as well as a Cannes Film Festival mention. The reader is informed that this music is "An expedition into inner self for the listener," along with the first-ever parental advisory warning on an album: "For mature audiences only." The back includes the bold statement "A Woodstock in Poetry," followed by a testimonial from Amiri Baraka: "*Right On!* is the beginning of new movies, where Black and 3rd World art is going. Poetry/image/music; this is the new electric drama form. Revolutionary revelation. All future movies will begin with this."

Luckily, the LP soundtrack isn't composed of recordings from the film, as the songs in the movie are shot in various outdoor settings while the band members jump about — resulting in substandard performances. Only one song is taken from the actual movie, while the rest were recorded under more controlled conditions at a show at New York's Cubiculo Theatre. Essentially this is a live album (using the film release as a cross-promotional tie-in) featuring Nelson, Luciano and Kain, accompanied by Carlos Cuebas on congas. Decades after they performed this concert, it still makes for intense listening. David Nelson's "Die Nigga!!!" engages in morbid humor:

Niggas love dying. Build big funeral homes so dead Nigga undertakers get rich burying dying Niggas with heartfelt shout-outs to those who've fallen on the battlefield. Niggas watch other Niggas die; they love it. Die Nigga. Niggas watched Emmett Till die, Niggas watched Mack Parker

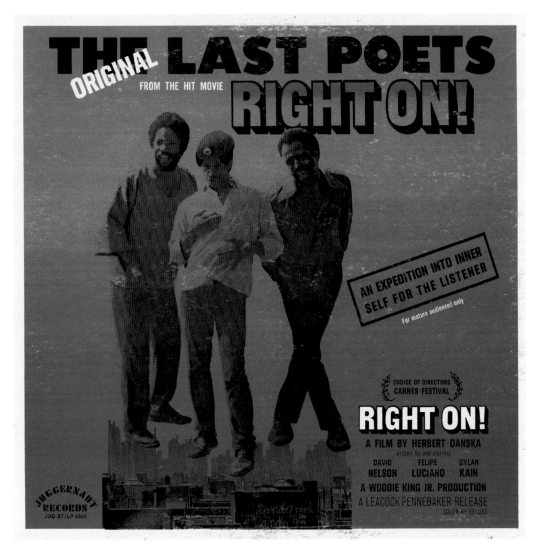

THE ORIGINAL LAST POETS

FROM THE HIT MOVIE

RIGHT ON!

AN EXPEDITION INTO INNER SELF FOR THE LISTENER

For mature audiences only

CHOICE OF DIRECTORS
CANNES FESTIVAL

RIGHT ON!

A FILM BY HERBERT DANSKA

written by and starring

DAVID   FELIPE   GYLAN
NELSON   LUCIANO   KAIN

A WOODIE KING JR. PRODUCTION

A LEACOCK PENNEBAKER RELEASE
COLOR BY DELUXE

JUGGERNAUT
RECORDS
JUG-ST/LP 8802

JOHARI AMINI: Johari Amini published her first works under her birth name Jewel C. Latimore. She was a poet and essayist who, through her numerous collections, *Images in Black* (1967), *Black Essence* (1968), *A Folk Fable* (1969), *Let's Go Somewhere* (1970) and *A Hip Tale in Earth Style* (1972), addressed the concerns of black females in society.

CLARENCE MAJOR: Clarence Major is a poet and novelist. His books include 1969's *All-Night Visitors* and 1979's *Emergency Exit*. He also compiled several anthologies of Black Arts Movement writing: 1969's *The New Black Poetry* and 1974's *The Dark and Feeling: Black American Writers and Their Work*. In 1971, he also edited *Black Slang: A Dictionary Of Afro-American Talk*.

DAVID HENDERSON: In 1962, David Henderson co-founded the Society of Umbra, which held writing sessions and gave public readings. In 1963, the collective began publishing *Umbra* magazine (with Henderson as editor), which became an outlet for emerging black writers (including some on the *Black Spirits* album). The first issue included SNCC's Julian Bond and a pre-fame Alice Walker. Over time, *Umbra* introduced the poet Nikki Giovanni, Ishmael Reed and future Miles Davis biographer Quincy Troupe. Henderson was also involved with one of the '60s premier counterculture newspapers: *The East Village Other*.

die, Niggas watched Medgar Evers die, Niggas watched James Chaney die, Niggas watched Bobby Hutton die. Die Niggas! So Black folks can take over!

The verses to all of Luciano, Nelson and Kain's poems are included inside the gatefold sleeve — and for those speculating about what the first Last Poets LP may have sounded like with Kain in that lineup, it's of note that he only dated his poetry on *Right On!*. The earliest was written in April 1968 and the latest a year later, so any of Kain's material could've appeared on the Last Poets' 1970 debut.

ABOVE: The gaudy colorization of what was obviously a black-and-white design recalls vintage "boxing posters," while the typography suggests Blaxploitation. However, the content of the recordings is anything but — as Amiri Baraka proclaimed, "Poetry/image/music; this is the new electric drama form."

He has appeared on Sun Ra recordings, and performed poetry on saxophonist Ornette Coleman's 1971 *Science Fiction* album.

NORMAN JORDAN: Norman Jordan is known as "West Virginia's most published African-American poet." He wrote a notable essay in 1969 for Amiri Baraka's journal *The Cricket*, in which Jordan suggested a definition of "Positive Black Music" (at least in the genre of free jazz). He formulated, "Black music, as well as constructive art, *must be free*, and at the same time it *must contain order*, a positive harmony on the physical, mental, and spiritual level."

ASKIA TOURÉ: Although listed as Aski Mohammad Touré on the *Black Spirits* album, he's better known as Askia Touré — a pioneer of the Black Arts Movement and the teaching of Africana Studies. Also an activist, he served with the Student Nonviolent Coordinating Committee's Atlanta Project and is a coauthor of SNCC's "The Basis Of Black Power: SNCC Position Paper" published in *The New York Times* on Aug. 5, 1966. It helped sway the Civil Rights movement toward the Black Power revolution. The SNCC declaration stated in part:

> *In an attempt to find a solution to our dilemma, we propose that our organization (SNCC) should be black-staffed, black-controlled, and black-financed. We do not want to fall into a similar dilemma that other Civil Rights organizations have fallen into. If we continue to rely upon white financial support we will find ourselves entwined in the tentacles of the white power complex that controls this country. It is also important that a black organization (devoid of cultism) be projected to our people so that it can be demonstrated that such organizations are viable.*

STANLEY CROUCH: Stanley Crouch is an outspoken cultural critic known for his essays on jazz, the dynamics of relationships between blacks and whites and the occasional novel. Most controversial are his commentaries on fellow African-Americans, including his denouncement of the separatist politics of Malcolm X and his ridicule of Toni Morrison's novels as "maudlin ideological commercials." Crouch's essays in the 1980s (continuing to this day) speak disparagingly of Miles Davis,

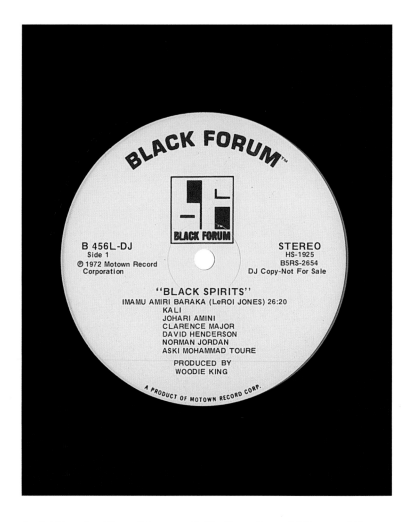

Amiri Baraka, Huey Newton, Spike Lee, Cornel West and Tupac Shakur. Whatever leftie thinking got Crouch invited to the poetry reading documented on *Black Spirits* changed in subsequent decades. Crouch has been known to punch journalists who've written negative reviews of his work. In his previous incarnation, Crouch recorded a prodigious spoken word album, *Ain't No Ambulances For No Nigguhs Tonight*, in 1969.

JACKIE EARLEY: Jackie Earley began performing theater and poetry during the Civil Rights movement, and remains active today. As a choreographer and dancer, she has performed with the Free Southern Theater, the National Black Theater and Karamu Theater. She continues to do poetry readings and has been published in various magazines and anthologies.

publications. In 1968, Neal and Baraka edited *Black Fire: An Anthology of Afro-American Writing*, a major tome for the Black Arts Movement. Still considered a seminal anthology, *Black Fire* featured decisive social critics, poets and playwrights including James Boggs, Ed Bullins, Sonia Sanchez, Stokely Carmichael, John Henrik Clarke, Harold Cruse, Henry Dumas and Hoyt Fuller.

KALI: The only poet appearing on *Black Spirits* that I couldn't find any detailed information about is named Kali, but the little I did find out about her is quite exceptional. At the time of the album's release (1972), Kali was a fifth-grade student at a public school in Manhattan! And even more impressive is that she had authored *Poems Of Kali* (under the name Kali Grosvenor), published by Doubleday in 1970.

There was a book simultaneously published by Random House (in conjunction with the Black Forum album) using the same title: *Black Spirits: A Festival Of New Black Poets In America*. Edited by Woodie King, who'd produced the poetry festival and accompanying album, the two-hundred-and-fifty-two-page book contains the fourteen poets who appear on the album and sixteen others, including Nikki Giovanni, Quincy Troupe and Ed Bullins. Presumably some of the others included in the book appeared at the Apollo Theatre as well, since the festival from which the album was culled lasted three days. Both the book and album are key artifacts of the Black Arts Movement.

IMAMU AMIRI BARAKA
IT'S NATION TIME (LP)

AMUS MOR: Despite being listed on *Black Spirits* as Amus Moore, the Chicago native is actually known as Amus Mor. He has also published under the name David Moore and can be heard reciting poetry on pianist Muhal Richard Abrams' 1967 landmark jazz album *Levels And Degrees of Light*.

LARRY NEAL: Larry Neal worked with Amiri Baraka in the mid-'60s to open the Black Arts Repertory Theatre School (BARTS) in New York. Neal's writings — 1964's "The Negro in the Theatre," 1965's "Cultural Front" and "The Black Arts Movement" in 1968 — were a guiding influence in defining the role of the arts in the Black Power era. His essays and poems nurtured the movement in *Liberator*, *Black Theatre*, *Negro Digest*, *Black World* and similar

Subtitled "African Visionary Music," Amiri Baraka's *It's Nation Time* was the seventh Black Forum LP, released alongside *Congressional Black Caucus* and *Black Spirits* in April 1972. *It's Nation Time* and Elaine Brown's record in 1973 are the only two albums of singing, songwriting and music released on Black Forum.

There are several sets of musicians on *It's Nation Time*, which Baraka divides into categories. On the songs featuring modern jazz veterans, he calls them the "New Music Group," which includes alto sax player Gary Bartz. Bartz' own visionary solo work along with his playing with Max Roach, Art Blakey and Miles Davis (during the trumpeter's electrifying *Live Evil* period).

Like Bartz, keyboardist Lonnie Liston Smith served time with Art Blakey's Jazz Messengers and Max Roach's ensemble before being called in July 1972 (a few months after the release of *It's Nation Time*) to play on Miles Davis' *On The Corner* sessions — a funky avant-garde electronic experiment that was greatly misunderstood upon its release. Smith also appears on Pharoah Sanders' illustrious "The Creator Has A Master Plan," recorded in February 1969 with vocalist Leon Thomas. In 1973, Smith stepped into his own with a series of solo albums on the Flying Dutchman label, starting with *Astral Traveling* and continuing with *Cosmic Funk* and *Expansions*.

Reggie Workman spent 1961 as part of John Coltrane's ensemble. After the bassist left Coltrane's employ, he found himself (like Bartz and Smith) serving his required time with Art Blakey's Jazz Messengers before playing with Yusef Lateef and Thelonious Monk. Along with Lonnie Liston Smith, he appears on Pharoah Sanders *Karma* album.

Also playing bass on *It's Nation Time* is Herbie Lewis, who appeared on early '60s albums by soul-jazz pianist Les McCann. By the latter part of the decade he was cutting tracks for McCoy Tyner and served with vibraphonist Bobby Hutcherson, with whom he recorded the 1969 Blue Note album *Now*, featuring Gene McDaniels on vocals. *Now* includes three songs co-written and sung by McDaniels, but those seeking the politically charged material that McDaniels would record five months later for his own *Outlaw* album will be disappointed. Hutcherson's *Now* is progressive — not militant — jazz, except for the closing song "Black Heroes" (written by saxophonist Harold Land). The song begins with McDaniels singing, "Folks all over the world are talking about freedom right now" then calling out for "Freedom Now!" with the names "Malcolm" and "Martin" interjected often.

Drummer Idris Muhammad played on various Blue Note Records grooves during the 1960s, including albums by Lou Donaldson, Reuben Wilson and the perennial crate-digger/DJ favorite Grant Green. For other songs on *It's Nation Time*, Baraka employed an entirely different set of musicians. In the notes, he alternates between calling them "Matchmakers 1619" and the "R&B Group." This group includes saxophonists James Wheeler and Phil Eley, trumpeter Jerome McGoggle, Khalid Ablal Shahid on electric piano, guitarist Ogden Lee Jr., bassist Sam Jordan

B 457 - L

IT'S NAT

African Visionary Music

and Lloyd Porter on drums. Augmenting the instrumentalists is singer Gwendolyn Guthrie.

The other musician categories listed on the album are "African Drummers," which consist of Akbar Bey, Pat Carrow, Charles Jones and Joe Armstrong, and seven female and two male vocalists named "The Spirit House Movers." These four groups are used separately and in various combinations throughout, with Baraka singing, chanting and rapping about the themes addressed on the back cover of *It's Nation Time*. The jacket copy reads:

> *These are projections of (image/sound) which represent the new life-sense of African men and women here in the west, it is the African man's vision/version of music. These words as emotion/feeling contact represent actual ways to live, the vision itself a version of life & how best we Africans live it ... This is the terrible terrible African badness in us, coming out us growin sweet & black everywhere!*

The album includes a glossary of terms, most of them in Swahili, including a doctrine of new nationalism (Kawaida) credited to Maulana [Ron] Karenga. There's also a definition of a Pan-African Nationalist, which summarizes the album's overall message as "a person who believes that Black people all over the world make up an African nation, that is, a group who has a common past, common present and hopefully, a common future based on a common way of life."

The album's lyrics are all written by Baraka and several pieces are new, written for the project with a few bits drawn from his vast published catalog. The books that Baraka drew from (published between 1968 and 1970) are *Tales, In Our Terribleness* and a volume titled the same as the LP *It's Nation Time*. A couple of others originally appeared in the 1971 *Spirit Reach* book.

James Mtume wrote some of the music (oddly, he doesn't play on the album). In 1972, he was Miles Davis' percussionist, appearing on Davis' most "out" albums, including *Big Fun*,

LEFT: The cover illustrates the notion that "African visionary music" must be rooted in history, culture and mythology. The people are headed toward the pyramid and the key of life, an Ankh (an ancient Egyptian hieroglyphic character which means eternal life).

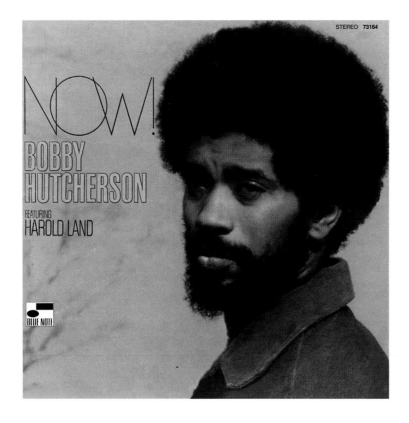

STEREO 73164

Get Up With It, Dark Magus, Agharta and *Pangea*. Despite Davis' pro-black, anti-white stance, he never aligned himself with any nationalist organization.

Among the highlights of the record, which blends soulful grooves, free jazz and tribal rhythms with singing, poetry and narratives, there's a weird and wacked-out version of The Supremes' "Come See About Me." Baraka takes that melody and phrase (repeated over and over), and uses it as a backing track for his own spiritual testimony. But the absolute triumph of the LP occurs in the middle of Side Two: "Who Will Survive America."

The song starts with question and answer from Baraka: "Who will survive America? Few Americans, very few Negroes and no crackers at all." A pulsating bass guitar underlines his statement

ABOVE: Remarkably, Gene McDaniels, who sings on the entire record, doesn't warrant a front-cover mention. During this era, Blue Note artists such as Eddie Gale and Horace Silver were incorporating vocalists with social political lyrics into the mix. Now it was Bobby Hutcherson's turn, and he was flaunting a righteous afro as well!

as he repeats, "Who will survive America? Few Americans, very few Negroes and no crackers at all." Baraka's voice drops out, while a female choir chimes in and repeats continuously: "Who will survive America? Very few Negroes, no crackers at all."

The whole ensemble kicks in, grooving and roaring like James Brown's backing band on stage at the Apollo, while the women's chorus keeps repeating their lines throughout the entire song: "Who will survive America? Very few Negroes, no crackers at all." Baraka dives back in, rapping like a mofo:

Will you survive America with your 20 cent habit? Your fo' bag jones, will you survive in the heat and fire of actual change? I doubt it.

Will you survive woman or will yo nylon wig catch a fire at midnight? And light up Stirling Street and your ass prints on the pavement. Grease melting in this brother's eyes, his profile shot up by a Simba, thinking who was coming around the corner was really Tony Curtis, and not a misguided brother, got his mind hanging out with Italians. Who will survive America? The Black future will. You can't, with the fat stomach between your ears, scraping nickels out the inside of nigger daydreams. Few Americans, very few Negroes and maybe no red Negroes at all. Who will survive America? Who will survive America?

The song continues to build in intensity, the women's chorus gaining enthusiasm, the band grooving, while Baraka becomes even more impassioned:

The stiff backed chalk lady Baptist in blue lace, if she shrinks from blackness in front of the church, following the wedding of the yellow robots will not survive, she is old anyway, and they're moving her church in the wind.

Baraka begins his own gospel-style call and response, calling out the question and answering it himself:

Old people? No! Christians? No! First Negroes to be invisible to the truth. 1944. Minnesota. No! No! Nothing of that will be anywhere. It will be burned clean; it might sink and steam up the sea. America might.

Baraka's vocals keep riffing along, shouting passionately over the chorus and band.

And no Americans, very few Negroes will get out and no crackers at all, no crackers at all, no crackers at all....But the black man will survive America. His survival will mean the death of America. Survive black man, survive black man, survive black man, (black woman too), survive black man, survive black man, black woman too, let us all survive, let us all survive .... We wish each other good luck.

It's easily one of the most memorable songs and strapping performances that I've uncovered researching this book. It ranks up there with Sly Stone's "I Want To Take You Higher" for balls-to-the-wall zeal.

In the 2003 Summer-Fall issue of the *African-American Review*, Baraka told Kalamu ya Salaam that while recording *It's Nation Time*, "We were obviously digging Martha and the Vandellas and digging Smokey, just like we were digging Albert Ayler, Ornette Coleman and Trane. To us it was just different voices in the same

family, different voices in the same community. The screaming and hollering in James Brown and the screaming and hollering in Albert Ayler was the same scream and hollering."

Reading Baraka's description, I realized that I could never find my own words to properly describe this ultimate mutation of free jazz, R&B and poetry. Baraka elaborates better than I can: "[On *It's Nation Time*] we had the chance to get the shit, plan it, go over it, and then go into the studio and get down with it. That's what I wanted to do. I wanted to go from rhythm and blues, to new music, to Africa at will."

ELAINE BROWN ELAINE BROWN (LP)
ELAINE BROWN "NO TIME" / "UNTIL WE'RE FREE" (7-INCH SINGLE)

Elaine Brown's self-titled album was Black Forum's eighth release (available in stores either in March or April, 1973 — there is conflicting data.) Brown joined the Southern California chapter of the Black Panther Party in April 1968. Her winning

men and women who had been working hard to establish the Panthers in the home turf of Ron Karenga and US. By the release of her 1969 debut album *Seize The Time* on the Vault label, Brown was Deputy Minister of Information for the Southern California chapter.

In 1971, Brown moved from L.A. to Oakland to become the editor of the Panther newspaper. With David Hilliard serving prison time, Eldridge Cleaver banished to Africa and Bobby Seale immersed in various legal battles, Brown became a crucial member of Newton's inner circle. She accompanied him on an historic journey to Communist China, meeting their government officials several months before Richard Nixon's much-heralded 1972 visit.

Eventually, as the original leaders began to leave the Party under various circumstances, Brown became the first and only woman to lead the Black Panther Party when Newton deemed her Chairman in August 1974. This was not an honorary title or a position in name only. Brown was calling the shots while Newton spent the next three years exiled in Cuba, avoiding the wrath of the courts over his accused involvement in the death of a young Oakland prostitute. Brown dutifully ran her post until Newton's return in 1977, upon which he was acquitted of the charges. At that point, Brown decided her tenure with the Party had run its course.

combination of street smarts, ass-kicking tenacity, political integrity and intellect made her a force to be reckoned with from day one. She quickly assimilated herself in the organization and became a key member of the Los Angeles branch. She joined Ericka and John Huggins, Bunchy Carter and other distinguished

During Brown's rise to power, another young woman was making waves over at Motown's executive offices. Suzanne de Passe was raised in Harlem, and by 1967 the 19-year-old hipster was involved in booking artists for the Cheetah, a fashionable New York club. De Passe, a big Supremes fan, began turning up at Diana Ross and Co. shows, catching the attention of Berry Gordy, whom she engaged in conversation. Gordy was enamored with this brash young woman who didn't hold back her opinions on how Motown's management needed a severe overhaul.

LEFT: In this portrait by Emory Douglas, Elaine Brown's face shows a vulnerability and sadness illustrative of the songs therein, including a tribute to Jonathan Jackson, George's brother. Although released as *Elaine Brown*, the album was originally titled *Until We're Free*. Huey Newton's inner sleeve notes refer to the album as *Until We're Free* — "the statement of a revolutionary in words and song."

Gordy brought de Passe to Detroit, where she wasted no time kicking ass and taking names. Although she initially alienated some of Motown's old guard, she brought a sense of youth to the aging company. She convinced the art department that the days of black artists with processed hair were over, and that The Temptations and others should appear on album covers with naturals (afros). Despite the rumors, de Passe never slept with Berry Gordy (he was too busy getting Diana Ross into the sack). De Passe, like Brown, was loyal, bright, confident and competent. Her brilliance and tenacity paid off when Gordy awarded her the presidency of Motown some fourteen years after she first walked into his office.

After their trip to China, Newton suggested that Brown record a follow-up to *Seize The Time*. Newton felt strongly that a black-owned company should release this new album, encouraging her to contact Motown. Ed Michel, a white supporter of the Black Panther Party who had produced recordings of the Chambers Brothers for Vault Records, knew Brown and helped arrange a meeting with Motown. By now, de Passe was Creative Director and based in Los Angeles, along with much of Motown's former Detroit staff. Despite the difference in their lifestyles — de Passe, the upwardly mobile record executive and Brown, the political activist and revolutionary — the two women found common ground. According to Brown's account in *A Taste Of Power*, that first meeting lasted five hours, during which de Passe expressed her admiration for *Seize The Time*. De Passe had received the album from Diana Ross' brother T-Boy, who loved Brown's songs.

As she had done on *Seize The Time*, Brown worked closely with arranger Horace Tapscott on embellishing the songs. Also on board from *Seize The Time* was illustrator (and Black Panther Minister of Culture) Emory Douglas, providing his distinctive cover art.

During the 1940s, Los Angeles-based Horace Tapscott studied piano and trombone. In the late 1950s, he joined vibraphonist Lionel Hampton's band as a trombonist, which brought him to New York, where he encountered the experimental style of John Coltrane. Tapscott found New York cold and expensive and soon returned to Los Angeles. Switching back to piano, he immersed himself in L.A.'s avant-garde jazz world, which was taking shape at the beginning of the 1960s. Tapscott became as well known for his outspoken opinions on race relations, politics and social ethics as he was for his maverick keyboard playing.

Based in Watts, Tapscott was determined to create an infrastructure for music within the Los Angeles ghetto community, and in 1961 he established the Pan-Afrikan People's Arkestra, a large ensemble of jazz musicians that he continued to lead until his death in 1999. The Arkestra was part of a collective that he called UGMAA (Union of God's Musicians and Artists Ascension), aimed at channeling artistic activity in the community into a sense of self-awareness and self-respect. Along with the Watts Writers Workshop, which birthed the proto-rap group The Watts Prophets, Tapscott's organizations were a cornerstone of Black Power in the Watts section of Los Angeles.

Chosen as the promotional single, "Until We're Free" has a radio-friendly sound of horns, handclaps and background singers. Brown told me in June 2010 that she didn't like the "jazzed-up" production of that song by co-producer Freddie Perren, who was doing a lot of disco at that time. By "jazzed-up," she obviously didn't mean *jazz*, but was referring to the glossy sheen he painted over her composition.

Although the album was released as *Elaine Brown*, it was originally called *Until We're Free* (one of the strongest compositions on the album). In fact, removing the title must have been a last-minute decision on Motown's part, as Brown still references the album today as *Until We're Free*. The March 24, 1973 issue of the *Black Panther Party Newspaper* provides further proof that Brown's album *Until We're Free* had been released two days earlier.

"Until We're Free" and "No Time" sum up what this album is all about, Elaine told the Black Panther Intercommunal News Service (BPINS) last week. "These two titles are our statement of the condition of our people at this moment in history," she explained. "If we're to survive, we have 'no time' to engage in so many of the human, personal, lovely things because of the horrors of today's reality, of so much of today's world. Not 'until we're free' can we know and experience freely all the beauty that surrounds us."

Elaine refuses to assert personal authorship of the songs. "I'm simply a chronicler, a notetaker and interpreter," she insists. "These songs were actually written through the experience of people in struggle." The song, "If We Do Not Die," she explains, grew out of her visit to Korea and was inspired by a visual presentation of the horrors of the anti-Japanese war of the Korean people. At that same time while in Korea Elaine learned of the death of Jonathan Jackson. [Brother of George Jackson]. The impact of these two experiences produced these lines: "There is a man/who stands in all our way/And his greedy hands/ reach out across the world/But if we slay this man/we'll have peace in this land/ and this glorious struggle will be done/And we shall meet again/If we do not die."

Huey Newton wrote the liner notes included on the inner-sleeve, which also references the album as *Until We're Free*. Newton wrote:

"Until We're Free' is the statement of a revolutionary in words and song — words erupting out of the manifold experiences of struggle, song flowing out of the pain and suffering of Black life in America. These are love songs expressing Elaine Brown's deep and abiding sense of oneness with all oppressed humankind, her devotion to her comrades-in-battle, her faith in the Victory that will be realized through the people's will, determination and effort, love songs that touch and stir the heart. A consuming talent, a total dedication and a proven commitment are combined in Elaine Brown, making her the first, genuine People's Artist America has produced.

Sadly, Brown's album marked the end of Black Forum, which certainly had nothing to do with her. It was inevitable that this sociopolitical detour of the Motown pop empire wouldn't last long. By 1973, the Black Power movement that had inspired the label was fragmenting and winding down. Ultimately, like most things in life, it came down to money. The Black Forum records couldn't sell in the quantities that Motown had become accustomed to via hit-makers like The Supremes, The Temptations and The Jackson 5.

Although the label only released a handful of recordings during its existence, apparently their original intentions were more ambitious. An April 3, 1971 article in the *Philadelphia Tribune* outlined an impressive release schedule, including two albums scheduled for later that year: *Black Unity* by James Baldwin and a selection of poetry read by Ted Joans titled *The Good Colored Man*. Additionally, they announced forthcoming releases by a diverse set of African-Americans: Eldridge Cleaver; SNNC co-founder and congressman Julian Bond; Richard Gordon Hatcher and Kenneth Gibson (mayors of Gary, Ind. and Newark, N.J.); Andrew Young (a key aide to King Jr. throughout the 1960s and a prominent politician in the following two decades); director of the NAACP Roy Wilkins; and a posthumous work by Whitney Young, who was head of the National Urban League from 1961 until his death just a few weeks before the *Philadelphia Tribune* article. None of these recordings was ever released.

Given the label's non-existent legacy, one can't help but feel that the records simply never reached their intended audience. As I wound up my interview with former Motown executive Miller London, I asked if he had any final comments about Black Forum. He replied, "The main problem was that Motown's network of regional record distributors simply didn't want to stock the albums. The distributors were of course hungry for the next Motown pop album, but getting them behind these political releases was difficult." ◉

3-10245

Columbia

HONKIES FOR HUEY

3

One of my favorite passages in David Hilliard's illuminating autobiography *This Side Of Glory* is his description of Honkies For Huey. White leftists began coming forward to support Newton during his trial stemming from the shooting of two Oakland policemen. This Berkeley-based organization printed up buttons saying "Honkies For Huey" and, Hilliard recalled in his book, at a meeting, one of them asked Eldridge Cleaver, "How do you think we honkies can help?"

On a related note, as Cleaver pointed out in his book *Soul On Ice*, the early 1960s Civil Rights protests by black students on Southern college campuses had inspired Northern white students to politicize themselves. He wrote, "In countless ways, the rebellion of the black students served as a catalyst for the brewing revolt of the whites." Indeed, a pre-Yippie Abbie Hoffman first got inspired as an organizer for SNCC, while a 1968 essay for *Esquire* magazine (on the Chicago Democratic Convention protests) written by notorious postmodernist William S. Burroughs stated, "Black Power: Find out what they want and give it to them. All the signs that mean anything indicate that the blacks were the original inhabitants of this planet. So who has a better right to it?"

Black Panther Field Marshall Don Cox got a taste of high society whites supporting the cause at the infamous Black Panther fundraiser chronicled in Tom Wolfe's 1970 *Radical Chic & Mau-Mauing the Flak Catchers*. Hosted by symphony maestro Leonard Bernstein, Cox' frank conversation shocked the celebrities assembled at Bernstein's Park Avenue mansion (including director Otto Preminger and anchorwoman Barbara Walters).

OPPOSITE: Bob Dylan's singles' picture sleeves had always featured his name and the song titles, but this unadorned black-and-white photo broke away from tradition: the stark image of Hurricane Carter stares back at viewers defiantly.

ABOVE: A poster that defines what this book is about features a 1971 "Revolutionary Intercommunal" event with appearances by key members of the Black Panther Party: Kathleen Cleaver and Huey Newton paid respect to other important Panthers jailed at that time, Bobby Seale and Ericka Huggins, plus comrade Angela Davis. Add in a performance by the Panthers' own singing group, The Lumpen, and one by hippie icons The Grateful Dead, and this poster symbolizes a diverse set of Black Power minds coming together, with support from the white counterculture. From the author's perspective, it's like a mini-Woodstock type of event.

While it's easy to bash these limousine liberals, I'm reminded of what Gene McDaniels told me when I first started writing this book. "Black people don't like blacks like me; it's only white liberals like you who think I'm cool."

DYLAN: THE SAGA OF GEORGE JACKSON AND THE BALLAD OF HURRICANE CARTER

Earlier, I mentioned Bob Dylan's "Ballad Of A Thin Man" and Huey Newton's insightful theories about race and society buried within the abstruse lyrics. In 1971, Dylan would address Black Power head on with "George Jackson," recorded just days after the political prisoner's tragic death.

George Jackson was arrested at age 18 for stealing seventy dollars during a robbery. Because he was black, he was sentenced to one year to life for a petty crime. By the time of his death in August 1971, he'd served eleven years. Like Malcolm X, he used his prison time to educate himself, writing the influential and best-selling book *Soledad Brother* in October 1970. (A second book, *Blood in My Eye*, was published posthumously.) Despite (and because of) his incarceration, Jackson was named Field Marshall of the Black Panther Party. He used his influence to sway prisoners to join the Party. More importantly, Jackson and the Panthers enjoyed a mutual admiration, emboldened by each other's tenacity. As Newton wrote during his own incarceration in San Luis Obispo on June 30, 1970, "George Jackson is a living legend throughout the prison system… Even some of the white 'racist' inmates have respect for him because they view him

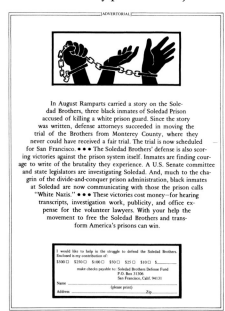

In August Ramparts carried a story on the Soledad Brothers, three black inmates of Soledad Prison accused of killing a white prison guard. Since the story was written, defense attorneys succeeded in moving the trial of the Brothers from Monterey County, where they never could have received a fair trial. The trial is now scheduled for San Francisco. ● ● ● The Soledad Brothers' defense is also scoring victories against the prison system itself. Inmates are finding courage to write of the brutality they experience. A U.S. Senate committee and state legislators are investigating Soledad. And, much to the chagrin of the divide-and-conquer prison administration, black inmates at Soledad are now communicating with those the prison calls "White Nazis." ● ● ● These victories cost money—for hearing transcripts, investigation work, publicity, and office expense for the volunteer lawyers. With your help the movement to free the Soledad Brothers and transform America's prisons can win.

I would like to help in the struggle to defend the Soledad Brothers. Enclosed is my contribution of: $500 □ $250 □ $100 □ $50 □ $25 □ $10 □ $_____ make checks payable to: Soledad Brothers Defense Fund P.O. Box 31306 San Francisco, Calif. 94131
Name _____ (please print)
Address _____ Zip _____

as a man who is totally straight. They know he is going to do exactly what he says he is going to do ... He refuses to compromise in any way to gain personal privilege. He has stood up and let himself be counted regardless of personal cost. George is a true revolutionary."

On Jan. 13, 1970, at California's Soledad Prison, when segregated prisoners were let into the exercise yard together, interracial tensions escalated into a riot. O.G. Miller killed three black prisoners, and a Grand Jury ruled Miller's actions as "justifiable homicide." Soon after, Soledad guard John Mills was attacked and killed in retaliation. Although there was no proof who had murdered Mills, George Jackson, Fleeta Drumgo and John Clutchette were singled out for their protest of Miller's acquittal and their political views. George Jackson, Fleeta Drumgo and John Clutchette became known as the Soledad Brothers.

On Aug. 7, 1970, just days after Jackson was transferred to San Quentin Prison in Marin County, Calif., his 17-year-old brother Jonathan Jackson burst into the Marin County Hall of Justice brandishing several weapons. He interrupted the trial of San Quentin inmate James McClain by arming McClain and two other prisoners, Ruchell Magee and William Christmas, who were scheduled to testify as witnesses. Demanding the release of the Soledad Brothers, the three inmates took the judge and four others hostage. As they attempted to escape in a van, the police killed Jackson, McClain, Christmas and the judge. Jackson was eulogized in Elaine Brown's song "Jonathan" on her 1973 Black Forum album.

George Jackson was stunned and depressed by his brother's death and, almost a year to the day, would meet his own demise

Easy to be black?

Experience the ghetto. Live on welfare. Be a target for police harassment. Try to buy in a white suburb.

Your challenge: To keep the land-hungry majority type from winning the game cheaply and quickly. To make changes. To redistribute the wealth and power. To shake up the status-quo.

The odds are against you. But when, and if, you get some odd breaks, it's time to stay loose and invent wild new strategies. You may use better resources, and risk yourself with more courage, than players who start well off but live uptight in fear of failure.

You may play the game again and again and never succeed, but BLACKS and WHITES, like life, is like that.

Designed for educational use, this game originated at the Univ. of Calif. at Davis. Players who chose to be black could

not win, or seriously effect the course of the competitive thing going on between white players.

But black and white students testing the game for PSYCHOLOGY TODAY, rewrote the rules of play. As students tend to do, they shook up the rigidities of the past and introduced free form alternatives into the game.

Black people, though still victims of discrimination, become the agents of change. A black player on welfare becomes a direct concern to other players. The idiom of money and property was enriched as much as possible with educational factors, Black-Power politics, and illogical luck.

BLACKS and WHITES. A PSYCHOLOGY TODAY GAME. $6.95 (plus 50c postage and handling). Dealer inquiries invited.

FREE! 2'x3' Full Color Poster with purchase of each BLACKS & WHITES game. This powerful visual statement from a past issue of Psychology Today is a regular $2 value. Act today! The supply is limited.

PSYCHOLOGY TODAY GAMES
P.O. Box 4762, Clinton, Iowa 52732

Please send me _____ BLACKS and WHITES game(s) (order #105) at $6.95 (plus 50c postage and handling). Please include my FREE Psychology Today poster—WHITE MAN'S WORLD. I enclose my check or money order for $_____ to cover the full amount of my purchase, and I understand that if I am not completely satisfied, I may return BLACKS and WHITES for a full refund. (New York and California residents please add applicable state sales tax.) P-51

NAME_____
ADDRESS_____
CITY_____ STATE_____ ZIP_____

at the hand of San Quentin guards. Somehow the authorities instigated a rebellion, which led to the death that day of three guards and two prisoners. Eyewitnesses say that Jackson had no gun (although authorities claim that his lawyer smuggled in a gun and gave it to Jackson, who hid it underneath an afro wig he was wearing!?) and that during the melee, Jackson, knowing he was the intended target, separated himself from other prisoners to keep the carnage to a minimum. On Tuesday, Sept. 21, 1971, the *National Evening News* on NBC confirmed the autopsy report showed that Jackson had been shot in the back by a bullet discharged at close range while he had knelt on all fours. George Jackson had been put down like a dog.

Bob Dylan was already politically involved: in 1963, he accepted a Thomas Paine Bill of Rights award from the Emergency Civil Liberties Committee (given to those individuals that the ECLC felt championed the cause of human rights) on behalf of SNCC and James Forman, whom he had mingled with, along with Julian Bond and Freedom Singer Bernice Johnson Reagon, earlier that year at SNCC voter registration drive. He also wrote topical songs in 1962 ("The Death Of Emmett Till") and 1963 ("The Lonesome Death Of Hattie Carroll") that specifically named African-Americans who had suffered gross injustice.

From 1964 Dylan spent the rest of the decade writing personal, surrealistic songs, such as "Like A Rolling Stone" and "Visions Of Johanna." And while Huey Newton's perceptive mind could extract a social protest message hidden within "Ballad Of A Thin Man," for most Dylan fans, much of his songwriting during the second half of the 1960s was curiously ambiguous. And yet, even when Dylan had supposedly stopped writing social-political commentary, with close listening, he was still at it. In "Outlaw Blues" from *Bringing It All Back Home* (March 1965), referring to the June 11, 1963, assassination of NAACP field secretary Medgar Evers, Dylan sang "I got a woman in Jackson, I ain't gonna say her name, she's a brown skinned woman, but I love her just the same." (It's also important to remember that Dylan was not the only white folk singer to write Civil Rights protest songs; many others did as well, most notably Phil Ochs with his 1965 seminal com- position "Here's to the State of Mississippi.")

On Nov. 4, 1971, Dylan quickly recorded a new song he'd written titled "George Jackson." In fact, he recorded two versions of it that day. One was a solo acoustic take — just Dylan with guitar and harmonica — that recalled the sound of a decade earlier. It's a plaintive performance that makes "George Jackson" sound like an instant protest classic, à la la 1962's "Blowing In The Wind." The song's other take was an up-tempo band version which included piano, drums, bass, steel guitar and two black female singers, result- ing in a more celebratory memorial to the slain martyr, similar to a New Orleans-style jazz funeral.

Just as Crosby, Stills, Nash & Young had chronicled the Kent State murders with "Ohio," Dylan insisted that "George Jackson" be released immediately, putting the topical song on the streets only two weeks after recording it. But Dylan also did something unusual. He released both versions on one single (the acoustic take on one side, the band version on the other) so that the radio stations (and his fans) couldn't get away with playing anything but "George Jackson." It was a formidable statement from a popular artist that had supposedly given up writing protest

material years earlier and, like all good topical songs, the lyrics were direct and poignant:

> *He wouldn't take shit from no one. He wouldn't bow down*
> *or kneel. Authorities, they hated him, because he was*
> *just too real. Prison guards, they cursed him, as they*
> *watched him from above. But they were frightened of*
> *his power. They were scared of his love.*
> *So they cut George Jackson down.*

For years, it's been more rumor than fact that Dylan met with Huey Newton and David Hilliard in December 1970. When biographer Anthony Scaduto asked Dylan about it in 1971, he replied, "What meeting? Why don't you talk to Huey about it?" Apparently Scaduto was unable to do so. Neither Newton nor Hilliard men- tioned it in their respec- tive autobiographies, so it remained more of a myth than anything else. In 2008, I asked Hilliard about the summit, and he confirmed that a meeting did take place among him, Newton and Dylan. He said it had been arranged by Emmett Grogan of the Diggers, a San Francisco-based white radical group who specialized in everything from guerrilla theatre to feeding starving hippies in Haight-Ashbury. The meeting took place at Jimi Hendrix' Electric Ladyland Studio in Manhattan. Supposedly the meeting didn't go well, with the Panthers and Dylan finding little common ground. "Let's just say," Hilliard summarized, "the Dylan that wrote 'Ballad Of A Thin Man' and Dylan the person are two totally different people."

The only other known interaction between "the spokes- man of a generation" and the Black Panthers occurred around the same time (late 1970) when the Committee To Defend The

Panthers wrote Dylan asking for a donation or a benefit concert for legal defense funds, and he responded with a check for $40. To be fair to Dylan, some time ago, while I was working with Hilliard on a potential collection of vintage Panther speeches and related music, I contacted Dylan's management about including "George Jackson." I expected either a "no" or a much-delayed reply. Within four days, I'd received a positive answer. Given Dylan's fame, his notorious isolation from the public and the deluge of requests his office receives each day, this quick and encouraging response spoke volumes about Dylan's feelings regarding the Black Power movement some thirty-five years later.

"George Jackson" wouldn't be the last topical song about the plight of a black American from Bob Dylan. He would step up one more time in 1975 with the anthem "Hurricane," detailing the story of boxer Rubin "Hurricane" Carter. Carter had entered into professional world of boxing in 1961. Because of his ultrafast fists, he became known as "Hurricane," inching closer to the world middleweight crown. In October 1966, Carter was in training for the world middleweight title when he was arrested for the June 17, 1966 killing of three white patrons at the Paterson, N.J. Lafayette Bar & Grill. Hurricane and John Artis had been arrested on the night of the crime because they fit a description of the killers (two Negroes in a car), but were released by a grand jury when an eyewitness had been unable to identify them as the gunmen. By the time of his second arrest, the state of New Jersey had two witnesses, Alfred Bello and Arthur Bradley, who claimed to have seen Hurricane and Artis at the crime. The prosecution had no real evidence against the two men except the possible motive that the murder was a racially inspired retaliation for the killing

of a black bar owner by a white man in another Paterson bar earlier that day. Bello and Bradley were both criminals who received reduced sentences in exchange for their testimony. On June 29, 1966, Hurricane and Artis were convicted of triple murder and sentenced to life imprisonment.

After years of defying the authorities within the prison walls, in 1974 Carter published his autobiography: *The 16th Round: From Number 1 Contender to Number 45472*. Cognizant of Dylan's support for black struggle, Carter sent him a copy. Dylan read it and paid the incarcerated fighter a visit. Dylan knew that he had to tell Carter's story as he had Hattie Carroll's, Emmett Till's and George Jackson's. After attempting to record it on July 30, 1975 with a large ensemble, including guitarist Eric Clapton and King Crimson alumnus Mel Collins on sax, Dylan nailed "Hurricane" on Oct. 24 with a more economical band. As with "George Jackson," Dylan demanded Columbia Records release it quickly, getting "Hurricane" out in early November.

The packaging had a couple of unique traits. Because of its eight-and-a-half-minute length, the song was split between two sides, resulting in "Hurricane" and "Hurricane Part Two." The record was presented in a picture sleeve that contained no text or artist credits, just a black-and-white photo of "Hurricane" in his fighting prime. The same image was used for the front and back, making both sides identical.

Unlike his early topical songs, "Hurricane" wasn't a folk ballad, but a high-energy rock anthem. The plentiful lyrics were sung quickly with great expression for maximum effect, incorporating Luther Rix' conga drumming to punctuate Dylan's point. In the words of Dylan scholar Paul Williams, "It is one of the most powerful recordings Bob Dylan has ever made."

The special ingredient in the song's sense of urgency is the gypsy violin of Scarlet Rivera. For eight-and-a-half minutes, the song never lets up, the violin weaving between, in, and around Dylan's expressive singing (he machine-guns out a novel's worth of lyrics in a short time). Energetic drumming keeps the song moving, while the rest of the band (including Ronee Blakley's spot-on harmony vocals) embellishes Dylan's message.

Over eleven fact-filled verses, Dylan outlines the bogus case that the prosecution had concocted with half-baked "eyewitness" testimony. Dylan drives home the fact that he's telling "the story of the Hurricane, the man the authorities came to blame, for somethin' that he never done, put in a prison cell, but one time he coulda been the champion of the world."

Dylan performed "Hurricane" throughout his 1975 tour, including a Dec. 7 show at the Clinton Correctional Institution (which included a press conference by Hurricane Carter before the concert) and a benefit at Madison Square Garden the following day. Billed as "Night Of The Hurricane," the Dec. 8 extravaganza featured a four-hour performance by Dylan and guests Roberta Flack, Joni Mitchell and Joan Baez. Despite the all-star cast, the most dramatic part occurred when Muhammad Ali walked onstage with a telephone and received a call from Hurricane Carter, which was broadcast to the entire audience. Carter said to the gathered masses, "I'm sitting here in jail and I'm thinking that this is truly a revolutionary act when so many people in the outside world can come together for someone in jail."

Despite receiving six months of freedom, partly in response to the publicity that Dylan generated, Carter and Artis would return to prison after a 1976 retrial (featuring more bogus testimony from Bello, who two years earlier had admitted he'd lied during the 1966 trial). Carter and Artis would not secure permanent release until 1985 and 1981 respectively.

JOHN LENNON GIVES BLACK POWER A CHANCE

Although John Lennon would become the most politically outspoken of The Beatles, Paul McCartney was the first Beatle to address African-American Civil Rights with his 1968 composition "Blackbird" on The Beatles' *White Album*. "Blackbird" was a beautifully simple ballad on which McCartney played acoustic guitar and sang (no other Beatles contributed to the recording). As McCartney told Barry Miles in the 1997 biography *Many Years From Now*: "I had in mind a black woman, rather than a bird. Those were the days of the civil-rights movement, which all of us cared passionately about, so this was really a song from me to a black woman, experiencing these problems in States."

John Lennon wrote a number of politically charged songs, including 1968's "Revolution" (which seemed to question the purpose of it all as much as it offered approval), 1969's "Give Peace A Chance" and 1971's "Power To The People" (the Black Panthers had popularized the slogan "All Power To The People" a few years earlier). But it wasn't until 1972 that Lennon specifically named people and events related to the Black Power movement in his songs. By the time of Lennon's 31st birthday on Oct. 9, 1971, he and Yoko Ono had moved from England to New York City, where they befriended Jerry Rubin and Abbie Hoffman (the outspoken and humorous founders of a white radical collective known as Yippies). During their first meeting, Ono told Rubin and Hoffman that she and Lennon considered the Yippie leaders to be "great artists." The ever-witty Hoffman replied "That's funny, we always thought of you and John as great politicians."

George Jackson's 1971 assassination on Aug. 3 triggered the Sept. 9-13 rebellion at Attica State Prison in New York, the bloodiest suppression of an inmate uprising in U.S. history. But they were protesting more than just Jackson's brutal death; the living conditions at Attica sucked. Each inmate was allowed only one shower per week and one roll of toilet paper per month! The facility had been built to hold twelve hundred, but had twenty-two hundred detainees, so overcrowding was a serious problem.

On Sept. 9, inmates freed a prisoner when it was rumored the guards would torture him, upon which he joined the others for breakfast. This sparked a confrontation with the prisoners securing large sections of the grounds, including the central command room. The inmates proceeded to take forty-two officers (including civilians who worked on the prison grounds) hostage and submitted a list of grievances, centered on the rights they'd been denied and the poor living conditions.

Over the next several days, the media began to arrive and get involved, including Tom Wicker of *The New York Times* and attorney William Kunstler (who had served as the defense lawyer at the Chicago 8 trial). New York Governor Nelson Rockefeller chose to ignore the situation. Commissioner Russell Oswald, who'd been leading discussions with the inmates, finally gave up and ordered the State Police to secure the prison. What ensued was nothing short of a bloodbath. When it was all over on Sept. 13, nine hostages had died from friendly gunfire and twenty-eight inmates had been killed. After the State Troopers left the scene, guards were allowed to beat the inmates in retaliation. The national media printed rumors that the inmates had slit the throats of the hostages as the shooting began, when in fact autopsies proved that the State Troopers' careless tactics had killed their own colleagues.

Exactly a month later, Lennon began writing a new song: "Attica State." Over the following weeks, Lennon and Ono finalized the song as it would appear on the June 1972 Lennon/Ono album *Sometime In New York City*. *Sometime In New York City* remains the most maligned and misunderstood album in Lennon's catalog (with the exception of Lennon and Ono's 1968 release *Two Virgins*, which was reviled for featuring both artists stark naked on the cover and had no discernable musical content). Fans and music critics alike have never been able to come to terms with the strident political messages contained within "Attica State" ("What a waste of human lives…Media blames it on the prisoners, but the prisoners did not kill, Rockefeller pulled the trigger") and "Angela" (in support of Angela Davis, who enjoyed a close relationship with George Jackson, mostly through an exchange of letters).

While I agree that *Sometime In New York City* isn't Lennon's most melodic or crafted collection, I stand behind this album as an astonishingly bold statement (including songs about John Sinclair, Jerry Rubin and Eldridge Cleaver) from a massively popular artist who had everything to lose by releasing something so controversial. Lennon compared it to a newspaper — it was rushed out quickly with performances that weren't perfect and lyrics that hadn't been fine-tuned — as he needed to get the message out while it was still topical. In fact, the cover resembled a newspaper, with song titles presented as headlines and lyrics designed like articles, with black-and-white photos to match.

I've saved the most contentious song for last: "Woman Is The Nigger Of The World," which not only kicks off the LP, but

was released as a single in April 1972, a few months in advance of the album. "Woman Is The Nigger Of The World" proclaims, "Yes she is, think about it. If she won't be a slave, we say that she don't love us. If she's real, we say she's trying to be a man.

ABOVE: This Japanese picture sleeve proves that, despite its controversial title, "Woman Is The Nigger Of The World," Lennon and Ono were committed to getting their message across the globe (via a 45 rpm single).

While putting her down, we pretend that she's above us...woman is the slave to the slaves."

Meant as a feminist anthem (much more than commentary on African-Americans in general), Lennon and Ono used the word "nigger" for its shock value and to ask the question: Were women of all races lower on the ladder of society than blacks overall? This would be debated again during the 2008 Democratic Presidential Primaries in the battle between Hillary Clinton and Barack Obama. Have Americans been waiting longer for a female president or a black one?

In the 2006 documentary *The U.S. vs. John Lennon* (which focused on the *Sometime In New York City* era), Angela Davis spoke about "Woman Is The Nigger Of The World": "It created a lot of controversy in all circles; I had a hard time listening to the song because of the way in which we all reacted to the public use of that word. But I certainly appreciated the intent, the content; the feminism in that song was quite remarkable."

Surprisingly, the song didn't do half-bad on the American singles charts — it peaked at #57 and remained in the Top 100 for five weeks. That said, I haven't heard the song played on any radio stations since.

THE MIKE DOUGLAS SHOW BRINGS BOBBY SEALE TO MIDDLE AMERICA

Not long before Lennon and Ono released *Sometime In New York City*, they appeared in the households of conservative Americans across the nation. *The Mike Douglas Show* beamed across America five days a week for ninety minutes, starting at 4:30 pm. The show's core audience was housewives, switching on Mike Douglas for light entertainment. Depending on when dad and the kids came home, they might catch part of the show as well.

During the entire week of Feb. 14-18, 1972, Lennon and Ono were full-time co-hosts with Mike Douglas. They did most of the talking and preselected the guests, including Yippie leader Jerry Rubin, consumer activist Ralph Nader, rock 'n' roll legend Chuck Berry, macrobiotic chef Hillary Redleaf and hippie comedian George Carlin.

On Thursday the 17th, the show included Chairman of the Black Panther Party Bobby Seale. In fact, a diverse representation

of the black community was broadcast into the homes of white America that afternoon. Two young black students came on first: Marsha Martin of Mills College in Oakland and Donald Williams from Stanford University. Marsha was Student Body President at Mills and she spoke of efforts to organize a National Black Youth Conference bringing together Black Student Unions from colleges across America.

Donald Williams was a medical student at Stanford and was helping to run a Sickle Cell Anemia Foundation in the Bay Area. Sickle Cell Anemia is a life-threatening condition in which red blood cells become misshaped, causing them to form clumps and not move through the bloodstream as healthy blood cells would. This disease is much more common in African-Americans than whites. According to the U.S. Department of Health, it affects one in every five hundred African-Americans, while it is virtually unknown to affect whites. Providing sickle cell anemia testing for thousands of people, many of whom couldn't afford to pay a doctor, was an important part of the Black Panthers' community work.

It was important to Lennon and Ono to present the Black Panthers in a positive light. Perhaps naively, they hoped to get racist or simply fearful white Americans to change their minds about the Panthers' activities. As Lennon said earlier in the week, when he mentioned Seale's forthcoming appearance, "They're really peaceful people and we're going to show that," and "We thought we'd give them a chance to show us what they're actually doing *now* and what they actually think *now*, not two years ago, or three years ago, but now and what their hopes are for the future."

Although the Central Committee was based in Oakland, the Panthers led a nationwide program within ghetto communities to feed hungry schoolchildren each morning, enlisting the cooperation of local churches. They gave away thousands of bags of groceries, hundreds of pairs of new shoes and provided free clothing to the poor. They ran free buses so that families could arrange to see their loved ones in prison; they arranged their own free twenty-four hour ambulance service to rush people to the hospital from black neighborhoods where white-operated ambulances often refused to go.

In a dignified and articulate manner, Bobby Seale captivated Mike Douglas and his co-hosts, using films of these

Panther-sponsored programs to reinforce his statements. When Lennon asked, "What is the philosophy of the Black Panther Party?" Seale replied; "we're into intercommunalism… we're not nationalists, nationalism is akin to superiority, is akin to racism…we want to inter-connect the communities of the world…we're not focusing on skin color, we're focusing on poverty."

Seale acknowledged that the media had long portrayed the Panthers as a violent group against whites, but that wasn't the reality. The reality was the Panthers' focus on these community survival programs. When Mike Douglas asked how the black community reacted to these efforts, Seale made it clear: "When you're giving away thousands of bags of groceries, people respond and show up!"

⚡ The JOHN SINCLAIR FREEDOM RALLY ⚡

The Feb. 17, 1972 *Mike Douglas Show* wasn't the first public appearance of Lennon and Seale together, although they didn't appear on stage at the same time. They both performed at the Chrysler Arena in Ann Arbor, Mich. on Dec. 10, 1971 at the John Sinclair Freedom Rally.

John Sinclair had played an essential part in spreading awareness of jazz and black culture in the Detroit area. He organized concerts and workshops, taught classes in jazz and poetry, and covered the regional music scene for *DownBeat*. Besides the *Fire Music* poetry collection, Sinclair published two books between 1965 and 1967 that honored Ornette Coleman (*This Is Our Music*) and John Coltrane (*Meditations*). These two volumes also celebrated Elvin Jones, Miles Davis, Marion Brown, Andrew Hill and Albert Ayler. These tributes came in the shape of poems that were essentially record reviews, capturing the essence of their music. In 1968, in the ultimate (if naive) white tribute to Black Power, Sinclair would form the infamous White Panther Party, which he anticipated

would become the "voice of the lumpen hippie, just like the Black Panther Party was the voice of the lumpen proletariat."

Fifteen thousand people attended the John Sinclair Freedom Rally in support of the MC5 manager and White Panther leader who'd been sentenced to ten years in prison for giving two joints to an undercover cop. The entire day's proceedings (including Lennon and Ono singing "Attica State") were filmed at Lennon's expense for a movie, *Ten For*

Two (a line from Lennon's song "John Sinclair"). The film was never officially released, but copies do circulate which include Bobby Seale's appearance. Seale makes a grand entrance, surrounded by half a dozen bodyguards who spread out around him. Several of them are dressed in full-length leather coats as if they'd just stepped off the set of *Superfly*.

The fifteen thousand hippies cheer wildly for Seale as he begins to speak. "With all these people here, I think the most appropriate, very human, revolutionary thing to first say, like we always say, is all power to the people." The crowd erupts. Over the next five minutes, Seale calls for the freedom of all living things, including animals and plants, equating environmental pollution with the oppression of all humanity. Seale suggests less talk and more action within the revolutionary struggle, mentioning that music can inspire the revolution. He wraps up by calling for the support of the Black Panthers' free food and medical programs, and claims that making everything "free" will spell the end of capitalism.

What effect, if any, Seale's appearance on *The Mike Douglas Show* had on the public's opinion of the Black Panthers can't be measured, but one thing is certain: John Lennon used his rockstar clout to compel Middle America to listen to the Black Power message. If anyone was entitled to wear a "Honkies for Huey" button, it was John Lennon in 1972.

1968 CHICAGO:
THE WHOLE WORLD IS WATCHING

To say that 1968 was a violent year would be an understatement. Here's a list of dramatic events leading up the Chicago Democratic Convention.

APRIL 4, 1968 Martin Luther King Jr. is assassinated in Memphis. Mass rioting occurs in over one hundred cities with large sections of ghettos in Washington, D.C, Chicago, Baltimore and Louisville burned and gutted.

APRIL 6, 1968 Bobby Hutton is killed by Oakland Police. Li'l Bobby was the Black Panther Party's youngest member, just 16 when he joined the Party two years earlier, shortly after the organization was founded. On the evening of April 6, two cars of Panthers (including Hutton, Eldridge Cleaver and David Hilliard) were driving around West Oakland when local police ambushed them. Cleaver would avoid a trial (and jail time) by going into exile in Algiers, while Hilliard would remain in the United States and face charges, spending several years in prison. As the first Panther shot down in the line of duty, Hutton lives on in the hearts of many surviving members of the Party and the Li'l Bobby Hutton Park in West Oakland honors his memory.

JUNE 6, 1968 Robert Kennedy is assassinated in Los Angeles while campaigning for the Democratic Presidential Nomination. Kennedy was seen as the great white hope who could bring together the diverse races and cultures in an attempt to end poverty and end the Vietnam War.

AUG. 26-29, 1968 Turmoil is brewing throughout the Democratic National Convention in Chicago. Incumbent President

---

On November 27, 1968, Eldridge Cleaver will be thrown back in jail.

The California establishment has reacted to the widening attention this man has received: fifteen days ago a judge of the California State Court of Appeals ruled that Judge Sherwin's ruling in Solano County last June, reinstating Cleaver's parole, was neither valid nor in due process.

Mr. Cleaver, senior editor of *Ramparts* magazine and lecturer in the widely publicized course on Racism in America at UC Berkeley, has been told by the Adult Authority that he will be returned to jail within sixty days of the Appellate court's ruling (September 27, 1968).

The political nature of Eldridge's persecution is clear and can be seen as a blatant attempt to silence him. Judge Sherwin, in his opinion granting habeas corpus last June, wrote:

> The uncontradicted evidence presented to this court indicated that the petitioner had been a model parolee. The peril to his parole status stemmed from no failure of personal rehabilitation, *but from his undue eloquence in pursuing political goals* . . . Not only was there absence of cause for the cancellation of parole, it was the product of a type of pressure unbecoming, to say the least, to the law enforcement paraphernalia of this state.

We must not allow this important voice to be silenced. The issue here is not the defense of the particular ideas espoused by Eldridge Cleaver, but the defense of any man's right to express unpopular ideas and to act on them politically. We are asking you to put aside any political differences you may have with Eldridge and to act as you might have acted when Dreyfus, Eugene Debs, Daniel and Sinyavsky, Tom Mooney, or Sacco and Vanzetti were similarly persecuted for political reasons and framed by frightened authorities.

We have formed the International Committee to Defend Eldridge Cleaver to keep Eldridge out of jail and to raise money for his defense. You can help by reproducing this petition and circulating it in your community, where you are employed, or in whatever social or professional organizations you participate. You can also help by placing ads in your local newspapers, protesting the action of the California courts and demanding that Eldridge remain free. And, finally, you can send contributions to help pay for the legal defense of Cleaver and for the further publicizing of his case. These contributions are urgently needed. Mail petitions, copies of ads or statements, and contributions to:

International Committee to Defend Eldridge Cleaver
495 Beach Street
San Francisco, California 94133

Checks should be made payable to the International Committee to Defend Eldridge Cleaver.

PETITION

TO: GOVERNOR RONALD REAGAN
HENRY KERR, CHAIRMAN
CALIFORNIA ADULT AUTHORITY
MEMBERS, CALIFORNIA ADULT AUTHORITY

RE: THE REVOCATION OF ELDRIDGE CLEAVER'S PAROLE.

We, the undersigned, recognize that ELDRIDGE CLEAVER, Senior Editor of *Ramparts* magazine, Minister of Information of the Black Panther Party, Presidential Candidate on the Peace and Freedom Party ticket, and author of the book *Soul on Ice*, is a victim of political persecution.

We see Eldridge Cleaver as a creative figure of recognized brilliance, a political leader of recognized importance, and a valuable member of society.

We also see his political suppression and intellectual persecution as similar to the actions of frightened authorities against such figures as Dreyfus, Eugene Debs, Daniel and Sinyavsky, Tom Mooney, and Sacco and Vanzetti.

We therefore state that the imprisonment of Eldridge Cleaver before he has been tried will serve to further prejudice any jury hearing his case, and that the imprisonment of Eldridge Cleaver before he has been tried will violate the principle that an individual is innocent until proven otherwise.

We demand, then, the continuation of parole for Eldridge Cleaver and an end to the harassment and intimidation bestowed upon him daily by the authorities of the State of California in general, and the County of Alameda in particular.

NAME	ADDRESS
NAME	ADDRESS
NAME	ADDRESS
NAME	ADDRESS
NAME	ADDRESS

ICDEC 495 Beach St., San Francisco, California 94133

I would like to join the efforts of all those who are working to defend Eldridge Cleaver from political persecution. Please add my name to the list of sponsors of the International Committee to Defend Eldridge Cleaver.

I enclose .... to assist the legal expenses and the Committee's campaign to publicize and promote Eldridge Cleaver's defense.

Name.. Date.................
Address ....
City .... State .... Zip.............
Profession .... Organization or Title.............

Lyndon B. Johnson announced on March 31, 1968 that he would not seek re-election. When Robert Kennedy announced his candidacy on March 16, he became a spoiler for anti-war Senator Eugene McCarthy, who had been unchallenged as the youth's candidate of choice. After winning Indiana and Nebraska (although he lost the Oregon primary), Kennedy won California and looked like a sure bet to beat the de facto choice of old-school Democrats, Vice President Hubert Humphrey, when an assassin took him down. With Kennedy dead, Johnson refused to attend the Chicago Convention.

Also attending was African-American Julian Bond, a founder of SNCC who became their communications director

A Panther-Yippie alliance was hatched, according to Jerry Rubin's 1970 book *Do It!*.

Eldridge's vision was coming true: young whites rejecting white society. "White" was a state of mind. Hippies were seeking a new identity. Young whites were blowing middle-class Amerika out of their minds and bodies with drugs, sex, music, freedom, living on the streets. They were filling the jails. They were not in the revolution merely to "support" blacks but were dropouts of white society fighting for their own freedom. Eldridge wanted an alliance between bad blacks and bad whites. Criminals of all colors unite. Brotherhood through common struggle and oppression. Equality under the pigs. Black-white unity becomes

a real thing only when whites are treated like blacks. Eldridge wanted a coalition between the Panthers and the psychedelic street activists.

Eldridge Cleaver, Rubin and fellow Yippie Stew Albert met in the Berkeley hills, smoked a ton of weed and co-wrote the

"Panther-Yippie Pipe Dream." Cleaver's part of the missive said, "Let us join together with all those souls in Babylon who are straining for the birth of a new day. A revolutionary generation is on the scene. There are men and women, human beings, in Babylon today. Disenchanted, alienated white youth, the hippies, the yippies, and all unnamed dropouts from the white man's burden, are our allies in this cause." Some time later, the Black Panther newspaper would run an article: "The Hippies Are Not Our Enemies."

By the time Rubin was compiling his *Scenarios of the Revolution*, Cleaver had fled the United States to Algeria, where he penned the introduction to Rubin's *Do It!* in November 1969. However, this was not to be Cleaver's last interaction with the hippie subculture; his exploits with the high priest of LSD, Timothy Leary, will be detailed later in this book.

⚡ The PANTHERS MEET the YIPPIES ⚡

(he oversaw their newsletter), as part of the Georgia Loyal National Delegation. The Loyalists were an insurgent group that successfully unseated the regular handpicked delegates. During the Convention, Bond was nominated for Vice President (as an alternative to Maine Senator Edmund Muskie, chosen by Hubert Humphrey), becoming the first African-American to be chosen by a major political party for that office. However, he had to withdraw, because at age 28, he was too young to serve under the constitutional minimum of 35. Bond also made his presence known outside the Convention, when he spoke in Grant Park to four thousand demonstrators on Aug. 27…

… Because the real shitstorm was happening outside the Convention: Abbie Hoffman and Jerry Rubin's Yippies, the Students For A Democratic Society (the SDS) were an activist group composed mainly of white college students in support of Civil Rights and against the Vietnam War) and a short-lived coalition who organized a march on the Pentagon in October 1967, MOBE (National Mobilization Committee to End the War in Vietnam), had organized mass demonstrations, inviting thousands of left-wing college students, hippies and outspoken radicals like poet Allen Ginsberg and novelist Norman Mailer. Politically savvy musicians such as the Jefferson Airplane and

POPPY RECORDS

GREGORY TALKS BLACK

POPPY RECORDS

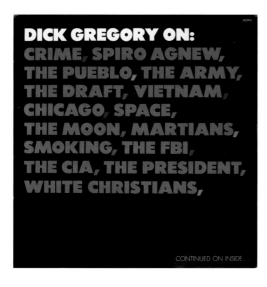

DICK GREGORY ON:
CRIME, SPIRO AGNEW,
THE PUEBLO, THE ARMY,
THE DRAFT, VIETNAM,
CHICAGO, SPACE,
THE MOON, MARTIANS,
SMOKING, THE FBI,
THE CIA, THE PRESIDENT,
WHITE CHRISTIANS,

CONTINUED ON INSIDE

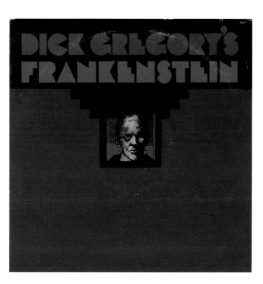

DICK GREGORY'S
FRANKENSTEIN

Country Joe & the Fish were slated to play, but dropped out as rumors of impending violence began to spread. In the end, the only musicians brave enough to weather the storm were those madmen from Michigan, the MC5 (managed by John Sinclair of the White Panther Party) and folk singer Phil Ochs, who was more committed to the revolution than he was to his music career. (John Sinclair and Wayne Kramer of the MC5 still enjoy a friendship with Black Panther David Hilliard to this day.)

The White Panther Party, despite its naive hippie drug-infused antics, was truly in awe of the Black Panther Party's skills and philosophy. Musically, this was reflected in an eighteen-minute discourse entitled "I'm Mad Like Eldridge Cleaver." In typical MC5 style, it's an avant-garde blues-based jam, building in intensity with acid rock overtones as vocalist Rob Tyner rages. The opening lines are "I'm mad out on the street, I'm frothing at the mouth, pissed." As the song builds, Tyner screams, "I'm mad, I'm mad, like Eldridge Cleaver is mad!" It's the sound of white hippies channeling the urban black man's angst against the authoritarian system. While whites can never know the black man's burden, the MC5 tried to empathize. "Cleaver" was a reworking of John Lee Hooker's "I'm Bad like Jesse James." Another song they took from Hooker's repertoire was "Motor City is Burning" (written by Al Smith), included on the MC5's seminal *Kick Out The Jams*. Rob Tyner added passionate words of his own, including praising the Black Panthers for their alleged role in the July 1967 Detroit riots.

Many books have documented the daily drama of the (mostly white middle-class) protesters and their nightly skull bashings by the Chicago Police, but it's important to remember the handful of blacks that also participated in the proceedings.

Comedian Dick Gregory paved the way for Richard Pryor and Chris Rock. And like Pryor and Rock, he was also a social commentator with monologues about race relations, use of the word "nigger" and the plight of Black America. Gregory's 1964 autobiography *Nigger* sold one million copies. Gregory was a strong-minded activist, and throughout the 1960s and 1970s, he not only used topical events and politicians for satire, but also disguised social critique as comedy. Gregory spent the early '60s marching for Civil Rights and spent as much time in jail cells as he did onstage. As Black Power made its ascension, Gregory joined in with his routines, delivering anti-establishment messages as poignant as those being made by the radical political leaders. Besides attacking Richard Nixon, Gregory also did bits praising Bobby Seale and the Black Panthers, ghetto life and the movement. Two of Gregory's more sublime moments can be found on the album *Frankenstein* recorded live at Bronx Community College on March 20, 1970. During the piece called "Black Power," Gregory says:

White folks in this country dirtied up the word black, not us…white folks in America corrupted power, not us… then one day we come through with two innocent words, "Black Power," and everybody go crazy…but if we had said

OPPOSITE: Generally, records with a political message sold in such small quantities that record companies rarely manufactured "promo only" packages such as this one, featuring a Dick Gregory button, poster, 7-inch single and press kit.

ABOVE RIGHT: Frankenstein's monster or King Kong can be seen as metaphors for black men and the fear of black men — America has created this monster (of Black America) and the monster is now turning against America.

*"Brown Strength"…everybody would have accepted that…
hell, we wouldn't be able to walk down the street without
white folks greeting us, "Brown Strength, my brother,
Brown Strength"…black folks took two innocent words
"Black Power" and everybody went crazy…we did not dirty
up the word "Black"…angel's food cake is white, devil's
food cake is dark…*

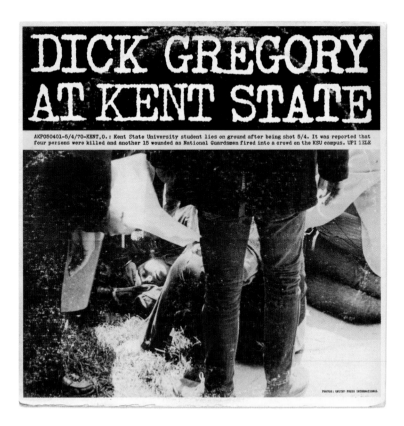

During the 1968 Democratic Convention, Dick Gregory was
on the Peace and Freedom Party ticket as their Presidential
candidate. (On the Nov. 5 ballot, Gregory, who had set up a
Peace and Freedom Party of his own to compete with Cleaver, would eclipse Cleaver, receiving forty-seven thousand and ninety-seven votes to Cleaver's thirty six-thousand, six hundred and twenty-three). He was living in Chicago and fronting marches by young white liberals who were attempting to take over Chicago's streets and parks. He gave speeches to tens of

thousands of anti-war protestors during the Convention. (On the
27th, Bobby Seale, who'd flown into Chicago as a guest speaker,
also addressed a crowd in Lincoln Park. He suggested people
defend themselves by any means necessary if attacked by the
police. Seale left Chicago soon after his speech, but his brief visit
would become more relevant later on.) Gregory's finest moment
that that week is captured in Howard Alk's 1969 documentary
American Revolution 2. The film crew followed Gregory, some two
thousand protesters and delegates, as they attempted to make
their way back to the Convention being held at the International
Amphitheater. When the National Guard stopped them, Gregory
announced that he was merely leading everyone to his own home
(which happened to be in the direction of the Amphitheater) and
that he had invited all these people to his house for a private
gathering. The National Guard didn't buy it, arrested Gregory
and kept the marchers from reaching the convention site.

While Gregory's actions had been captured on film for later
viewing, television cameras had captured the previous evening's
events for the entire country to witness as it occurred. For seventeen minutes, live on TV and repeatedly rebroadcast, the Chicago
Police brutally beat and clubbed, Maced and forcibly arrested
hundreds of demonstrators (most of them white middle-class
college kids) and bystanders.

LEFT: *Cleaver for President*: Power to the people; Black Power to black people. Con-
sistent with Black Panther ideology, the call for giving Black Power to black people
does not exclude giving power to all people — something to keep in mind when
running for president.

RIGHT: The Civil Rights movement intersects with the middle-class anti-war movement; soldiers are now firing on white students in the same fashion as they'd been
firing on black protesters for years.

As the demonstrators began to fight back, the police violence escalated, with billy clubs cracking open the skulls of young students. Across America, demonstrators' family and friends watched the bloodshed on TV as it was happening. In the midst of the chaos, the demonstrators became aware of the television crews broadcasting their beatings and began chanting, "The whole world is watching, the whole world is watching." Finally, white Americans were witnessing what black Americans had experienced for years: police brutality in their own homes.

THE CHICAGO 8 TRIAL
AND GRAHAM NASH

The demonstrations that week led to an infamous trial that began on Sept. 24, 1969, and continued for the next five months. Originally it was called "The Chicago 8 Trial" after the eight defendants that were charged for conspiracy to start riots: Rennie Davis, Dave Dellinger, John Froines, Tom Hayden, Abbie Hoffman, Jerry Rubin, Lee Weiner and Bobby Seale. The U.S. government had handpicked these defendants as a cross-representation of the subversive counterculture: the Yippies, SDS and MOBE leaders, anti-war activists and a token representative of the Black Power movement. Having Bobby Seale called as a defendant was beyond bullshit, as he was the one person out of the eight who didn't personally know the others (Seale had met Tom Hayden earlier, but not in relation to the Democratic Convention), nor had he or any other Black Panther been involved in any of the meetings planning the activist advance on Chicago. It was apparent that Seale had only been brought up on charges because he was a prominent member of the Black Panthers,

which the Nixon administration had declared Public Enemy #1. As Dick Gregory perceptively pointed out on his *Frankenstein* album as part of a monologue titled "Chicago Trial":

Bobby Seale walked into that courtroom in Chicago as Dumeek and humble as a man can walk and said "Judge, your honor, my lawyer is out in San Francisco being operated on, would you postpone my trial?"… And the whole world knew his lawyer was being operated on. Everybody in the world had read that Attorney [Charles] Garry had been operated on. Judge said, "No boy, you go to trial today." "OK, your honor would it be OK if I acted as my own lawyer?" The Judge said, "No, you use their lawyer." The trick behind that was Bobby Seale was indicted with seven other folks, five of whom he never met and didn't know. Why would he use the lawyers of strangers? That's why he was raising so much hell. You dig it?… Bobby Seale trying to defend himself, ended up shackled to the chair, hands cuffed, mouth taped. In a courtroom where the worldwide press is watching. You dig?… If a man trying to defend himself in a courtroom where the world wide press is watching ends up getting shackled to the chair, hands cuffed, mouth taped, what do you think is happening in these courtrooms in America where there ain't nobody looking?

On Oct. 29, Seale was silenced with a gag in his mouth after demanding his right to an attorney of his choice or the right to his own defense. On Nov. 5, a mistrial was declared for just Seale, and a new trial was proposed specifically for him. The Chicago 8 became the Chicago 7. Seale was then sentenced to four

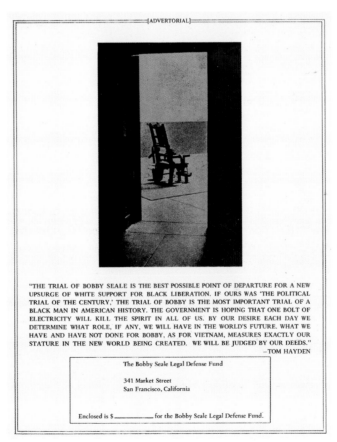

A New Single By
GRAHAM NASH
"CHICAGO"
———
"SIMPLE MAN"
Atlantic 2804 Produced by Graham Nash

From The Forthcoming LP
'Songs For Beginners'

Atlantic SD 7204

Direction: The Geffen Roberts Management Co.

ABOVE: As discussed in the text, English-born rock star Graham Nash wrote a song about Bobby Seale's participation in the Chicago 8 trial and wound up with a hit single in the process. Notice that the ever-vigilant Nash is reading the paper — keeping up with the news, current events, politics. Even in his hotel room, on tour, he's reading and working on that next topical song. Photo courtesy of Joel Bernstein.

years for contempt of court, a sentence that was eventually overturned, and he was never convicted of any conspiracy charges. In terms of media coverage and notoriety, the Chicago 8 Trial had the profile and controversy of the 1992 trial of Rodney King.

"Chicago" by Graham Nash represented the Chicago 8 debacle and the injustices inflicted on Bobby Seale through a pop song. Released as a 45 (and featured on Graham's solo album *Songs For Beginners*) during the height of Crosby, Stills, Nash, & Young (CSN&Y)'s success, it was the most successful single of Nash's solo career, hitting the Top 40 charts in the summer of 1971 for four weeks. It also didn't hurt the song's notoriety when Nash included a version on CSN&Y's live album *4 Way Street*, which was released just a month before *Songs For Beginners*. Interestingly, the version of "Chicago" on *4 Way Street* was recorded live in that city on July 5, 1970, and was one of the first public performances of the topical song, having been demoed by Nash on April 30, 1970.

Crosby, Stills, Nash, & Young had been invited to perform a benefit in Chicago for the trial's defense fund by Wavy Gravy (infamous for his amusing stage announcements at Woodstock). Apparently, Stills and Young were apathetic about participating, and Nash was inspired to make his plea for their participation by writing the song, as well as stating his dismay of the trial's proceedings.

In Nash's own words, in Dave Zimmer's *Crosby Stills & Nash: The Authorized Biography*:

"I saw Bobby Seale get chained and gagged and bound and put on the witness stand. And everyone goes, 'Here, now we're going to have a fair trial.' That was total bullshit and that's where [the song] 'Chicago' came from, which I actually wrote to Stephen [Stills] and Neil [Young]... 'Won't you please come to Chicago, just to sing?'"

Although CSN&Y didn't play the benefit, Nash's song, which might not have been written if they had, drew more attention to

Bobby Seale's circumstances in the long run, especially among rock music fans and FM radio listeners. By the time the song was released in 1971, the trial was over, but Nash's stardom propelled the song's popularity and repeated airplay throughout the first half of the 1970s. Eventually, the song entered into the pantheon of what is now considered "classic rock," with "Chicago" remaining in print decades after its release, effectively carving Seale's tribulations into a permanent part of the pop culture vernacular.

"Chicago" begins with a syncopated drumbeat and a haunting, single-note organ riff accenting the offbeat. Several decades later it would be artfully looped and sampled by black female rapper Medusa, and featured in the 2004 movie *Freestyle: The Art Of Rhyme*. Nash's lyrics come right to the point in the first verses:

> *Though your brother's bound and gagged and they've chained him to a chair, won't you please come to Chicago just to sing?*
> *In a land that's known as freedom, how can such a thing be fair? Won't you please come to Chicago for help that we can bring?*

Although the song up until this part is somber, Graham weaves an uplifting anthem into the tune.

> *We can change the world, re-arrange the world.*

Nash reprises this theme at the end as a "sing-along" chorus with gospel vocalists Clydie King (who later sang on Dylan's born-again LPs *Saved* and *Shot Of Love*) and Dorothy Morrison (who shared the bill with CSN&Y at the Big Sur Folk Festival in 1969; she was the lead vocalist on the Edwin Hawkins Singers' "Oh Happy Day" in April of that year).

As the singers repeat the exuberant slogan *We can change the world, re-arrange the world*, Nash interjects his dismay with the judicial system:

> *It's dying — if you believe in Justice.*
> *It's dying — if you believe in Freedom.*
> *It's dying — let a man live his own life.*
> *It's dying — rules and regulations, who needs them?*

And then, as wonderfully naive as Lennon's "Give Peace A Chance," Nash suggests with a blend of hope and resignation in his voice:

> *Open up the Door.*
> *Somehow people must be free, I hope the day comes soon.*

Graham Nash's "Chicago," along with Bob Dylan's "Hurricane" and "George Jackson," as well as John Lennon & Yoko Ono's media-grabbing efforts, brought Black Power struggles to the attention of whites who might have otherwise ignored the situation. ⭘

SEIZE THE TIME

ELAINE BROWN

BLACK PANTHER PARTY

ELAINE

vault STEREO 131

SOUL ON WAX:
The Black Panthers on Record

4

Songwriter/pianist Elaine Brown and R&B vocal group The Lumpen promoted Black Panther ideology by writing and recording songs. It was not uncommon for them to perform at Party-sanctioned events, while their records helped spread the word to a wider audience. Key Panther spokesmen Huey Newton, Bobby Seale and Eldridge Cleaver recorded albums of speeches and interviews.

THE LUMPEN: From the middle of 1970 to early 1971, the Black Panthers supported a music group known as The Lumpen (short for Lumpen-proletariat) composed of Party members. Minister of Culture Emory Douglas suggested the name, inspired by the phrase coined by (the godfather of Communism) Karl Marx in the 1800s. Lumpenproletariat described the working class that couldn't realize class-consciousness, rendering them worthless for revolutionary struggle. Huey Newton felt that given the changes in society and economics since Marx's lifetime, the Lumpenproletariat could now be a resourceful part of the revolution. Newton suggested that the disenfranchised inhabitants of the ghetto had potential to become the popular class, the revolutionaries that the Black Panthers sought to organize.

Starting with the third issue of the Black Panther Party newsweekly in 1967 until the late 1970s, Emory Douglas' illustrations, cartoons and artwork were an essential part of the weekly paper, most notably his creative interpretations of the police drawn as pigs. As the ideological position of the party changed from combating cops to organizing the community with free food, sickle cell testing and other programs, Douglas

OPPOSITE: Featuring a cover illustration by the Black Panthers' Minister of Culture Emory Douglas: one may not notice that the hand gripping a Soviet-made AK-47 (a symbol of solidarity with the North Vietnamese) is wearing nail polish. There's obviously a strong woman behind these revolutionary songs.

shifted to illustrations of brothers and sisters from the community: the Lumpenproletariat. A wide selection of his work is gathered in the 2007 book *Black Panther: The Revolutionary Art of Emory Douglas.*

The Lumpen were originally four rank-and-file Party members whose work assignments included assembling the weekly newspaper at the print shop in San Francisco. To help pass the time, they'd harmonize and sing along with the radio while they worked. Inspired by Elaine Brown's song album *Seize The Time* (with cover art by Emory Douglas), Lumpen member Bill Calhoun penned two songs, a spiritual tune he called "No More" and an energized R&B number, "Free Bobby Now" (also known as "Bobby Must Be Set Free"). With the encouragement of Emory Douglas, the two songs were recorded. The 7-inch single was pressed and distributed by the Party rather than a conventional record company. The Lumpen were continuing a centuries-old tradition of using music to motivate and educate, as well as document, a resistance movement. Also, as Lumpen member Michael Torrance pointed out, "Some folks don't read, but everyone listens to music."

When they weren't performing, members of The Lumpen band were down in the trenches with other rank-and-file Panthers, taking care of the daily duties. They were truly "the people's band." Their repertoire expanded as they reworked songs by Sly & the Family Stone, The Impressions and The Temptations into provocative revolutionary anthems. Stone's "Dance to the Music" became "Power to the People" while the traditional "Ol' Man River" evolved into "Ole Pig Nixon."

In November 1970, the Lumpen toured America, singing in Boston, New York, Washington, D.C. and other cities as the opening act for speaking engagements by Black Panther leaders. Before the tour, a nine-song concert was recorded at Merritt College in Oakland on Nov. 10, 1970, in hopes of releasing a live album, or at least having the material broadcast on the radio. Neither ever occurred, as the temperament of the recordings was just too hot to handle. Radio program directors couldn't imagine hearing The Lumpen lead hundreds of people shouting in unison: "Death to the fascist Pigs!"

It was disconcerting to hear The Temptations song "It's Summer" reworked with these lyrics: *There's bullets in the air, snipers everywhere, for freedom.*

The master tapes of this 1971 concert have disappeared, although lo-fi cassettes still make the rounds amongst the dedicated few. The Lumpen, like The Temptations and other Motown acts, wore matching outfits as singing front men. They didn't play instruments and used a backing band, which they called The Freedom Messengers. Noted Bay Area DJ, author and scholar Rickey Vincent has done extensive research on The Lumpen that he graciously shared with me. His forthcoming book will dig even deeper into the crucial history of this oft-overlooked band.

Ungagged at last!

SEIZE THE TIME BOBBY SEALE
The Story of the Black Panther Party and Huey P. Newton

$6.95, now at your bookstore RANDOM HOUSE

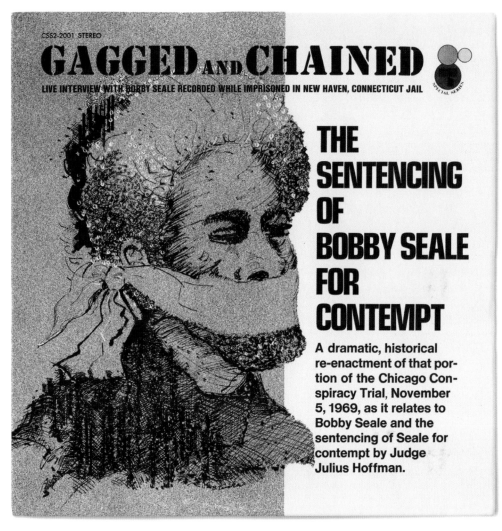

CSS2-2001 STEREO

GAGGED AND CHAINED

LIVE INTERVIEW WITH BOBBY SEALE RECORDED WHILE IMPRISONED IN NEW HAVEN, CONNECTICUT JAIL

THE SENTENCING OF BOBBY SEALE FOR CONTEMPT

A dramatic, historical re-enactment of that portion of the Chicago Conspiracy Trial, November 5, 1969, as it relates to Bobby Seale and the sentencing of Seale for contempt by Judge Julius Hoffman.

BOBBY SEALE: Along with Huey Newton, Bobby Seale co-founded the Black Panther Party and was the Party's Chairman (and one of its most popular spokesmen) from 1966 to 1974. The drawings (cameras were not allowed in the courtroom) of a bound-and-gagged Bobby Seal during the Chicago 8 Trial media circus sit alongside Huey Newton's "wicker chair" and the clenched-fist salute at the 1968 Olympic Games as indelible images of the Black Power era. Seale's courtroom antics became immortal, resulting in one of the most oddball recordings featured in this book.

In 1970, a company called Certron Corporation Music Division released a double album: *Bobby Seale: Gagged and Chained*. The front cover declares, "Live interview with Bobby Seale recorded while imprisoned in New Haven, Connecticut Jail." Indeed, the first couple minutes contain a brief opening statement from Seale. Seale mentions his contempt of court charges stemming from his request to have the lawyer of his choice or be allowed to defend himself as outlined in the American Constitution. Seale describes Judge Hoffman as "a fascist, a racist, and a pig" and that all the defendants "have no alternative but to stand up and act like men, act like human beings and act like free men."

Given his cruel and unusual punishment during that trial — he was "gagged and chained" to his chair, as well as hit several times in the genitals by the courtroom police — he accurately defends his right to call the judge a pig. The LP cover: "A dramatic, historical re-enactment of that portion of the Chicago Conspiracy Trial, November 5, 1969 as it relates to Bobby Seale and the sentencing of Seale for contempt by Judge Julius Hoffman."

ABOVE: Courtroom sketches of Bobby Seale "gagged and chained" are some of the most vivid images of the infamous Chicago 8 Trial. It was these illustrations that turned public opinion against the ultra-conservative judicial system.

PLAYBOY INTERVIEW: # ELDRIDGE CLEAVER

a candid conversation with the revolutionary leader of the black panthers

Eldridge Cleaver has been called the first black leader since Malcolm X with the potential to organize a militant mass movement of "black liberation." Whether he will succeed in forging it, whether he will remain free—or even alive—to lead it and whether, if he does, it will be a force for racial reconciliation or division remains to be seen. But there is no denying that Cleaver, like Malcolm X, has great impact on the young in the ghettos: They know his own ghetto origins; they identify with his defiance of the establishment and with his advocacy of self-defense; and, unlike SNCC's fiery former chieftain Stokely Carmichael, Cleaver offers them a growing organization to join—the Black Panther Party, of which he is minister of information. Carmichael, in fact, has recently joined the group himself. From their base in Oakland, California, the Panthers have established chapters in New York, Detroit, San Francisco, Los Angeles, Cleveland and San Diego, with a membership estimated at anywhere between 1000 and 5000.

Immediately identifiable by their black berets, black jackets and the empty .50-caliber shell worn on a rawhide thong around the neck, the Panthers are increasingly evident at community meetings, in churches, on the streets— every place they can manifest their concern for organizing masses of black people. Police departments, along with many white citizens, consider them highly dangerous, but some civic officials disagree. New York City Human Rights Commissioner William Booth, for exam-

ple, credits members of the Black Panther Party with helping "relieve tensions in the community." In any case, they are a force, and their leaders— Cleaver and Huey Newton, the Black Panthers' jailed minister of defense— enjoy rising support among radical young whites as well as in the black ghetto. But Cleaver, even more than Newton, generates the kind of magnetism that creates converts as well as enemies. As Jeff Shero, editor of Rat, a New York underground newspaper, puts it: "The heroes aren't Tim Leary and Allen Ginsberg anymore; they're Che Guevara and Eldridge Cleaver."

But not to everyone. Among opponents of his program and philosophy—in addition to those expectable proponents of the code phrase "law and order"—are many deeply concerned intellectuals, honest liberals and antiviolence workers for racial peace. Cleaver is accused of advocating justice via violence, which these people see as a tragic and dangerous contradiction. More importantly, perhaps, they have charged him with intensifying racial hostilities to the detriment of black Americans by alienating white sympathy and support for the cause of black equality; and with providing racists—in and out of uniform—with precisely the provocation that can lend legal legitimacy to suppression. That he has also alienated many dedicated integrationists is a fact he would be among the last to deny.

There are many, however—integrationists and otherwise—who regard Cleaver as far more than a revolutionary gang

leader. By many in the intellectual community, he is considered a writer and theoretician of major dimensions. This past fall, he was invited to give a series of lectures at the University of California in Berkeley—precipitating a fierce conflict about his "moral character" between the university on the one hand and its board of regents, Governor Reagan and the state legislature on the other. The chief reasons for this brouhaha: Cleaver's leadership of the Panthers and his 1968 book of explosive essays on the American racial dilemma, "Soul on Ice," which has sold more than 56,000 copies. Among the many laudatory reviews was that of Richard Gilman in The New Republic, who called it "a spiritual and intellectual autobiography that stands at the exact resonant center of the new Negro writing . . . a book for which we have to make room—but not on the shelves we have already built."

This sudden thrust to national prominence has been achieved by a man of 33 who has spent most of his adult life in jail. Born in Little Rock, Cleaver grew up in the Los Angeles ghetto. After several convictions for possession of marijuana, he was sentenced in 1958 to a 14-year term for assault with intent to kill and rape. By the time he was paroled in December 1966, Huey Newton and Bobby Seale had formed the Black Panther Party in Oakland. Cleaver soon joined them. Since then, he has taken time out to write not only his book but several articles in Ramparts, of which he is a senior editor, and to campaign this

"If we don't get justice in the courts, we'll get it in the streets. If atrocities against us continue unpunished, if police aggression is not stopped, more and more blacks may have to fight gunfire with gunfire."

"Our basic demand is for proportionate participation in the real power that runs this country—decision-making power concerning all legislation, all appropriations, foreign policy—every area of life."

"What can whites do? Be Americans. Stand up for liberty. Stand up for justice. Stand up for the underdog; that's supposed to be the American way. Make this <u>really</u> the home of the free."

What follows after Seale's introduction is an audio documentary, with a narrator describing the highlights of the trial leading up to Nov. 5 accompanied by actors recreating the defendants', the lawyers' and the judge's statements pulled from court transcripts. Despite their well-meaning intention, the recreations are flat and dull (Judge Hoffman and the defense attorneys) or, in the case of Seale, silly and ludicrous. For those looking for a dignified, yet accurately humorous portrayal of the proceedings, I'd recommend the 2007 film *Chicago 10* directed by Brett Morgen.

ELDRIDGE CLEAVER: Along with Bobby Seale, Eldridge Cleaver was the Black Panthers' best-known spokesman. Cleaver began sparring with the legal system as early as 1954; his book *Target Zero* contains a mug shot from the California Prison System taken that year. That sentence was for possession of marijuana. A couple of years later, Cleaver returned to prison, this time on rape charges, chronicled in his 1968 book *Soul on Ice*. Cleaver was released from prison in December 1966 and joined the staff of the San Francisco-based *Ramparts* magazine. Originally launched in 1962 as Catholic literary magazine, it soon shifted its focus to more radical exploits. *Ramparts* can take credit for influencing Martin Luther King Jr. to begin speaking out against the Vietnam War, as well as helping to arrange Cleaver's 1966 parole.

In early 1967, Huey Newton heard Cleaver speaking on the radio and was blown away by his oratory prowess. According to Bobby Seale, Newton immediately went to the station demanding Cleaver join the Panthers. Knowing Cleaver was a skilled writer, Huey made Cleaver editor of the newspaper

ABOVE: *Playboy* Magazine, well known for its tastefully done sexual photographs as well as spearheading a consumer-based culture, was also a transformative force in American politics. The seductively successful glossy actively challenged the conservative mindset by keeping up with controversially progressive racial activists, integrating thoughtful interviews with outspoken radicals like Eldridge Cleaver with its sensual content.

OPPOSITE: The grooves of the vinyl seem to radiate like sound waves from Cleaver's open mouth. His photo in the center of the LP also suggests a "bull's eye" — a lot of people wanted Cleaver dead.

DIG

More Record Company

ELDRIDGE CLEAVER
RECORDED AT SYRACUSE

and bestowed upon him the title of Minster of Information. Seale was initially skeptical of Cleaver's involvement, but once he saw Cleaver get shit done, he declared, "This nigger here is where it's at."

On July 28, 1968, in Syracuse, N.Y., Cleaver addressed the Peace & Freedom Party, a newly formed political group that had chosen him as their presidential candidate despite the fact that he was too young to be legally elected and ineligible to vote because of convictions. Therefore, his name was not allowed to officially appear on the ballot. Nevertheless, Cleaver gave an impassioned speech that day, recorded by the More Record Company from San Francisco. They released the album *Dig: Eldridge Cleaver At Syracuse,* which included informative liner notes by Reginald Major, then the Director of the Educational Opportunity Program at San Francisco State College. In 1971, Major wrote *A Panther Is A Black Cat,* one of the first books to explore the origins and goals of the Black Panther Party.

Over the course of the album, Cleaver discusses the Democrat and Republican Pig parties and mentions that President Johnson is a pig who could end the Vietnam War by just picking up the phone and calling his brother pig in the Pentagon. Also:

We are gonna organize the Black Panther Party all the way across this country, we're gonna develop the coalition all the way across this country, we're gonna build the Peace & Freedom Party and the Black Panther Party here in Syracuse, and if the chief of police and the mayor here don't like it — they can go to hell or be wait to be sent there!

But Cleaver's speech includes more than just inflammatory rhetoric. He also delivers thoughtful ideals. "Every man, woman and child on the face of planet earth has the right to the highest and the best and the most beautiful life that technology and human knowledge and wisdom is able to produce. Period. So we start from there." Later pressings of the record featured Cleaver's name in large red letters, along with the slogan *Soul On Wax.*

RIGHT: Similar to *Esquire, The New York Times* ran an informative piece about the Black Panthers mixed with satire. The photo caption is priceless: "Our other man in Algiers." This statement infers a couple of things that are quite humorous: the first being that the establishment considers Eldridge Cleaver "their representative." The second one is, at that time, the U.S. government had a tenuous relationship with Algiers at best, so the only other American of note hanging out there was acid guru Timothy Leary!

Our Other Man in Algiers   Contents—Page 21

As detailed elsewhere, an April 1968 skirmish between the Oakland police and Eldridge Cleaver, David Hilliard and Bobby Hutton led to the sudden death of Hutton, the eventual imprisonment of Hilliard and the November 1968 fleeing of Cleaver, who'd spend the next seven years in exile, settling briefly in Cuba before moving on to Algiers, where he established an international office of the Black Panther Party. The international section in Algiers became a refuge for other Panthers, black soldiers gone AWOL from the U.S. Army and the high priest of LSD, Tim Leary. By early 1970, Leary had been charged with possession of two roaches, which had been reportedly planted by a cop searching the ashtray of Leary's car. The court awarded him ten years for less than a half-ounce of marijuana. Leary escaped from prison in September 1970 and made his way to Algeria with the aid of the Weather Underground. Founded by the most radical members of the SDS, The Weathermen took their name from Dylan's song "Subterranean Homesick Blues," which has the lyric "You don't need a weatherman to know which way the wind blows." The Weathermen's 1969 founding manifesto called for a "white fighting force" to be aligned with the "Black Liberation Movement" and other radicals to achieve "the destruction of U.S. imperialism."

According to Leary's 1973 book, *Confessions Of A Hope Fiend*, Yippie Stew Albert had been sent over by Abbie Hoffman and Jerry Rubin to help prepare Leary's new surroundings in Algeria. Leary wrote, "Eldridge was pleased by my arrival. He urged that we join him, assured that he could help obtain political asylum for us. There was much that we could do together, unify the American Revolution, etc."

However, the reality of living around Cleaver was trying, and ideological differences surfaced. Things came to head when the mercurial Cleaver placed Leary under house arrest. Not long after, the Pacifica Radio network in California (Berkeley's KPFA, KPFK in L.A.) received the following reel-to-reel tape for broadcast from Cleaver:

Today is January the 12th, 1971. Since September of 1970, Dr. Timothy Leary and his wife Rosemary have been with us here in the inter-communal section of the Black Panther Party in Algeria. During that time much confusion has been generated, partly because of our own silence on the subject. As to the relationship between the Black Panther Party and Dr. Leary and his wife, I want to take this opportunity to set forth our position on that and also to make a few observations on the drug culture as a whole inside the United States. Specifically as it relates to the process of carrying out a revolutionary struggle against the fascist imperialist empire of the United States of America. A couple of months ago, I was talking to Dr. Leary about how we would deal with his case, how we would integrate him into our operation here. What role he could play, how he could function and specifically how he should be projected to the press in terms of his public image.

His suggestion was because of the difference in psychology of this part of this world, particularly he was referring to Europe, that we had to use terms, concepts and images that they could relate to. He stated that he thought he should be projected as the Aristotle or the Socrates or the Sartre of the American Revolution. I think that kind of symbolizes or typifies how Dr. Leary has constantly tried to relate to us. That he seems to take himself seriously as the high priest of the revolution. And that he, in some sense, sees himself as sort of a secular god around which the universe is constructed. Around which the revolutionary movement inside the United States revolves. And also after many discussions with him on the subject of drugs and the relevancy of drugs, specifically LSD, acid, as a weapon in a revolutionary struggle.

I've come to the conclusion that Dr. Leary is irrevocably wed to the idea of the beneficial aspects of LSD in the context of a revolutionary movement. That he would rather die than give up the idea of changing American society by dosing everyone with LSD. Well, this is not a principle or suggestion that we in the Black Panther Party can in any way endorse. Because we think it's absurd and unrealistic as an approach to carrying out our struggle. Leary seems content to continue advising people to "turn on, tune in, and drop out." And that he really means it when he says that freedom means getting high. While this in direct conflict with the needs of the American revolution. We feel that we need people with clear heads, sober people who have their wits about them because we're confronted with murderous fascist pigs.

Over the next twenty minutes, Cleaver rails against the drug culture, with the exception of marijuana, "because there are many of us who like to get high on marijuana once in a while." However, he makes it clear that people should not engage in revolutionary activity while under the influence of drugs of any type. He also emphasizes the historical importance of drugs in the past, as a progressive step in destroying the uptight status quo of American culture. But he now feels that the drug culture is no longer useful to the revolutionary struggle and that it's time to get down to the serious business of destroying the Babylonian empire.

Cleaver finally delivers the punch line: that on Jan. 9 he issued the order to take Leary and his wife to an undisclosed location and to confine them there until further notice. Cleaver implies that Leary is under house arrest, but doesn't actually use that phrase. Cleaver struggles to find the right terminology, and finally says; "I don't really know the term to use, but we'll just say that on January the 9th, we busted Leary — Leary is busted!"

Leary summarizes the event in *Confessions Of A Hope Fiend* as an ordeal that only lasted four days, and he was treated with a "stylish, professional courtesy that no white police could manage." Leary felt his being kidnapped was "part of an overall tactic on Cleaver's part to seize control of the militant revolution, to polarize and separate the political from the military, to become the toughest spokesman from the left."

Cleaver played this exploit to the fullest, with the *Paris Herald Tribune* carrying a front-page story

RIGHT: Throughout the late '60s and early '70s, *Playboy* Magazine was a cornerstone of hip American pop culture. Beside the playfully nude women, there were the annual music polls (listing the popular jazz and rock musicians of the day), and insightful articles by the likes of Norman Mailer and Jack Kerouac. Showing that the Black Panthers had truly "arrived" was an interview with Huey Newton next to the Playmate of the Month.

in which Cleaver claimed responsibility and authority over all Americans in Algeria, creating a stir in public and private circles. Meanwhile, relations between Huey Newton and Cleaver were

PLAYBOY INTERVIEW: HUEY NEWTON
a candid conversation with the embattled leader of the black panther party

When most of the American public first heard of him, it was as a name on a button, a graffito scrawled on subway walls: FREE HUEY. Huey, it turned out, was Huey P. Newton, "defense minister" of the Black Panther Party, a paramilitary organization (founded by him and "chairman" Bobby Seale) with a flair for self-publicity and inflammatory sloganeering. He became a martyr for black militants—and a cause célèbre for white liberals—after being convicted of and imprisoned for manslaughter following a 1967 shoot-out with Oakland police that many called a frame; he swore he wasn't even carrying a gun.

But being in trouble with the law—and carrying guns—was nothing new for Huey Newton. Son of a Louisiana sharecropper and Baptist minister who had almost been lynched for "talking back" to his white bosses, Huey was in a more or less uninterrupted state of war with his teachers in elementary school, started breaking open parking meters when he was 11 and was arrested at 14 for gun possession and kept in juvenile hall for a month.

Though almost illiterate until his last year of high school in Oakland—to which his family had moved when he was two —Newton taught himself to read and write and, in 1959, entered Oakland City (now Merritt) College. There he met

Donald Warden, head of the Afro-American Association, hung out with members of a socialist labor party and, in 1961, was introduced to the Black Muslims. "Malcolm X was the first political person in this country that I really identified with," says Newton. "If he had lived and had not been purged, I probably would have joined the Muslims. As it is, his insistence that blacks ought to defend themselves with arms when attacked by police became one of the original points in the program of the Black Panther Party."

When he wasn't in class or at meetings during this period, Huey was spending his spare time burglarizing homes in Berkeley, passing forged checks, engaging in credit-card hustles and other activities for which he was occasionally caught—but never tried, for lack of evidence. His first jail term, in 1964, was for assault with a dangerous weapon: a steak knife. Huey and other witnesses present claimed it was an act of self-defense. In any case, he served eight months—two of which were spent in solitary confinement in a cell the other inmates called the "soul breaker"—and drew an additional three years' probation.

In 1965, out of jail and back at Merritt College, Newton joined Seale and a handful of other blacks in forming the Soul Students Advisory Council, which pushed for the rights of black students.

But since the Watts uprising some months earlier, the Oakland police had been patrolling the black ghettos with shotguns and rifles at the ready; Newton and Seale felt a militant response was needed and, in October of 1966, created the Black Panther Party for Self-Defense. "The party was formed as an alert patrol—an armed one," says Newton. "We wanted to show that we didn't have to tolerate police abuse, that the black community would provide its own security, following the local laws and ordinances and the California Penal Code." By then a prelaw student at Merritt, Newton had carefully researched the code and found that it was perfectly legal for a citizen to carry a loaded, unconcealed gun.

The alert patrols were an instantaneous success from the standpoint of gaining publicity, which is what the Panthers needed most. In a series of dramatic confrontations with police, Newton refused to surrender his weapon—and threatened to use it in self-defense if they tried to take it away. The impact on black crowds was electric; they weren't used to seeing a black man refuse to submit to a white policeman, let alone jack a round of ammunition into the firing chamber of an M-1, as he did once in the face of a squad of officers who then backed off and docilely went away.

But the event that launched the party

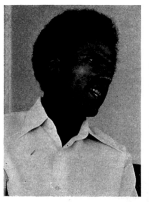

CANDICE BERGEN

"Eldridge Cleaver's rhetoric allowed the police to murder many of our members without great community protest. If we'd had an organized people, they wouldn't have been able to get away with it."

"Our ambition is to change the American Government. I think that ultimately it will be through armed violence, because the American ruling circle will not give up without a bitter struggle."

"While I was handcuffed on a stretcher, the police kept beating and spitting on me. I was bleeding internally, so I started spitting back—lungsful of blood right in their faces."

breaking down for reasons both real and imagined. Leary would make his exit to Switzerland, where he would cross paths with the Krautrock band Ash Ra Tempel in August 1972 and record an album titled *Seven Up*. Leary contributed vocals to Ash Ra Tempel's mixture of ethereal and blues-based melodies. Leary's libretto was based around a "mind map," stepping through the various stages of perception, culminating in the supreme level of "white light" at which point you travel no further, as consciousness and identity disintegrate.

HUEY NEWTON: Taking advantage of the fact that Cleaver was out of the country, the FBI stepped up their COINTELPRO (Counter Intelligence Program). The FBI's search-and-destroy mission was to deepen the growing ideological divide between Cleaver and Newton's philosophies. Cleaver called for an escalation of armed battles with police, while Newton felt it was time to set aside weapons and focus on the various programs initiated by the Party: free breakfast for children before school, free bags of groceries for the poor, sickle cell testing and other community services.

Meanwhile, the FBI sent bogus messages between various Panthers with suggestions of mutiny and assassinations. With the entire Black Panther Party under duress, paranoia was easy to fuel. By early 1971, Newton had expelled Cleaver and the entire International office. Newton and Cleaver would continue to do battle publically, with Newton denouncing Cleaver in the Black Panther newspaper and Cleaver issuing tape recordings condemning Newton as the right wing of the Party. Across the United States, the Panthers began to fragment, with Newton vs. Cleaver factions cropping up. Expulsions continued with the dramatic exit of co-founder and Chairman Bobby Seale in August 1974. Newton ran to Cuba, following his arrest for supposedly killing a prostitute. Elaine Brown became Chairman of the Black Panther Party, the first and only woman to do so. Brown oversaw the Party

until July 1977, when Newton returned to America to stand trial. The following year, Newton was acquitted of murder. By this point, the Party was running on fumes.

There was a book of poems and two albums directly associated with Huey Newton issued during his lifetime. In 1975, while Huey Newton was exiled in Cuba, City Lights, publisher of Beat classics such as *Howl*, put out *Insights*, twenty pages of Newton's succinct, poignant poems that reflected on prison, wisdom, ego, consciousness and knowledge. The book also included twenty-five poems by Ericka Huggins. Huggins was an editor of the Panthers' newspaper and educational director of the Intercommunal Youth Institute, an elementary school run by the Party in East Oakland. Ericka's husband John Huggins had been assassinated by US members on the UCLA campus in 1969, and her writing spoke of her continued commitment to the movement, including tributes to Jonathan Jackson and Bunchy Carter, and lyrical observations about East 14th street in Oakland.

In 1970, Paredon Records released *Huey Newton Speaks*. The cover declares, "The founder of the Black Panther Party speaks of struggle, revolution, philosophy, prison, racism, and death," followed by "Interviewed July 4th, 1970 by Mark Lane in the California State Prison at San Luis Obispo." Below that was a quote from Newton, "In the new world the most important thing will not be a social status or a material possession, it will be love and harmony between men."

Paredon founders Barbara Dane and Irwin Silber, in a December 1991 interview conducted by Jeff Place, discussed the origins of the Newton album. Dane and Place were close friends with lawyer/activist Mark Lane and he was extremely interested in Newton's legal situation. He'd been trying for some time to interview Newton, but had been continually turned down by prison authorities who were denying permission as a way of keeping Newton out of the public eye. Finally, Lane was able to secure an interview with the help of Charles Garry, Newton's attorney. Garry accompanied Lane to the prison and is credited as a co-interviewer. Dane mentions that because Newton had been held in solitary for a couple years, nobody had been able to interview him, and that Paredon had no direct communication with Newton except through Lane and Garry. Nevertheless, they were eager to release an album of Newton speaking. Newton had told Lane that he could release the interview in any form he wished in order to help popularize Newton's legal case. So, Paredon produced an album, sending Newton a copy upon its release as well as distributing it via the Black Panther Party.

Lane's interview is a remarkable snapshot of a period when Newton was locked down in his cell twenty-one hours per day for weeks at a time. Yet, over the course of three days, Newton emerged calmly for a total of twelve hours to participate in these interview sessions. Lane said, "I have never met a man more at peace with himself: more free. He is less a prisoner than any man I have ever met."

In this interview, Newton discussed his refusal to work inside the prison for their usual pay of 2-to-10¢ per hour. He demanded a minimum wage of $1.65 per hour, for which he counter-offered to pay back the prison system $1,500 a year for his room and board. The bureaucracy running California couldn't put their head around this concept, so Newton refused to participate in their work program. When asked about his post-prison plans, Newton replied one of his duties would be helping Cleaver return to the United States. (At the time, Newton and Cleaver were still comrades.) Unbeknownst to any of the participants at the time, Newton would be released just a month after this interview was conducted.

Seven minutes of the flipside is devoted to a press conference that Newton gave on Aug. 22, 1970 in Manhattan after his release. He told the assembled newsmen that his trial had helped motivate the Party to battle against oppression of all kinds, as well as give the Black Panthers solidarity with the people of Vietnam

engaged in fighting American troops. The prison interview continues on the remainder of Side Two, in which Newton articulated a deep knowledge of global revolutionary movements. For a 28 year-old raised in the Oakland ghetto (before the Internet age), having never traveled outside of America (at that point), Newton was incredibly acute and worldly.

In 1972, Folkways Records released an LP titled *Huey!/Listen, Whitey!*, which featured two different recordings. The *Huey!* side was subtitled *Black Panther platform with Seale, Cleaver, Rap Brown* and taken from the soundtrack of the documentary film *Huey!*. The record begins with rank-and-file Panthers outside of the Alameda County Courthouse pronouncing, "We're going to be here and stay here until Huey P. Newton is set free. If he is not set free, the sky is the limit!"

It then shifts to the Free Huey Rally at the Oakland Auditorium on Feb. 17, 1968 — the same event captured on Stokely Carmichael's *Free Huey* album. The *Huey!* side of this record is like a companion piece, as it includes sound bites from the other personalities who spoke that night: H. Rap Brown, Eldridge Cleaver, Bobby Seale, attorney Charles Garry, Bob Avakian of the Peace & Freedom Party and even Huey Newton's mother. She thanks everyone for attending her son's birthday celebration, with an overwhelming response. Bobby Seale also receives a charitable round of applause, as he exquisitely explains the Party's previously outlined ten-point platform.

H. Rap Brown fuels the crowd when he declares, "the only thing that's gonna free Huey is gun-powder!" After Brown speaks, edited snippets of Carmichael's oration are heard — the same speech that appears in its entirety on the *Free Huey* album. But on this *Huey!* LP, there's no acknowledgment that Carmichael is speaking, nor any mention of him anywhere in on the LP jacket. Actually, many of the speakers are misidentified or not listed at all. This recording is easily one of the most disappointing releases detailed in this book, one not worthy of Newton's legacy.

The other side of the album is titled *Listen, Whitey!* (subtitled *Black communities reaction to the assassination of Dr. Martin Luther King*). *Listen, Whitey!* is also taken from the soundtrack of a documentary film. It opens with a radio announcer: "This is WWRL 1600 on the dial in New York." The DJ begins taking "on air" phone calls from listeners, who comment on the best way

PAREDON P1004

HUEY NEWTON SPEAKS

The founder of the Black Panther Party
speaks of struggle, revolution, philosophy,
prison, racism, and death
Interviewed July 4th, 1970
by Mark Lane in the California State Prison
at San Luis Obispo
"In the new world the most important thing
will not be a social status or a material
possession, it will be love and harmony
between men."—Huey Newton

seize the time!

ELAINE BROWN

BLACK PANTHER PARTY

to immortalize King Jr.'s legacy. Some feel they should continue King Jr.'s nonviolent tactics, others think it's time "to stand up as men, to face force with force when necessary."

The record switches to another radio station, Washington D.C.'s WPGC. Interspersed between radio broadcasts (recorded the week of King Jr.'s assassination) and an overdubbed narrator (for the purposes of the documentary film) are a cross-section of unidentified black men and women from all walks of life voicing the senselessness of King Jr.'s death. Several of them anticipate an increase in strength and a rise in popularity of Black Power now that King Jr.'s era has passed. As an aural snapshot of the week of King Jr.'s death, these recordings are much more compelling than the side celebrating Huey Newton.

ELAINE BROWN — *SEIZE THE TIME*: Black Panthers Bunchy Carter and John Huggins had been murdered in January 1969 on the UCLA campus during a scuffle with members of US. Chief of Staff David Hilliard went to Los Angeles to attend Carter's funeral where he heard Elaine Brown sing the Thomas Dorsey gospel song "Precious Lord." Later that evening, Hilliard summoned Brown to sing her own songs, accompanying herself on piano. She performed three of her compositions: "The Panther," "The Meeting" (written about an encounter with Eldridge Cleaver) and "Assassination" (written in jail following the murders of Carter and John Huggins). Hilliard decided "The Meeting" should become the Black Panther Party National Anthem, ordering cassettes of the song to be distributed amongst members and for the lyrics to be memorized. He commanded Brown to record an entire album of her songs, and thus her 1969 album *Seize the Time* (issued on Vault Records) was born, which the Black Panthers' newspaper called "the first songs of the American revolution."

Brown brought in Horace Tapscott to oversee the proceedings. As she describes in her book *A Taste of Power*, "The piano and horn arrangements of Horace Tapscott blended wonderfully with my messages, with 'their' songs which my hand wrote. Under Horace's direction, his jazz orchestra lifted my unembellished piano-playing."

Brown spoke with writer Denise Sullivan for the magazine *Ptolemaic Terrascope* about the origins of the record:

This guy gave us a party, he was a VP at ABC/Dunhill Records and I asked him, "How do I get an album made?" and he said he knew a guy at Vault Records. We recorded it direct to disc, without any playback and no tracks. Horace's whole orchestra had to be there. That guy was fired from ABC/Dunhill and could never find another job and was blackballed; he lost his job, his house, his marriage, his whole life, just because he helped us in that way.

Brown described how she knew Tapscott:

I first met Horace at the Watts Happening Coffeehouse, he was very involved in black music. He always thought music was an answer [...] Tapscott gave me a sense as singer-songwriter; he validated me. He was a true jazz musician and great pianist. His musicianship was so big — in an Alice Coltrane tradition of piano playing — and he could sit down and orchestrate a song just as you sang it.

While I was researching this book, several people told me that they were disappointed that *Seize The Time* wasn't a bitching funk album, along the lines of Betty Davis' (Miles Davis' ex-wife). They are missing the point. Black Power wasn't just about the groove. It was more about the message. Brown's influences included Bob Dylan and a strong dose of classical music — as she mentioned in the *Ptolemaic Terrascope*:

I think Huey Newton liked my music because its classical quality gave dignity to our movement, it wasn't just dancing in the street, not that there is anything wrong with Martha and the Vandellas because we loved that...Someone accused me of not having a black sound and I wasn't sure what that meant. I just wanted to make the most beautiful

OPPOSITE: Very few album covers ever designed have dispensed with song titles and other essential information on the back cover. However, Elaine Brown's 1969 LP did exactly that. The album effectively had two front covers — the seminal Emory Douglas illustration on the front lets the viewer know exactly what the record was all about, and this back cover photo of Brown which offered an equally striking, but far less militant image.

sound I could make and do the most beautiful thing I could do to honor our people.

Broadside was a small, influential folk-music publication that began in 1962. Its mimeographed pages blended handwritten music notation (often freshly written topical songs by the likes of Bob Dylan, Phil Ochs and Tom Paxton), typewritten text, hand-drawn illustrations and news clippings from other magazines. With its cut-and-paste layout, *Broadside* resembled the indie-rock fanzines of the 1980s. Many of the political songs that made their debut in the magazine were recorded by the artists-composers for inclusion in a series of *Broadside* compilation LPs released by the Folkways record label.

The June 1970 issue dedicated an entire page to Elaine Brown's *Seize The Time* album, including lyrics and musical notation of the title track. There's even a review reproduced from another publication known as the *Grass Roots Forum*, which compares her singing to Nina Simone's, "but with more clear headedness, as she builds up dramatic effects with her voice and the persistent rhythm and support of her instrumental backing." The review makes it clear that this "isn't an album of sweet, or passionately crooned love songs," and quotes Brown as well: "I used to write about flowers, butterflies and love — that kind of bullshit." The reviewer praises Brown for humanizing and glorifying the dedication of a Black Panther member, as well as for her expressive "admonitions to the rest of us to wake up and get with it." The review wraps up with a PO Box address in San Francisco for the "Ministry of Information," from which you can order the album for $3.50.

Also in 1970, Carola Standertskjöld, a Finnish singer of American jazz and pop standards, covered Brown's song "Seize The Time," accompanied by a "big band," on Scandinavian television. The clip of this cross-cultural moment, which featured large-scale reproductions of the *Seize The Time* album artwork (as well as photos of Huey Newton) as part of Standertskjöld's stage props, is available on YouTube.

During those years, Elaine Brown did live performances in support of the Party. Her appearances include an Oct. 11, 1970 show billed as a "Seize The Time" benefit in honor of Bobby Seale, in which The Lumpen also performed. There's brief (but silent) video footage from the early '70s of Brown playing a Fender Rhodes piano in an unidentified Oakland location and a short

film (with sound) of Brown singing, which I presume to be shot in Los Angeles circa 1969-70.

In 1973, Bobby Seale ran for Mayor of Oakland and Brown for City Council. Throughout the winter and spring, they actively campaigned with the support of the Party, who covered their activities in the Panther newspaper. On Dec. 1 of that year, they appeared at San Francisco's Glide Memorial Church. Led by the Rev. Cecil Williams, the Methodist Church was (and is) a cornerstone of the Bay Area black community. Throughout the 1960s and '70s, Glide was both a place of worship and refuge for the politically oppressed — offering a safe place for a diverse cross-section of society, from the Hookers Convention to the American Indian Movement to the Black Panthers. The church also served as a rallying point for the anti-Vietnam War movement and housed speeches by Bill Cosby and Angela Davis. There's a recording of Brown playing piano and singing at Glide that day. Sister Ruth Jones makes an introduction:

It is with a great deal of pleasure for me to bring to you a woman — many of you have seen and heard, it has not happened before, that a woman who knows what it means to struggle for all people, who knows how to take the stand that this woman has taken, therefore, she has decided that she would run for the city of Oakland council seat. Without anything further, I would like to introduce to you, our next, we hope, city councilwoman Elaine Brown!

The crowd roars with approval, Brown thanks the Glide community and the Rev. Cecil Williams for inviting her and says, "We have two selections that we'd like to do." She begins to play a grand piano, accompanied by her compelling voice: "I'd like to hold some child forever, hide his eyes from it all, yes, hold some black child and rock him, but outside it's raging and there's no time to hold."

Brown performs "No Time," the opening song from her Black Forum album, and the audience cheers as the song comes to a close. With little pause, she launches into an engaging performance of "Very Black Man," a song of pride from *Seize The Time*. Again, the crowd responds enthusiastically, a reflection of Brown's successful merging of music and political commentary. Bobby Seale follows with a passionate campaign speech, discussing the corruption of the Nixon administration vs. the Black Panther Party's bid for Oakland mayor and city council. Seale's speech concludes with "All Power to the people!" "Right On!" as the church choir launches into "Reach Out and Touch (Somebody's Hand)."

A March 1973 issue of the Panther newspaper mentions that four hundred people attended Brown's birthday celebration held at her campaign headquarters in downtown Oakland, in which significant endorsements for her campaign were announced. Mentioned amongst the Bay Area Democratic Party organizations that supported her were a couple of individuals, including movie producer Bert Schneider. The newspaper also reported that live performances by "the 'get down' sounds of In One Piece, the mellow moods of Love, Power and Strength (backed by United Black Artists), and the dance routines of Shades of Soul kept the entire affair jumping with joyful enthusiasm and a fresh air of commitment and confidence."

In keeping with the Party's support of Brown's music, the same issue dedicated a page to her lyrics in commemoration of her March 2nd birth date. A "Happy Birthday Elaine" headline was followed by these words: "The talents and creative abilities of popular community leader Elaine Brown extend far beyond her winning efforts to organize meaningful social programs for the people of Oakland. Indeed, Elaine is also an accomplished singer and songwriter, possessing a singular, consummate ability to translate the feelings and desires of our people into a truly beautiful, haunting artistic form."

The newspaper included the complete lyrics to "Assassination" and "Very Black Man" featured on *Seize The Time*; two songs from her recent Black Forum album, "No Time"; and the title track "Until We're Free." Although the album cover had no title (other than *Elaine Brown*) — the album was called *Until We're Free*, which is how Huey Newton's inner-sleeve notes refer to it, how the Party newspaper referenced it several times during 1973 and how Brown still refers to it decades later.

On Friday July 27, 1973, Elaine shared the bill with Ike & Tina Turner and Graham Central Station at the Oakland Auditorium as a benefit for the Party's community programs. An August 1973 issue of the Party newspaper mentions that the Bishop Norman Williams Quintet performed some "very mellow jazz" in their opening set, and that the group, led by tenor saxophonist Brother Norman Williams, remained on stage to backup Brown, "who proved why Brother Huey Newton has called her 'the first, genuine People's Artist America has produced.'"

The concert review states Brown's full and resonant voice filled the auditorium and that "Elaine sang and occasionally accompanied herself on piano. Many of the songs she did were taken from her new album ["Until We're Free" released by Motown], and all were written by Ms. Brown herself. From her swinging opening number, to the soft and sweet love ballad, 'No Time' which she dedicated to 'all people involved in the struggle for the liberation of all oppressed people,' Elaine Brown's performance was a joy to behold." ⊙

Flying Dutchman

STEREO   FDS-105

AIN'T NO AMBULANCES FOR NO NIGGUHS TONIGHT

STANLEY CROUCH

LOOK OUT WHITEY!
Black Power's Gon' Get Your Mama!

Like the Panthers, members of SNCC turned up on a variety of albums, some as singers and/or songwriters, while others gave speeches. Angela Davis released two albums of interviews, and inspired many tribute songs recorded by rock, jazz and soul artists during the "Free Angela" era. Several black female poets made their entrance onto the scene with books and recordings that reflected on their personal lives as well as the turbulent world around them. The Watts Prophets presented a universal message about fusing politics and humanity, while Kain of the Last Poets recorded a solo album that exploded with musical diversity.

VIOLENCE IS AS AMERICAN AS CHERRY PIE: SNCC RECORDINGS

STOKELY CARMICHAEL AND THE DIALECTICS OF LIBERATION: The Congress on the Dialectics of Liberation was held at the Roundhouse in July 1967. Amongst music fans, the Roundhouse in London is a notable venue where American bands like The Doors and the Patti Smith Group made their British debuts in 1968 and 1976, respectively. The Roundhouse is also an essential part of pop culture history. In October 1966, progressive rock pioneers Soft Machine and Pink Floyd performed at the launch party for the underground newspaper *International Times*.

OPPOSITE: In 1995, movie producer Lynda Obst told The New Yorker that back in the day, "Stanley cultivated this gangster look with a little cigarette hanging from the corner of his mouth" (which is very evident on the front of this 1969 album). Crouch, appearing inside a "bombed out" brick building, symbolizes that ambulances won't go into "war zones" such as the Watts Riots.

Over two weeks in July 1967, the Roundhouse hosted lectures in the politics of modern dissent, in which existential psychiatrists, Marxist intellectuals, anarchists and political leaders gathered to debate social issues. Amongst the speakers were Stokely Carmichael and Allen Ginsberg, joined by a diverse mix, including German philosopher Herbert Marcuse talking about liberation from the affluent society, Scottish psychiatrist R. D. Laing on social pressures, Marxist economist Paul Sweezy on the future of capitalism, and Julian Beck (director of The Living Theatre, a highly influential experimental drama group), who lectured on money, sex and the theater. Amazingly, each of the speakers at the Congress on the Dialectics of Liberation was accorded his own album. A total of twenty-three different recordings were released from the conference. Carmichael had two

⚡ MALCOLM X ⚡

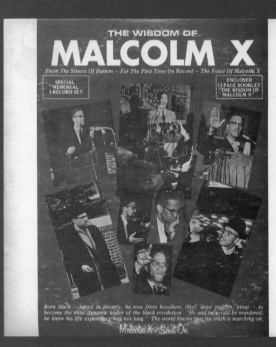

Malcolm X is the father of Black Power — and with his assassination on Feb. 21, 1965, he became the first martyr of the movement as well, especially among Black Nationalists. While nobody would deny the inspiration of Martin Luther King Jr.'s nonviolent protest, it was X's doctrine of obtaining Civil Rights "by any means necessary" that turned on Huey Newton, Bobby Seale, Eldridge Cleaver, Stokely Carmichael and Amiri Baraka, amongst others. David Hilliard wrote in his 2006 book *Huey: Spirit of the Panther*, "'Here was a man,' Huey used to tell me, 'who combined the world of the street and the world of the scholar.'" The original full name of the Black Panther Party was the Black Panther Party for Self-Defense, inspired by Malcolm X's words, "It doesn't mean that I advocate violence, but at the same time, I am not against using violence in self-defense. I don't call it violence when it's self-defense, I call it intelligence."

Eldridge Cleaver described X's influence on prisoners in *Soul on Ice*: "Malcolm X had special meaning for black convicts. A former prisoner himself, he had risen from the lowest depths to great heights. For this reason, he was a symbol of hope…" In his autobiography *Ready for Revolution*, Carmichael recalled

STEREO · SD 795

LEFT: The cover clearly recalls the many faces of Malcolm X, the complex figure that he was and the tremendous personal and ideological changes that he was going through during the last year of his life.

ABOVE: After Malcolm X was assassinated in 1965, posthumous album releases in the late '60s, such as this one, helped market his legacy to the burgeoning youth movement; the album contains speeches given to young people in Ghana, England and the United States. The way his name encircles the album cover echoes how his powerful rhetoric encircled the globe.

albums of his own: *Black Power — Address to Congress* and *Black Power — Address to Black Community*. Pressed in small quantities and privately distributed, these albums make even the rarest LPs featured in this book seem easy to find. Carmichael, along with Ginsberg and R. D. Laing, was included on a group dialogue album taken from the symposium: *Dialectics Of Liberation: Public Meeting And Discussion*.

The night before Carmichael was scheduled to speak, news of John Coltrane's passing reached him. In Carmichael's mind this could not be ignored, so he began with an announcement and requested the attendees rise and "observe a period of silence for this great black artist and cultural warrior." As Carmichael later recalled, "A few people seemed surprised, vaguely discomfited. But in truth, I really wasn't asking them.

the first time he'd seen Malcolm X speak up close: "What Malcolm demonstrated that night in Crampton Auditorium on the Howard campus was the raw power, the visceral potency, of the grip our unarticulated collective blackness held over us. I'll never forget it."

While earlier figures such as Marcus Garvey come into play, no single protagonist of the era had more influence on Black Power than Malcolm X. To this day he remains ripe for rediscovery by students and historians. His ideas and concepts have been recycled, especially by Black Nationalists. With good reason — he often strikes a resonant chord.

> *If I have a cup of coffee that is too strong for me because it is too black, I weaken it by pouring cream into it. I integrate it with cream. If I keep pouring enough cream in the coffee, pretty soon the entire flavor of the coffee is changed, the very nature of the coffee is changed. If enough cream is poured in, eventually you don't even know that I*

had coffee in this cup. This is what happened with [Martin Luther King Jr.'s August 1963] March on Washington. The whites didn't integrate it, they infiltrated it. Whites joined it, they engulfed it, they became so much a part of it, it lost its original flavor. It ceased to be a black march, it ceased to be militant, it ceased to be angry, it ceased to be impatient. In fact, it ceased to be a march.

Years later, Amiri Baraka summarized the impact of Malcolm X's death on culture and politics: "And for many of us, the assassination of Malcolm X was the end of what we called 'Downtown' as the center of 'new learning.'" Itfs meaning was altered and diminished. In the wake of this assault on the Afro-American people and the concomitant rising of the Black Liberation Movement, there was an even sharper emergence of Black Nationalism.

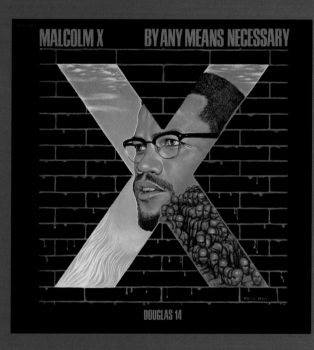

DOUGLAS 14

ABOVE: There is something "Christ-like" about Malcolm X's image: visions of hell, fire, blood dripping from the brick wall, "the lost souls," which may well be Africans packed into slave ships.

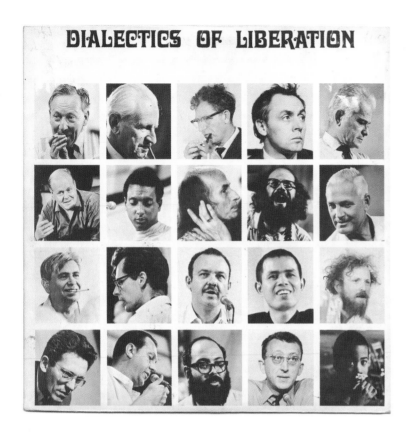

DIALECTICS OF LIBERATION

It was a matter of respect. They stood. That established; I went to work."

Carmichael's lecture hit hard.

I'm always amazed when I pick up a newspaper and read that "England today decided to give the West Indies their independence." That's totally absurd, you cannot give independence to anyone. You cannot grant anyone their independence. If it's independence, they just take it; and that is what white America is going to learn. No white

liberal can give me anything. The only thing a white liberal can do for me is help civilize the other whites, because they need to be civilized.

H. RAP BROWN: In May 1967, H. Rap Brown became Chairman of SNCC, replacing Stokely Carmichael, who had chosen not to seek a second term so he could focus on spreading "Black Power" throughout the ghettos of the North. Like Carmichel, H. Rap Brown was a clever and ass-kicking orator. As Carmichael jokingly told reporters when Brown took over, "You'll be happy to have me back when you hear from him, he's a bad man."

Soon after, at a speech in Jersey City, Brown announced, "We must wage guerrilla warfare on the honky white man." A week later in Cambridge, Maryland, Brown decreed, "If America doesn't come around, then black people are going to burn it down." After parts of Cambridge were torched in July 1967, Brown was charged with inciting to riot and arson. In February 1968, during Huey Newton's birthday rally in Oakland, attended by Carmichael and H. Rap Brown, Eldridge Cleaver announced an alliance between SNCC and the Panthers, naming Carmichael as honorary Prime Minister and Brown as Minister of Justice. By the summer of '68, that alliance dissolved as SNCC became suspicious of the Panthers' intentions. They accused the Panthers of wanting to take over SNCC, while the Panthers insisted they wanted the more experienced SNCC leaders to oversee a merger. During this era, SNCC changed from the Student *Nonviolent* Coordinating Committee to the Student *National* Coordinating Committee. In 1969, Brown wrote the book *Die Nigger Die!*, chronicling his (at that point) brief-yet-turbulent life, interspersed with his acerbic views on America's political structure. According to his book, "Rap" was a nickname he picked up during his school days because he could rap. "The name stuck because my brother Ed would always say 'That my nigger Rap,' 'Rap my nigger.'"

ABOVE: A prime example of a privately pressed record that emerged during this era of material deemed too academic for the masses. These are the insurrection-fomenting and sometimes furry faces of contemporaneous existentialist dissent in the fast-forwarding multi-cultural and artistically progressive late '60s: Ginsberg, Laing and Beck, alongside Stokely Carmichael and Bateson, ferociously challenging homogeneous notions of reality and the poetry of commerce.

OPPOSITE: Although there is no direct connection between the performances of H. Rap Brown and Leon Thomas on this record, Brother Brown and Brother Thomas are fighting the same thing — only with different weapons (spoken word vs. song). H. Rap Brown appears contemplative (not as if he is screaming), the fist is not a Black Power Salute, but closed in a moment of reflection. Perhaps he's thinking of his fallen SNCC comrades, Featherstone and Payne.

Brown went underground in March 1970 while out on bail. He resurfaced in October 1971 after seventeen months on the FBI's "Ten Most Wanted List," engaging in a gun battle with New York City cops, which left him hospitalized. He spent the next five years (1971-76) in Attica State Prison. During that time Brown converted to Islam, changing his name to Jamil Abdullah al-Amin. Since 2002, he has been imprisoned for allegedly shooting a policeman. H. Rap Brown became an immortal voice of the turbulence of the '60s when he declared, "Violence is as American as cherry pie."

In 1970, the Flying Dutchman label released *SNCC's RAP*, an LP that combined two separate recordings: H. Rap Brown speaking on Oct. 22, 1969 at Long Island University and Leon Thomas performing on March 15, 1970 at the Fillmore East. This isn't a direct collaboration between Brown and spiritual jazz singer Thomas. Instead, Brown's October '69 speech is broken into four segments, separated by two excerpts of Thomas' March '70 concert. There's a final fragment where the album switches clumsily back and forth between Brown's and Thomas' performances. Using today's digital editing technology, that section would have been seamless. The tapes were assembled hastily at Electric Ladyland (Jimi Hendrix' personal studio) by engineer Eddie Kramer and SNCC's Communications Department. The LP was rush-released to rally support for Brown, who'd gone underground.

Julius Lester's liner notes clarify the concept:

This record is augmented by the sound and words of Leon Thomas and what more can be said behind that? He adds another dimension to the concepts articulated by Rap, showing the roots from which we've come, and all the variations therein.... Brother Brown and Brother Thomas are saying the same thing, only with different weapons. There is no better example of a brother functioning in the struggle on the level he happens to be on than Leon Thomas. He has turned his voice into a revolutionary weapon. And, that's what it's all about.

Lester also explains why Brown had disappeared.

With the appearance of this record, many will wonder, 'Where is Rap? Is he alive?' He has not been seen or heard of

since the first week of March 1970, when he disappeared at the time of the murders of Ralph Featherstone and William "Che" Payne in Bell Air, Maryland, where he was to have gone on trial for inciting to riot in Cambridge, Maryland. To those who might ask themselves such questions, it is clear that they have not internalized the revolutionary thought of H. Rap Brown. Where he is, what he is doing, whether he is alive or dead is not the question. The question is: What're you doing, brother? What're you doing, sister? And that is the only question. When Rap Brown wants us to know what he's doing, he'll let us know. In the meantime, Black folks still ain't free. And as baaaaad a dude as Rap is, ain't no way he can fight no revolution by his lonesome. Is there?

Elsewhere in this book, I discuss Leon Thomas' anti-war rant, "Damn Nam (Ain't Goin to Vietnam)" from his *Spirits Known and Unknown* album; a live version is included on *SNCC's RAP*, along with a brief Thomas number entitled "Um, Um, Um." The back of *SNNC's RAP* states, "This album is dedicated to the memory of William 'Che' Payne and Ralph Featherstone." Both were SNCC members who had died in the line of duty. The March 23, 1970 issue of *Time* gave the government's explanation of their death.

Two black militants were killed when their car was blasted to bits while they were riding on a highway south of Bel Air, Md. The dead were Ralph Featherstone, 30, and William ("Che") Payne, 26. Featherstone, a former speech therapist, was well known as a Civil Rights field organizer and, more recently, as manager of the Afro-American bookstore, the Drum & Spear, in Washington. Both were friends of H. Rap Brown, whose trial on charges of arson and incitement to riot was scheduled to begin last week in Bel Air. Reconstruction of the car's speedometer indicates it was traveling about 55 miles an hour when it blew up.

Police believed that Payne had been carrying a dynamite bomb on the floor between his legs and that it accidentally exploded. A preliminary FBI investigation supported that theory. Friends of the dead men contended that white extremists had either ambushed the pair or booby-trapped their car, perhaps trying to kill Brown. But police pointed out that Featherstone and Payne had driven in from Washington without notice, cruised around Bel Air briefly and seemed to be headed back. That assassins could plot and move so quickly defies belief.

However, the magazine's final paragraph about the event seemed to argue against its own right-wing slant.

Although Featherstone had not been known as an extremist, friends said that he had grown markedly more bitter in the past year. Police cited a crudely spelled typewritten statement found on his body: "To Amerika:* I'm playing heads-up murder. When the deal goes down I'm gon [sic] be standing on your chest screaming like Tarzan. Dynamite is my response to your justice.

Decades later, the question remains: Why would an educated man like Featherstone leave a note written in that ignorant tone? And how did that piece of paper miraculously survive a dynamite blast? The whole episode stunk of the FBI's COINTELPRO campaign to destroy the Black Power movement.

The album itself is classic H. Rap Brown. He humorously offers white people advice on how to help the movement by suggesting they douse themselves in gasoline, light it and jump on President Nixon. But Brown does more than just elicit a laugh; he inspires. He describes the difference between "being educated" and "being trained." A "trained" person is someone who is programmed how the programmer desires. An "educated" person is able to relate what they see and hear to their own experience. Notably, Brown uses a music example. He cites Isaac Hayes' rendition of Jimmy Webb's "By the Time I Get to Phoenix" — a song that Hayes was able to make his own thing. Because Hayes is "educated," he was able to relate that song to his own experience. Brown then summarizes by telling the students at Long Island University that they are being "trained" by the white man to serve the political needs of whites. It is their responsibility to become "educated" to a political base that is relevant to the lives of black people.

FREEDOM IN THE AIR: Several years before Brown was running SNCC, when it was still the Student *Nonviolent* Coordinating Committee with John Lewis and Julian Bond at the helm, SNNC released an album with a totally different vibe than *SNCC's RAP*. Released on their own label as catalog number SNCC-101, *Freedom In The Air: A Documentary on Albany, Georgia 1961-1962* features traditional hymns and modern gospel, as well as the sermon "As the Eagle Stirreth Her Nest." There are also local townspeople eloquently stating their feelings on social issues, and impassioned

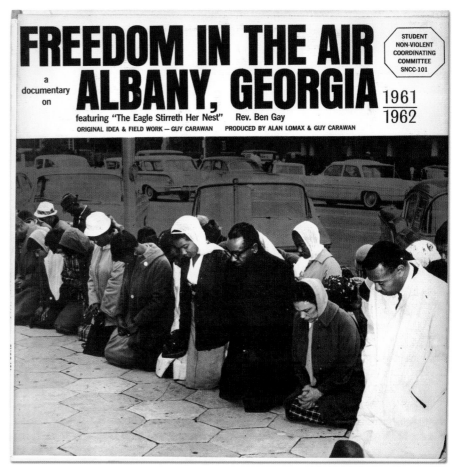

OPPOSITE: The photo shows citizens praying in protest in downtown Albany, Ga.; "just like an eagle stirs her nest, so that her young ones will have no rest" — this was the early days of SNCC, when they rustled the leaves of dissent in a "proper" manner with local clergy involved. Later, Carmichael and H. Rap Brown would bring a "badass" element to SNCC proceedings.

student organizers voicing their impatience, all captured on tape by Guy Carawan, a white folk musician and musicologist.

Carawan is credited with introducing the song "We Shall Overcome" to SNCC members in 1960. Originally a union organizing song based on an African-American spiritual, it became an anthem of the Civil Rights movement. As the liner notes for *Freedom In The Air* attest, "SNCC were the catalysts. Not only did they stir up the nest but they helped show the people in what direction to fly."

JULIUS LESTER: After attending college in Nashville in the late 1950s, Julius Lester migrated to New York City, where he immersed himself in the Greenwich Village scene as a traditional singer and guitarist. He began writing articles for the folk music journal *Sing Out!* and in 1965, co-authored a book with seminal folkie Pete Seeger detailing Leadbelly's twelve-string guitar technique. Throughout this era, Lester had casually crossed paths with SNCC, which culminated in an official capacity in 1966. Hired as SNCC's house photographer, Lester was sent to North Vietnam in May 1967 to document conditions there. A few months later, he visited Cuba as part of a contingent of songwriters organized by *Sing Out!* and singer/activist Barbara Dane. Stokely Carmichael arrived in Cuba at that same moment and was summoned by Fidel Castro. Over a period of several days, Carmichael, Castro and Lester drove around the Sierra Maestra Mountains talking endlessly and taking photos.

As an interesting aside, one of Lester's photos taken of impoverished Alabama plantation workers appears on the cover of the *Movement Soul* album: *Live recordings of songs and sayings from the Freedom Movement in the Deep South*, released by the ESP label in 1966. The album contains forty short sound bites of interviews, singing, testifying and rallies. Among the voices featured are SNCC members Willie Ricks, James Forman and John Lewis. While not the first book to use "Black Power" in the title, Richard Wright's 1954 chronicle of his trip to the African Gold Coast (before Ghana won independence from the United

RIGHT: The photographs represent several dimensions of the movement, from gospel singing to protest speeches, and also serves as a reminder that soul music did not emerge from Memphis or Detroit, but from the Deep South.

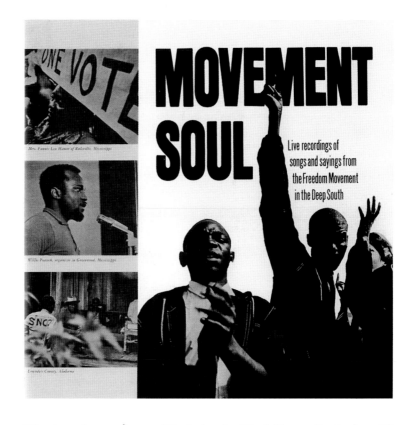

Kingdom in 1957) was titled simply *Black Power*. Lester's 1968 *Look Out Whitey! Black Power's Gon' Get Your Mama!* was an early document of the emerging movement. Although Lester claims that his was the first book to explore the American Black Power movement, he was beaten to the punch a year earlier by Stokely Carmichael's *Black Power: The Politics of Liberation in America*. Co-written with Professor Charles V. Hamilton, Carmichael's book became a manifesto of black solidarity that remains in print today via its original publisher, Vintage Books.

Nevertheless, *Look Out Whitey! Black Power's Gon' Get Your Mama!* stirred up some shit. Its aim was not only to document the historical roots of the movement via Marcus Garvey, but to needle the white community about what was brewing. During winter 1967, Lester wrote the book in SNCC's office, helmed by new chairman H. Rap Brown. Brown supported Lester's endeavors and offered to shop the book, bringing the manuscript to Dial Press. A year later, they also published H. Rap Brown's *Die Nigger Die!* Long out print, Lester's manuscript complements Carmichael's in detailing the history and theories of SNCC.

Lester spoke to writer Tim Tooher in 2006:

The role that music played at the time of mobilizing people and getting people involved in the Civil Rights movement and the anti-war movement was critical. Without music I don't think either movement would have been as successful. I was very aligned with SNCC and Malcolm X politically then. I had very little use for Dr. King.

BERNICE REAGON: Bernice Johnson Reagon is founder of the celebrated Sweet Honey in the Rock, a Grammy award-winning a cappella ensemble that has performed traditional African-American songs around the world since 1973. In 1961, a young Bernice Reagon left her birthplace of Albany, Ga. to join the SNCC Freedom Singers. Over the next decade, her journey encompassed songs of the movement, Black oral culture, traditional songs of the South and contemporary African and American protest songs.

She recorded her first solo album, *Folk Songs: The South*, for Folkways Records in 1965. In 1975, Paredon Records issued *Give Your Hands to Struggle: The Evolution of a Freedom Fighter: Songs by Bernice Reagon.* Paredon was co-founded in 1970 by white blues/jazz/folk singer Barbara Dane. Besides her diverse musical legacy, including a groundbreaking album *Barbara Dane and the Chambers Brothers* released by Folkways in 1965, Dane is a staunch Civil Rights and labor movement activist. As Dane wrote in the liner notes of a 2005 CD reissue of the *Barbara Dane and the Chambers Brothers* album, "In 1965 when this music was made, there were very few recordings

However, the Black Panthers were less impressed with Lester's discourse, with Huey Newton and Eldridge Cleaver reportedly threatening Lester in print.

Although he'd first started (much like Bob Dylan), performing work songs and traditional numbers, Lester began composing his own material. By the time he was approached by Vanguard Records (home to Joan Baez, Richard & Mimi Farina, et al.) to record his self-titled debut in 1965 (and a follow-up album entitled *Departures* in 1967), he had his own repertoire. As a singer/songwriter, Lester became sort of an African-American version of Phil Ochs — fearlessly confronting political situations in song, but with a distinctive black perspective that no white songwriter could approach.

LEFT: Julius Lester was a departure from the traditional blues-inspired black sound. Lester transformed himself (somewhat) into a black version of Phil Ochs, singing topical protest folk songs. Lester is an urban folkie; he's not a rural bluesman.

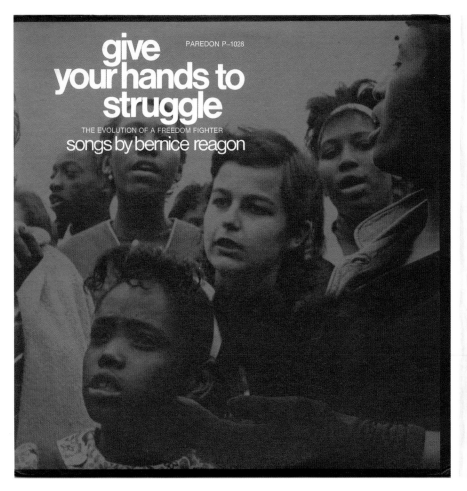

ABOUT BERNICE REAGON:

I was born in Albany, Georgia, and grew up in the Baptist Church where my father, Rev. Jessie Johnson, was minister. I have linked political struggle with music since 1961, when I joined the Albany Movement in Georgia. It was there as a song leader that I saw first-hand how Black culture has always supported people involved in struggle.

I left home and school in 1962, to sing with the original Freedom Singers of SNCC (Student Non-violent Co-ordinating Committee). Later, I moved from the songs of the Movement to the larger area of Black oral culture, attempting to find ways to use this material in the institutions where Blacks found themselves during the mid 60s. I helped Anne Romaine, a white country singer from Atlanta, Georgia, to organize the Southern Folk Festival, which brought Black and white traditional musicians to audiences throughout the South. I helped develop

the first Soul Roots Festival, which presented Black traditional materials to Black college campuses, institutions which often had made little space for such materials.

My work with public schools in Atlanta involved teacher-training workshops and the development of a year-long program which utilized Black traditional oral materials, along with the members of the Black community who had preserved those materials, in the teaching of our history to children. During the development stages of Black Nationalism and Pan Africanism, I organized the Harambee Singers, a group of Black women whose repertoire represented a link between Black traditional materials and contemporary African and U.S. protest songs.

More recently, I have received my PhD. in Oral History from Howard University, and live in Washington, D.C. with my two children, Toshi and Kwan. I continue to sing, teach, research, compose

© PAREDON RECORDS / PO BOX 889 / BROOKLYN, NEW YORK 11202

(continued on next page)

on the market which mixed black and white musicians and there were no album covers showing mixed groups of any kind. Aside from small jazz groups, not many live performances were mixed either."

From 1970 until the mid-'80s, Dane, with co-founder Irwin Silber (editor of folk music magazine *Sing Out!* from 1951 to

ABOVE: Though this album was recorded in 1975, it contains Black Nationalist songs that Reagon composed in the late '60s, along with traditional gospel songs that she had learned years before as a child. The young people featured in this cover photo symbolize Reagon's beginnings, i.e. *The Evolution of a Freedom Fighter*. Interestingly, inside the LP's sleeve notes, it was changed to "the evolution of a freedom singer."

1967), oversaw the release of fifty albums that represented leftwing and liberation movements from around the world. Besides social-protest singers, Paredon released oratory from Huey Newton, Fidel Castro and Puerto Rican independence leader Albizu Campos.

Although not recorded until 1975, several songs on Reagon's album were written in the late '60s. She annotated the inspiration of each composition in a booklet included with the LP. Her notes for "Ballad of Featherstone and Che" mentioned the March 1969 death of her friends, SNCC members Ralph Featherstone and Che Payne. Reagon cited the album *Malcolm X Speaks* and his speech "Ballots or Bullets" as the stimulus to write her song "Had, Took and Misled." Her commentary for a song entitled "In My Hands" addressed the ever-widening gap (especially for young African-Americans) between the original Civil Rights movement and the emerging Black Nationalist crusade:

> *In 1968, I was asked who I would vote for: Hubert Humphrey or Richard Nixon. I tried to answer that question with "In My Hands." At the time, I was becoming increasingly involved in the Black Nationalist movement. Black people were looking to their own community for solutions, rather than to the traditional American symbols and institutions. I was still too close to the Civil Rights movement to be able to evaluate what had been accomplished. I was critical of the conservative traditional Black leadership, and emphatic about my own responsibilities to help build a world that would not have to kill a Malcolm.*

The album features no instrumentation save Reagon's voice, but by overdubbing herself she created a wall of sound. As

producer Barbara Dane told Smithsonian archivist Jeff Place during a December 1991 interview:

> *And as a singer I want to tell you, watching her work was an absolute revelation, and I consider her a real tour de force. I don't know anybody else who's done anything like it. She overdubbed all the voices and made this whole album, as you will hear, very texturally involved and interesting without retaking anything. I mean everything was first take, first take, first take! All the way through the album, which indicated to me that she had a clear grasp of what she wanted to hear.*

DETERMINING THEIR OWN DESTINY:
ANGELA DAVIS AND OTHER SIGNIFICANT PARTICIPANTS

ANGELA DAVIS: It's a common misconception that Angela Davis was a member of the Black Panther Party. She wasn't — she was a member of the American Communist Party. However, the Panthers and Davis crossed paths, especially in support of political prisoner George Jackson. Davis enjoyed a personal relationship with Jackson, exchanging passionate letters that coincided with Davis befriending his mother and brother Jonathan in hopes of starting a crusade to set the Soledad Brothers free. While Davis spoke at rallies in defense of Jackson, his brother Jonathan hatched other plans (which may or may not have involved Davis).

As detailed elsewhere, on Aug. 7, 1970, George's younger brother Jonathan burst into the Marin County Hall of Justice brandishing weapons, resulting in several deaths, including his own. Davis apparently purchased some of the guns and she became the target of a nationwide search. Placed on the FBI's "Ten Most Wanted List," she was caught in late 1970 and imprisoned. With Jonathan Jackson dead, the government needed a scapegoat, so Davis was charged with all the events of Aug. 7,

LEFT: Gotta love an album with a photograph of an angry black man titled *Ballots or Bullets*, released on "First Amendment Records." One can only hope that someday President Obama will step up to the plate.

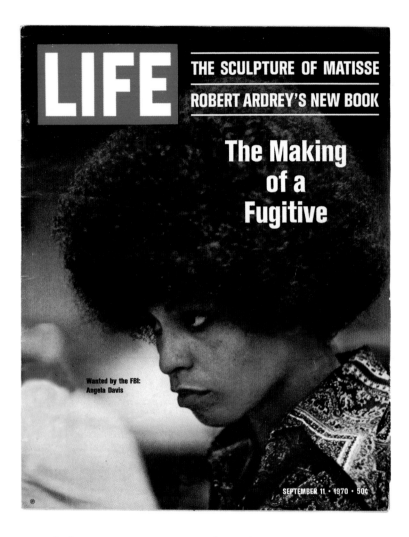

Wanted by the FBI:
Angela Davis

SEPTEMBER 11 · 1970 · 50¢

In 1971, Flying Dutchman Records released *Soul and Soledad*, which featured an interview with Davis conducted by San Francisco radio commentator Art Seigner. The discussion focused on George Jackson and the Soledad Brothers case, for which Davis was a major spokesperson. The interview was conducted on June 2, 1970, two months before Jonathan Jackson had burst into a Marin County courtroom. Yet the album wasn't released until the height of the "Free Angela" movement, making it of historical note. In the words of Julius Lester, who wrote liner notes, Davis "almost anticipates what was to happen to her." On the recording, Davis and Seigner occasionally interact with the Soledad Brothers' defense attorney Don Wheeldin, who provides specific details about their case. Decades later, Angela Davis comes off as dry and boring, with few "sound bites" to recommend, except as an academic exercise. Davis does make a strong analogy between the Soledad Brothers and Bobby Seale, then on trial in New Haven, Conn., for a trumped-up murder charge for which he was later acquitted. As Julius Lester points out, one could argue that Davis was arrested (like Seale) not because she was guilty of a crime, but because she was political.

Also released in 1971 was *Angela Davis Speaks* (by the Folkways label), serving as a soundtrack for a WABC-TV documentary *Angela: Like It Is* and based on a concept by Joe Walker (who also penned the album's liner notes), the New York editor

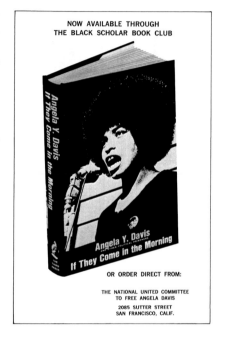

NOW AVAILABLE THROUGH
THE BLACK SCHOLAR BOOK CLUB

Angela Y. Davis
If They Come in the Morning

OR ORDER DIRECT FROM:

THE NATIONAL UNITED COMMITTEE
TO FREE ANGELA DAVIS
2085 SUTTER STREET
SAN FRANCISCO, CALIF.

1970: kidnapping, conspiracy and murder. Much like the "Free Huey" movement, "Free Angela" posters and lapel pins became symbolic for the oppression of black Americans across the country. A jury of eleven whites and one Mexican American acquitted her of all charges on June 4, 1972. Her attorneys proved that she had not helped execute the courthouse mayhem.

ABOVE: Although it's doubtful that she would ever agree, Angela Davis should really thank the FBI for placing her #1 on their "Ten Most Wanted List" in August 1970, a month before this LIFE article. It changed her from an outspoken academic into a popular folk hero. Decades later, she still commands large speaking fees at universities across the nation due to magazine articles like this.

OPPOSITE: Davis' trademark afro fills up the entire sleeve, but one is also drawn towards her facial expression, which shows her ready for action. The album is titled *Soul and Soledad*: black expression trapped inside the prison walls.

**SOUL AND SOLEDAD
ANGELA DAVIS**

of the nationally distributed newspaper *Muhammad Speaks*. Walker's idea was to ask people on (image #94 Angela A front) the streets of Harlem what questions they'd like to pose to Davis. Since no cameras were allowed in prison, the film contains visual clips of Davis from other sources while she gives her answers. During this interview, Davis comes across better than on the *Soul and Soledad* album, providing an inspired and more succinct dialogue.

Other sections of the LP include interviews conducted by ABC TV's Gil Noble with Joe Walker describing how the *Muhammad Speaks* interview came about (published in its entirely in their Jan. 1, 1971 issue); attorney Margaret Burnham providing insight into Davis' extradition to California to stand trial; and comments by Charlene Mitchell, a member of the New York Committee to Free Angela Davis.

The album concludes with the question: "Do you think Angela Davis will get a fair trial?" posed to African-Americans on the streets of New York: some reply that because she's black she won't get a fair shake, while others are confident that the momentum of support surrounding her will succeed in the end.

CARL STOKES:
THE MAYOR AND THE PEOPLE

Carl B. Stokes was the first black mayor of a large American city, serving Cleveland from 1968 to 1971. While mayor, Stokes recorded an album for Flying Dutchman, *The Mayor and The People*. During his mayoral term, Stokes provided city hall jobs to blacks and women. He was not afraid to spar with the Cleveland city council and police department. He initiated a funding program called Cleveland: Now! that revitalized decaying Cleveland neighborhoods. Inside Stokes' album were comments written by *Village Voice* columnist Nat Hentoff, in which Stokes told him, "Here I am. I'm a black mayor and I run a white city better than most white mayors can run a city. But I'm still black. However, I am here until November 1971 and can't nobody do anything about it. But if the system were to break down, they'd have me out of here tomorrow morning."

Some sources claim that Stokes was threatened with prosecution by the Federal government for corruption and that he was privately advised that if he declined another term, they'd drop the potential charges. Stokes didn't seek reelection and hit the college lecture circuit. In 1972, Stokes landed the first black anchorman position in New York City, for WNBC-TV. During his tenure at WNBC, he won a New York State Regional Emmy for his coverage on the opening of a Paul Robeson play on Broadway.

FREE ANGELA!

Angela Davis was accused of supplying the guns used by George Jackson's brother Jonathan in the Marin County shootout, which earned her placement on the FBI's Top 10 Most Wanted List (for a period of two months starting on Aug. 18, 1970). While she was on the run, *LIFE* Magazine put her on the cover, painting her in a fairly sympathetic light for a mainstream publication. In 1972, she was acquitted of all charges, but not before becoming an icon to black (and white) radicals throughout the world.

Mick Jagger, who often gave lip service to the Black Power movement but never actually gave financial aid, wrote a song about Davis: "Sweet Black Angel," which appeared on the Rolling Stones album *Exile On Main Street*. While Lennon and Ono's song focused on her political struggles — "Angela they put you in prison, Angela, they shot down your man" (referring to George Jackson) — Jagger focused on the Angela Davis posters that were cropping up in college dorm rooms and displayed at rallies. In typical Jagger fashion, he noted her sex

appeal: "Got a pinup girl, got a sweet black angel, up upon my wall."

Although Jagger and Lennon were the most famous musicians to compose tributes to Davis, they weren't the only ones. During the early '70s, several artists recorded tributes to Davis, including Santana, who performed a funky instrumental workout entitled "Free Angela" on their 1973 live album *Lotus*. Often thought to be a Santana composition, it was recorded a year earlier as "Free Angela (Thoughts and all I've got to say)" by keyboardist Todd Cochran, who (under the pseudonym Bayete) released it on the Prestige Records album *Worlds Around The Sun*. Joined by jazz vibraphonist Bobby Hutcherson and other jazz-funk stalwarts, Bayete uses a pumping keyboard riff and a strong drum pulse as a platform to chant "Free Angela" before the rhythmic drive breaks down and the song enters an ethereal and reflective phase. The crosscultural Santana band wasn't a stranger to the cause, having performed a benefit for the Black Panthers at the Berkeley Community Theatre on Feb. 6, 1970.

Among the many tribute recordings to Davis, one of particular interest is Larry Saunders' "Free Angela" from an album of the same name. Saunders was an obscure singer known as "The Prophet of Soul" who cut several hard-to-find

albums at the Muscle Shoals Recording studio in Alabama with drummer Roger Hawkins, bassist David Hood, pianist Berry Beckett and guitarist Jimmy Johnson (the same musicians appear on seminal Aretha Franklin recordings). Saunders' tune is swinging soul-jazz, with a flute as the driving force, which seems remarkably lightweight given the topic at hand. Meanwhile Saunders croons, "Free Angela...our sister...sitting in jail with no bail...how can she get a fair

ABOVE: A quintessential image of the times, Angela Davis captured in full anger mode, with prison bars superimposed over it. Most surprisingly, this record originated in Muscle Shoals, Ala. Released by the Sound Of Soul label based in Richmond, Va., the *Free Angela* album was sold by The National Committee to Free Angela Davis to help raise funds for her defense.

trial when even the president condemn the black child…oh, Free Angela."

Released by the Sound Of Soul label based in Richmond, Va., the *Free Angela* album was sold by The National Committee to Free Angela Davis to help raise funds for her defense. While the rest of the LP doesn't specifically address Davis, it does consist of politically charged material by Saunders, Dickie Wonder and Tyrone Thomas, recorded at Muscle Shoals and nearby Fame studios. Among the highlights are Saunders' "This World," which uses a flute more effec-

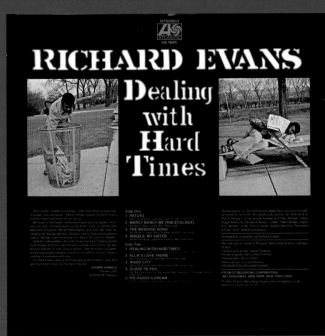

tively than on "Free Angela," providing a strong opening for lyrics that address "killing our innocent brothers…they talk of peace at the United Nations, trying to bring peace among all nations…they talk about war and demonstrations."

Saunders is also responsible for the lost masterpiece "Old Uncle Tom is Dead," which rivals "What's Going On" in the category of socially charged soul. Moody and gospel-styled, one impassioned vocalist keeps repeating "Old Uncle Tom Is Dead" over and over. Meanwhile, piano and organ vamp underneath some fervent testifying by another singer about the yesteryears of cotton-picking and the emergence of King Jr., culminating in a plea for black and white brothers to unite and stop fighting.

On her 1973 Warner Brothers album *Phew*, Claudia Lennear (best known as a backing singer for Joe Cocker, Leon Russell and Ike & Tina Turner) sang her ballad "Sister Angela," accompanied by the murky psychedelic-soul of the Dixie Flyers' Jim Dickinson and Tommy McClure, Lennear's song declared that the "Alabama angel deserves freedom still" and that "she'll give them hell until" they set Davis free.

Richard Evans was the house producer for Chess Records' Cadet imprint. In yet another Angela Davis tribute, Evans played bass and composed and arranged material for Marlena Shaw, Ramsey Lewis and Jack McDuff. The flute weaving through Evans' "Angela, My Sister" gives it a Herbie Mann flavor, while the wah-wah guitar and strings are lifted from the *Shaft* soundtrack.

The liner notes by Yvonne Daniels of WSDM-FM state:

Born black — raised in Chicago — later becoming a musician, arranger, and composer. These things qualify Richard Evans to know what hard times are all about… [on] Angela where Richard holds a direct, honest, and hip conversation with you. Richard Evans — with a lot to say and a lot of roles to play getting it said. I hear you Richard. Rap on.

Herbie Hancock's *Mwandishi* contained a long instrumental, "Ostinato (Suite For Angela)," paying tribute to Angela Davis. The suite blends bass clarinet and trumpet flourishes over a solid rhythmic thrust of Fender Rhodes piano, bass and two drummers. Two guests provide support to this jazzy testimonial: Santana member Jose "Chepito" Areas on congas and timbales and guitar hero Ronnie Montrose. In February 1972, Hancock's ensemble participated in a "Free Angela Davis" benefit that included performances by Malo, Taj Mahal and poet Maya Angelou at the Berkeley Community Theatre.

LEFT: Richard Evans doesn't need the newspaper to know these are *hard times*; the only function of the newspaper is to use it as a blanket, as street people often do. In fact the times are so hard, he's got a bass but no amplifier.

Flying Dutchman

STEREO FDS-130

THE MAYOR AND THE PEOPLE

CARL B. STOKES

A BLACK SUITE FOR STRING QUARTET AND JAZZ ORCHESTRA BY OLIVER NELSON

The Mayor And The People was a twenty-six-minute press conference that comprised one side of the record. It's a provocative listen as a young black man poses a question about the genocide of African-Americans. Stokes replies that, yes that is possible; there is evidence that internment camps are being prepared across America to potentially hold militant blacks and other radicals, in the same way that Japanese Americans were detained during World War II. However, Stokes advises that violence is not the solution, because if there's a violent black uprising, the United States Government has the upper hand with the resources of the CIA and the military. They have tanks and missiles and they'll use them if they have to.

Stokes continues reinforcing the notion that "blacks must work within the confines of the system" and argues that eventually the system will be righteous. He offers an example in regards to the Black Panther Party in Chicago. He says that despite the tragic killing of Fred Hampton, all attempted murder charges against the surviving members of the Black Panther Party vs. the Chicago Police shootout were dropped. Stokes condemns the fact that no white policemen were charged for the assassination of Hampton, but points out that at least no blacks had to suffer the indignity of being prosecuted. Stokes claims this as a "victory" and perhaps it is — as he says, it could have been worse, with all Panthers involved ending up in prison. But it still seems like an odd choice to claim victory, when Fred Hampton and fellow Panther Mark Clark were murdered in cold blood. There was no "shootout"; the police merely burst in and started firing, giving the Panthers no chance to defend themselves. Stokes defends his stance by stating that the end results are preferable to a violent race war that could've broken out on the streets of Chicago after the Hampton massacre.

The other side of the Stokes album carries a different title: *A Black Suite For String Quartet And Jazz Orchestra by Oliver Nelson.* Nelson arranged an eighteen-minute musical suite in which Stokes recites several spirituals, including "Take This Hammer" and "Precious Lord." Stokes also stoically reads three Langston Hughes poems, "Mother To Son," "I Too Sing America" and "I Dream A World." Nelson's music provides a dramatic backing to Stokes' voice, as well as instrumental interludes between the spoken bits. Dramatically, the record ends with Stokes performing "Paint It Black," not the Rolling Stones' 1966 song, but a poem from Gil Scott-Heron's debut album, *Small Talk at 125th and Lenox.*

As Nat Hentoff states inside the gatefold jacket, "There has never been an album like this in the history of American politics — or recordings. A mayor of a major city reading poetry and spirituals on one side of the album — and on the other, engaging in what may well be the most candid press conference any government official has conducted in recent memory."

STANLEY CROUCH SAYS
AIN'T NO AMBULANCES FOR NO NIGGUHS TONIGHT

As discussed elsewhere, Stanley Crouch is a right-leaning curmudgeon par excellence with an tendency to put down other African-Americans, including Malcolm X, Huey Newton, Spike Lee and Cornel West. However, in a previous lifetime (the late 1960s), Crouch's heart and soul were in a different place. At that time, Crouch could be spotted wearing the occasional dashiki and extolling the virtues of Amiri Baraka. He wasn't above sticking it to the man himself, and one story has him bullshitting the administration of Pomona College in California to make him a tenured English professor when he had no undergraduate degree of his own. In the words of Amy Alexander in a 1999 Salon. com article, "It was the height of the student activist movement, and Crouch played the role of radical black militant like a pro."

One of Crouch's students at Pomona was Lynda Obst (producer of the movie *Sleepless in Seattle*), who in 1995 told Robert Boynton of *The New Yorker*: "Stanley cultivated this gangster look with a little cigarette hanging from the corner of his mouth" (which is very evident on the front of his 1969 album, *Ain't No Ambulances For No Nigguhs Tonight*). She also told Boynton, "He had a real tough Panther walk — a cross between Ike Turner and Bobby Seale, that crackled with energy, all coming from his head. It was very physical and intellectual, which, of course, also made it very sexual."

OPPOSITE: The people's mayor: Stokes being mobbed by his adoring fans after the groundbreaking election of the first black mayor of a major white city — an America that could have been. Hence Stokes draws from the work of Langston Hughes: "I Too Sing America" and "I Dream A World." The photo reflects people testifying like they are in church, raising their hands in praise.

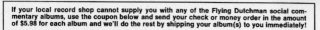

Murder at Kent State
FLYING DUTCHMAN HAS THE SOUND OF THE TIME

The repression: New York Post columnist, Pete Hamill and poetess Lois Wyse, run down the tragedy of Kent State in a way that shakes you up and gives you new food for thought. The album is narrated by Rosko.

MURDER AT KENT STATE/FDS—127

Robert Scheer, then an editor of **Ramparts**, spent **A Night At Santa Rita** after being busted at the People's Park confrontation and lived to tell the tale.

A NIGHT AT SANTA RITA/FDS—111

The war: Massacre At My Lai, a series of penetrating articles by Pete Hamill shows us in glaring relief what Vietnam is doing to the country. The album is narrated by Rosko with James Spaulding, flute; Ron Carter, bass.

MASSACRE AT MY LAI/FDS—118

Black Amerika: Prize-winning poet Stanley Crouch (his work is anthologized by LeRoi Jones and Larry Neal in **Black Fire** lets you know where he and his people are at by rapping and reading from his poetry and forthcoming novel. **Ain't No Ambulances For No Nigguhs Tonight,** the title poem, tells more about Watts and the "riots" than a shelf full of commission reports.

AIN'T NO AMBULANCES FOR NO NIGGUHS TONIGHT/FDS—105

If your local record shop cannot supply you with any of the Flying Dutchman social commentary albums, use the coupon below and send your check or money order in the amount of $5.98 for each album and we'll do the rest by shipping your album(s) to you immediately!

FLYING DUTCHMAN PRODUCTIONS, LTD., 1841 Broadway, New York, N.Y. 10023
Enclosed is my check or money order for the following album(s): MURDER AT KENT STATE UNIVERSITY (FDS 127) □ A NIGHT AT SANTA RITA (FDS 111) □ MASSACRE AT MY LAI (FDS 118) □ AIN'T NO AMBULANCES FOR NO NIGGUHS TONIGHT (FDS 105) □
NAME_____
ADDRESS_____
CITY_____STATE_____ZIP_____

Flying Dutchman

Distributed in the United States exclusively by Mainstream Records, Inc.
Distributed in Canada by Polydor Records

During this era, according to poet Garrett Hongo in *The New Yorker*, Crouch was an expressive orator. "He had these chant like lines that resembled Whitman, but they were in a black street vernacular that was eloquent and pissed off — He'd run this rap, with quotations from Shakespeare and Melville, riff on Langston Hughes and Cecil Taylor, and then relate it all to that day's news."

It was *this* Stanley Crouch that recorded the Flying Dutchman release, *Ain't No Ambulances For No Nigguhs Tonight*, which gets its title from the response that a black resident of Watts allegedly received during the 1965 riots after phoning for assistance. The Flying Dutchman record label was founded in 1969 by maverick producer Bob Thiele, the man behind the great Coltrane albums on Impulse!. As the 1960s came to a close, Thiele's relationship with ABC (who owned Impulse! at that time) petered out and he decided to start his own label. Although Flying Dutchman eventually became a very successful label distributed by Atlantic and then RCA (resulting in releases by Gil Scott-Heron, Leon Thomas, Oliver Nelson and Lonnie Liston Smith), when the label first started, the independent jazz label, Mainstream Records, distributed it. In fact, Crouch's release was only Flying Dutchman's fifth and bears the Mainstream logo rather than Atlantic or RCA.

Although primarily known as a jazz imprint, Flying Dutchman dove into politics with *Massacre at My Lai* (documenting the atrocities of the Vietnam War), *A Night at Santa Rita* (a commentary on prison conditions) and *Murder At Kent State University* — all three based on essays written by *New York Post* columnist Pete Hamill, featuring narration by NYC radio personality Rosko, accompanied by bassist Ron Carter and flutist James Spaulding.

In his 1995 memoir, *What A Wonderful World*, Thiele recalls having discussions with Amiri Baraka, Stanley Crouch and music critic Frank Kofsky, inspired by the frenzied music that Coltrane was recording for Impulse!. Thiele mentions that he and Crouch would "argue for hours and hours about the black movement and the music." Evidently, at the time, Crouch shared Kofsky's oft-expressed and documented opinion that Coltrane was a militant. Thiele wrote "I purchased master recordings by Angela Davis and H. Rap Brown to release on Flying Dutchman during this period, and my combative good friend Stanley Crouch enlivened the proceedings with his memorably titled poetry album, *Ain't No Ambulances For No Nigguhs Tonight*, which did not immeasurably cut into the record sales of the *Mary Poppins* soundtrack released at around the same time."

Although the liner notes were written on April 17, 1969 by K. Curtis Lyle did not mention the recording's location, it's obvious that Crouch is speaking to an auditorium of college students. In 1966, Lyle became a founding member of the Watts Writers Workshop (the same organization that birthed the Watts Prophets). In 1969, he moved to St. Louis to help establish the Black Studies program at Washington University and has continued to publish poetry. In 1971, Lyle blended rap-styled narration with the avant-jazz music of saxophonist Julius Hemphill on the album *Collected Poem For Blind Lemon Jefferson*, released on Hemphill's St. Louis-based Mbari label.

Crouch begins by asking the assembled audience a series of historical music questions. "Anybody know who 'Fats' Navarro was? Anybody know who Bud Powell was? Anybody know who 'Bird' was?" There's almost no response. Crouch then counters these questions by asking if they are familiar with white jazz musicians such as Dave Brubeck, Stan Getz and Benny Goodman. These musicians get a bit more recognition from the audience, but not much. Crouch then folds Janis Joplin into the equation (eliciting much more response from the crowd), followed by Betty Carter (no response). Crouch explains:

A bold new publishing venture begins today.

Soul on Ice is an angry book by an eloquent young Negro. Cleaver brilliantly analyzes the forces that shaped his life. But more important he contributes understanding of our increasingly violent racial eruptions and chronic urban explosions.

"Cleaver is simply one of the best cultural critics now writing...one of the discoveries of the 1960's"
Maxwell Geismar

"...An even more valid diagnosis of the nature and future of our civilization than all the discussions of our affluence and military power."
Kenneth B. Clark

"...He's a very talented man."
Norman Mailer

The first in a new series of important contemporary books jointly sponsored by Ramparts Magazine and McGraw-Hill.

Other titles in the series: **MARRIED PRIESTS AND MARRIED NUNS**, by James P. Colaianni $5.95
A LAYMAN'S GUIDE TO NEGRO HISTORY, compiled and edited by Erwin A. Salk $5.95
THE CIA FILE, by the editors of Ramparts $5.95
McGRAW-HILL

What I'm trying to say is, in reference to black art and black music, most black people know more about white people and imitation black people, imitation black artists than they know about black artists. That is that, we have not only had our greatest artists hidden from us, but the white man has thrown imitators of those artists at us, and we know them even better than the ones who really did

the first thing...What I'm saying again is, that people like Janis Joplin, who is like an imitation nigger is more well known by black people than black blues singers who she's trying to copy. And that sound that Janis Joplin is trying to get has nothing at all to do with white musical tradition, white musical sound or white musical emotional projection. And that she, and The Beatles, and the Rolling Stones and the rest of those people are imitation niggers and that is the reason why they are successful.

Over the course of the next forty minutes, Crouch recites poetry, including the "Ambulances" title piece inspired by the Watts Riots, a lengthy narrative titled "Blue Moon, The Hog in the Spring; A Boogie Tune" and shorter poems, "Pharoah" (for Pharoah Sanders) and "After The Rain" (about the spirit of John Coltrane). Mixed between the poetry is additional social commentary. For example, in *Soul On Ice*, Eldridge Cleaver pointed out that Chubby Checker gave the white man his body back; "That is to say, that the whole kind of sexuality that was being projected through 'The Twist' was something that white people weren't too much doing."

BLACK, BROWN AND BEAUTIFUL:
OLIVER NELSON

Also released by Flying Dutchman was Oliver Nelson's *Black, Brown and Beautiful*. Unlike the spoken word of H. Rap Brown and Stanley Crouch, Nelson made his statement musically. Nelson was a saxophonist and composer, having recorded many albums on Impulse! and Prestige. He eventually switched to the newly formed Flying Dutchman, for whom he recorded

BLACK, BROWN AND BEAUTIFUL
OLIVER NELSON

STEREO FD 10116

SIDE ONE
AFTERMATH
Soloists: JOHN GROSS—tenor sax
            JOHN KLEMMER—tenor sax
REQUIEM
Soloists: PEARL KAUFMAN—piano
            OLIVER NELSON—piano
LAMB OF GOD
Soloist: PEARL KAUFMAN—piano
MARTIN WAS A MAN, A REAL MAN
Soloist: OLIVER NELSON—alto saxophone

SIDE TWO
SELF-HELP IS NEEDED
Soloist: FRANK STROZIER—alto saxophone
I HOPE IN TIME A CHANGE WILL COME
Soloist: OLIVER NELSON—soprano saxophone
3, 2, 1, 0
Soloists: BOB BRYANT—trumpet
            ROGER KELLAWAY—piano
BLACK, BROWN AND BEAUTIFUL
Soloist: OLIVER NELSON—alto saxophone
REQUIEM, AFTERTHOUGHTS
            ROY HAYNES, JOHN GUERIN—drums
            CHUCK DOMANICO—bass
            ROGER KELLAWAY—piano
            OLIVER NELSON—soprano saxophone

Produced by BOB THIELE

SOUND MIXER: AMI HADANI
FRONT COVER PHOTOGRAPH: CHARLES STEWART
BACK COVER & LINER PHOTOGRAPHS: IRV GLASER
DESIGN: ROBERT FLYNN
ALTO SAXOPHONE COURTESY YAMAHA, LTD.
SOPRANO SAXOPHONE COURTESY PRIMA INSTRUMENT CO., LTD.
A PRODUCT OF FLYING DUTCHMAN PRODUCTIONS, LTD.
PRINTED IN U.S.A.

The concept that this country is moving towards two separate societies is true. Our country is Racist, the Churches have failed completely. Uncle Tom is gone forever and the Black, Brown and White Militants are here to stay." Nelson goes on compare the Nazi invasion of Poland to the National Guard quelling the riots in American cities with gunfire following the assassination of King Jr. He states further, "that America must change before the Silent Majority elects a George Wallace for their President — which will bring about the inevitable holocaust."

SOUL AND MADNESS
AMIRI BARAKA

For a man who takes himself extremely seriously, Amiri Baraka gives his music short shrift. His 1997 autobiography doesn't mention any of his albums, and his website also omits them, despite detailing his many accomplishments. In a previous section, I focused on his 1972 album *It's Nation Time*, but Baraka released several recordings before that. In 1964 (as LeRoi Jones), Baraka appeared on the self-titled debut of the New York Art Quartet. The band included trombonist Roswell Rudd and drummer Milford Graves (who'd go on to record several albums for ESP as well as perform on Sonny Sharrock's landmark *Black Woman*). Baraka appeared on one song, reciting "Black Dada Nihilismus," taken from his second book of poetry *The Dead Lecturer*. The song's violent imagery was controversial, causing *The New York Times* to write that Baraka's poem was a "call for black revolutionaries to rape and murder in the service of liberation."

In November 1965, Baraka (still known as LeRoi Jones) recorded drummer Sunny Murray, accompanied by saxophone maverick Albert Ayler, trumpeter Don Cherry and others in New York City's improvisation scene. Titled *Sonny's Time Now,* the

throughout the 1970s. *Black, Brown and Beautiful* is far from the cutting-edge music recorded by his former Impulse! label mates Archie Shepp or John Coltrane. The instrumental big-band music is fairly mundane, although Nelson's self-penned notes from Nov. 20, 1969, reveal that Nelson was feeling socially disobedient while composing the album.

ABOVE: Not just '"Black and Beautiful," but *Black, Brown and Beautiful* — uniting browns and blacks, but also calling attention to diversity within the black community itself.

LP featured Baraka reciting a poem on one track. This session become the debut release on Baraka's own label, Jihad Records.

In 1968, he released two albums on Jihad. One was a play he'd written entitled *A Black Mass*. It had been written in 1965, when the Nation of Islam was still a heavy influence on him. After Malcolm X's murder, he distanced him from the Nation of Islam as a means of expressing his allegiance to X. Around this time, Baraka co-founded the Black Arts Repertoire Theatre School in Harlem, where he and other members of the Black Arts Movement taught writing and acting. A couple of times a week, Sun Ra gave musical instruction and "scientific philosophical musings on the Universe." Baraka eventually left Harlem and opened The Spirit House, an arts and performance space in Newark, N.J.

RON KARENGA and US

Ron Karenga was the founder of the organization US, which intended to bring traditional African culture into daily American black life, to create a defiant Afro-American culture and infuse black people with "blackness." The meaning of US has been debated, with the Panthers and others suggesting it meant "United Slaves," but Karenga told Amiri Baraka it simply meant "US" vs. "THEM." Karenga personally gave each US member a Swahili name of his choosing (Ron Everett awarded himself the status of "master teacher" and "the original nationalist" in the Swahili language when he became Maulana Ron Karenga). Karenga also insisted his followers memorize passages in the Swahili language, and encouraged celebration of traditional African holidays, including the weeklong Kwanzaa, which occurs between Christmas and New Year's Day. Karenga created the Kawaida doctrine, which outlined his seven principles of the black value system. There was also a blending of the philosophies of Elijah Muhammad, Marcus Garvey and Malcolm X in Karenga's rhetoric, coupled with the ideologies of Lenin, Stalin, Marx and Mao. Karenga's ideology presented a fresh comprehension of African-American history and laid out a blueprint for raising the political consciousness of black people by restructuring their values.

Panther member Bunchy Carter began organizing a Los Angeles chapter of the Panthers not long after the L.A.-based US was established. The groups' ideological differences, coupled with Karenga's need to maintain *his* turf, led to tension between the two groups, with US members threatening and attacking Panthers making their way around Los Angeles. Misinformation fed to each group by the FBI heightened hostilities. On Jan. 17, 1969, Panthers Bunchy Carter and John Huggins were slain on the UCLA campus. The two US members accused of the shooting were brothers (George and Larry Stiner). After their conviction, they escaped from San Quentin Prison on March 31, 1974.

Amiri Baraka claims that Ron Karenga was in New York with him at the time of the actual shooting. Regardless, in Baraka's words, US developed "a foxhole mentality" in its public campaigning and community organization to dodge possible violent skirmishes with the Panthers. In short, they were afraid of getting their asses kicked. The function of US was now security and defense, with all development and growth on hold. According to Baraka, Karenga had a machine gun on a tripod sitting in his living room floor facing the front door, and was addicted to "chill pills" to keep sedated.

It was here in 1968 at The Spirit House that Baraka invited Sun Ra & his Myth Science Arkestra, actors he knew from the Black Arts Repertory Theatre School (such as Yusef Iman) and his second wife Sylvia Robinson (aka Amina Baraka) to record a performance of *A Black Mass*. Sun Ra's dramatic score combined with the highly animated actors makes one synopsis of the play seem apt: "An evil white beast is accidentally created by a black magician." Baraka once described *A Black Mass* as "a play of mine, on the mad scientist Jacoub's creation of white people, as told by Elijah Muhammad with Sun Ra's Myth Science Arkestra." Unless someone is a Sun Ra freak, I don't consider *A Black Mass* required listening. In fact, Baraka doesn't appear on the album; his involvement was directing the play and producing the recording.

What is essential is Baraka's other 1968 Jihad release, *Black & Beautiful, Soul & Madness*. On this album, Baraka is accompanied by an a cappella quintet known as the Jihad Singers, who provide a Motown-inspired, doo-wop backing to Baraka's spoken word prophesying. The Jihad Singers ensemble included Russell Lyle (from Eddie Gale's *Ghetto Music* and *Black Rhythm Happening* albums) on sax and flute, and Baraka's comrade Yusef Inman on vocals and congas — also a member of the performance troupe The Spirit House Movers.

a black mass

by **Amiri Baraka** (*LeRoi Jones*)
Sun Ra and the **Myth Science Arkestra**

RIGHT: Amiri Baraka once described *A Black Mass* as "a play of mine on the mad scientist Jacoub's creation of white people, as told by Elijah Muhammad with Sun Ra's Myth Science Arkestra." In the autobiography of Malcolm X, it is spelled as Mr. Yacub (the mad scientist). Here is the image of Jacoub/Yacub as the alchemist, all of his ingredients mixing up, "Though he was a black man, Mr. Yacub, embittered toward Allah now, decided, as revenge, to create upon the earth a devil race — a bleached-out, white race of people."

The first song on the album, "Beautiful Black Women," used the refrain and melody of Smokey Robinson's 1965 hit with the Miracles "Ooo Baby Baby" as a base for Baraka's passionate tribute to *the* sisters. The next song "Black and Beautiful (Miss Natural Soul)" continued the R&B-styled testimony to the female persuasion. On songs "Form Is Emptiness" and "Madness," Baraka & Co. move away from R&B into free jazz territory, which the liner notes describe as new music with "dangerously contemporary" lyrics. On "Madness," with a chorus of screaming behind him, Baraka declares, "the white man at best is corny."

In a 2003 interview, Kalamu ya Salaam asked Baraka, "What made you think, or feel, that putting a piece out like 'Beautiful

Black Women' with the Smokey doo-wop, that the people who would dig that, would also dig something like 'Form Is Emptiness?'" He replied:

> *Because they go into deeper shit in their churches, number one. These people [avant-garde artists] think they out; they need to dig these Negroes in these churches jumping up and down with their eyes rolling around in their heads smoking cigars. I haven't seen anybody doing that on stage. All that whooping and hollering and rolling on the floor and kicking their feet in the air, and starting to scream about Jesus. You ever seen somebody wild with Jesus? That's what I was saying about James Brown a long time ago. Poets were thinking they were getting out there, but they had better check out James Brown. His voice was further out than Ornette [Coleman] and them because James's voice had more himmy, dimmy, shimmy scrappers in it. To me it was just a release of the whole consciousness.*

Baraka had described The Original Last Poets' *Right On!* as "where Black and 3rd World art is going." In the liner notes to *Black & Beautiful, Soul & Madness*, the same reference is made: "[The songs] are aimed at the third world, a world breaking out from under the unholiness of holy holy ugliness. Black music will tell it and be about itself, so that the unity music can begin in earnest. We're crying, 'Black Man Black Man, The White Man Owns You.'"

REDD FOXX IGNITES RICHARD PRYOR'S CONSCIOUSNESS

Throughout 1968, Redd Foxx mentored Richard Pryor, giving him gigs at the Redd Foxx Club in Los Angeles, as well as lecturing him about Malcolm X, whom Foxx had known personally. Malcolm X's assassination in 1965 had left Pryor apathetic, but now he was infatuated with Malcolm X's legacy. Pryor decided to go underground, putting live performances on hiatus and moved to Berkeley in '69 to immerse himself in the counterculture. Pryor spent his days reading X's essays, while playing Marvin Gaye's *What's Going On*. He soaked up the politically charged Bay Area atmosphere and began rethinking his comedy under the influence of non-comedians Angela Davis and Huey Newton. When Pryor resurfaced in Los Angeles in 1971, his newfound voice gained an audience with African-Americans who shared his admiration for the Black Power movement.

Starting in January 1972, Redd Foxx would find commercial success as the star of the TV sitcom *Sanford and Son*, set in the Watts neighborhood of L.A. While using *Sanford and Son* as a comedic expression of ghetto life, Foxx made financial contributions to the Black Panther Party.

ABOVE: Along with the street corner and the barbershop, the front porch is a critical site of learning in the black community. It's notable that Baraka and his vocal group are sitting on the front porch of The Spirit House, observing the neighborhood, telling stories and making critical connections to the African-American lifestyle that surrounds them.

Sisters Are Doin' It For Themselves:
AFRICAN-AMERICAN WOMEN'S POETRY

Black female poets of the era were often overshadowed by their male counterparts. However, both Nikki Giovanni and Maya Angelou became world renowned, while the likes of Sarah Webster Fabio and Jayne Cortez deserve a wider audience than they've received thus far.

WANDA ROBINSON: Poet Wanda Robinson's first experience as a writer was composing letters for neighborhood Baltimore girls whose boyfriends were fighting in Vietnam. She charged 25¢ to talk about love on their behalf. As the '60s progressed and Robinson entered college, her writing turned more political, although it still focused on male-and-female relationships. Inspired by singer Arthur Prysock's 1969 LP, *This Is My Beloved*, a collection of romantic poems by Walter Benton set to music by Mort Garson, Robinson recited her poetry into a tape recorder while playing albums in the background.

Classmates at the Community College of Baltimore were impressed, as were local DJs who played her recordings on the air. Soon, the 20-year-old received a phone call from Perception Records in New York. Perception was known for releasing jazz

(Dizzy Gillespie and James Moody were among its stable of artists), while Perception's sister label Today Records focused on soul, such as the band Black Ivory. While she was in New York, they offered Robinson access to their tape library, suggesting she pick prerecorded tracks. She chose several pieces from the Harlem-based R&B group Black Ivory, hence the name of Robinson's 1971 debut, *Black Ivory*. Although the liner notes claim that the poems are taken from Robinson's book *The Daze of Wine...Without Roses*, she never got around to publishing it. Her second album for Perception, 1973's *Me and a Friend*, was assembled from session outtakes from *Black Ivory* and released without her input. By that time, Robinson had dropped out of music and was in the process of changing her persona to Laini Mataka.

While others have placed Robinson in the same league as the Last Poets, I'd file her work in the category of mediocre, freshman-year of college love poems, supplemented by extraneous background music. Given the origins of her poetry, that's exactly what it is! In 1977 she self-published *Black Rhythms for Fancy Dancers* under the name of Laini Mataka. In subsequent decades, she's become a respected figure of black consciousness, with works published by Baltimore's Black Classic Press (who have also reprinted George Jackson's *Blood in My Eye* and Bobby Seale's *Seize the Time*).

SARAH WEBSTER FABIO: Sarah Webster Fabio earned a master's degree in language arts at San Francisco State College in 1965. Soon after, she began teaching at Merritt College, where the student body included Bobby Seale and Huey Newton. The burgeoning Black Power movement excited Fabio, as her own poetry passionately voiced the African-American experience. She began presenting her work with jazz accompaniment, and in 1966 was invited (with Langston Hughes) to Dakar, Senegal to perform at the First World Festival of Negro Art. Fabio's tenure

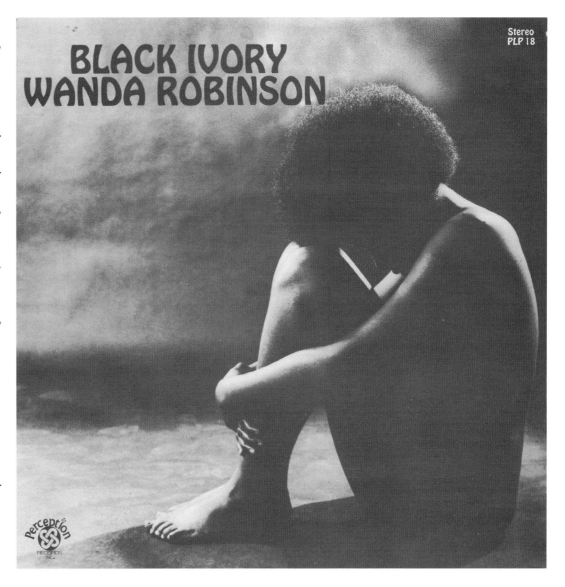

ABOVE: The cover photo reveals Wanda Robinson's guarded vulnerability, much like her poetry. Her work expresses heartbreak and sadness; her body language suggests the same. Funk diva Betty Davis probably wouldn't be snapped in this pose.

at Merritt College from 1965 to 1968 was instrumental in seed-ing the Black Arts Movement (creative literature combined with politics) into the minds of young black students in Oakland.

In 1968, she published her first poetry collection, *Saga of a Black Man*. In '69, she followed up with *A Mirror, A Soul*. Between 1968 and 1971, she lectured at the University of California at Berkeley, helping to establish their Black Studies Department. In 1972, she released her debut album *Boss Soul* on Folkways

Records, utilizing members of her family on guitar, bass and congas. On the title track, supported by a tribal conga rhythm, Fabio's cadence and delivery is engaging and warm as she name-checks, "those who gave soul a special hue; Malcolm, Coltrane, Monk, Marcus [Garvey], Stokely, Sarah, Nina, [W.E.B.] Du Bois, Gwen, Muhammad Ali, Aretha, and then that little LeRoi cat [Amiri Baraka] and his words built into OBAC's wall of respect to shout from the brick front, 'Black people, calling all black people, wherever you are, Urgent! Come on in.'"

Fabio's "Panther Caged" is an unaccompanied poem for Huey Newton in which she recites:

> *Huey, idol of America's clear-eyed youth, you who have dared to take up arms against the evils of our time, what can you see that we cannot, that would prompt you to make, barely visible — a sign with up thrust fingers of V for victory and this with a transcendent flicker of a smile.*

RUBY DEE: Also on Folkways were two volumes of *What If I Am a Woman? Black Women's Speeches Narrated by Ruby Dee*. Dee is an actress who appeared in the movie *A Raisin in the Sun* and the TV miniseries *Roots*. She was a member of CORE and SNCC and, along with her husband Ossie Davis, was a personal friend of Martin Luther King Jr. and Malcolm X. In fact, Ossie Davis gave the eulogy at X's funeral in 1965. Volume One of *What If I Am a Woman?* featured Dee reciting speeches about slavery and women's rights originally written in the 1800s. Volume Two contained Dee recreating then-current selections: "It is Time for a Change," the March 1969 inaugural address Shirley Chisholm, the first black Congresswoman, gave before the House of Representatives, and a reading of Angela Davis' "I am a Black Revolutionary Woman," a statement from Davis' 1971 imprisonment. Ossie Davis appears throughout Volume Two, introducing each of Dee's six performances.

MAYA ANGELOU AND CAMILLE YARBROUGH: Poet/novelist/actor Maya Angelou is one of America's great Renaissance women. During the early 1960s, Angelou lived in Egypt and Ghana working as a journalist and teacher. While in Ghana, she befriended a visiting Malcolm X, whom she followed to America in 1964 to join his Organization of African-American

Unity. Shortly after, Malcolm X was murdered and the coalition dissolved. Angelou was then asked by King Jr. to serve as the Northern Coordinator for King's Southern Christian Leadership Conference. King Jr.'s 1968 assassination was overwhelming, and she felt lost until her friend, author James Baldwin, encouraged her to work on a collection of autobiographical stories, published as *I Know Why the Caged Bird Sings*.

Many more autobiographical works and poetry books would follow over the decades. Angelou would even co-write songs with singer/pianist Roberta Flack. In 1969, she recorded her own album for the GWP Records label. *The Poetry Of Maya Angelou* captures the iconic writer at her most outspoken. Many of the poems included were subsequently published in Angelou's 1971 volume, *Just Give Me A Cool Drink Of Water 'Fore I Diiie*, while the LP itself was re-released on Perception Records in 1972. On unaccompanied poems like "The Calling Of Names," Angelou recites, "He went from being called a Colored man after answering to 'hey nigger', now that's a big jump, anyway you figger." The rioting of the '60s is the subject of several poems. "Revolt"

discusses the looting and burning of stores, "Some thought the Friendly Furniture Mart burned higher, when a leopard print sofa, with gold legs (that makes into a bed) caught fire, an admiring shout from the waiting horde, said 'Absentee landlord, you got that shit.'"

"Lighting (By a hundred watts)" illustrates the era, "Whole blocks burning like brand new stars, policemen driving their bulletproof cars, saying 'Chugga, chugga chigga, let's shoot that niggah, trying to out-run us, he can't get that far.' "National

LEFT: The back cover of Maya Angelou's 1969 album. In contrast to her current image as a joyous, laughing storyteller, her stories of the late '60s were of a more militant and angry nature. She's also wearing a classic afro of the era.

ABOVE: Ruby Dee is using her voice to channel the dual burdens of being black and being a woman in history (not just society). She's rubbing her neck to alleviate the stress, while her facial expression is showing the acceptance and suffering of this combined role.

Guard nervous, with his bright new gun, thinking 'Rumble, rumble, rumble, they ain't even humble, what is that they shouting? Burn, Baby, Burn?"

Composer Ed Bland provides incidental music between several of the poems. Despite the contemporary tone of Angelou's poetry, the music is classic bebop performed by a jazz quartet. However, Bland would add "modern" arrangements to records by soul-jazz guitarist Phil Upchurch, hippie rockers Country Joe & the Fish, and most notably for inclusion in this book, *Iron Pot Cooker*, the seminal 1975 album by Camille Yarbrough.

Yarbrough's "Take Yo' Praise" was a melodic slice of sensual female black pride that was sampled by Fatboy Slim for his 1999 hit, "Praise You." Some readers may remember Fatboy's groove, but everyone should seek out Yarbrough's original on Vanguard Records. Yarbrough was not just a singer/songwriter, but also an actress who'd appeared in a production of Lorraine Hansberry's *To Be Young, Gifted and Black* as well as a cameo in the Blaxploitation movie *Shaft*. Many songs on her album began as politically charged poems used for Yarbrough's early '70s one-woman/spoken word stage dramatization, *Tales and Tunes of an African-American Griot*.

JAYNE CORTEZ: Jayne Cortez was pivotal in the Black Arts Movement. At the suggestion of SNCC's James Forman, she went to Mississippi in 1963 to participate in voter registration drives. Returning to Los Angeles, she founded a Friends of SNCC chapter. Wanting to focus on the artistic side of the movement, Cortez started facilitating writing and drama workshops in Watts in 1964 (the year she ended a decade-long marriage to

jazz maverick Ornette Coleman). Cortez' relationship with the infamous L.A. ghetto continued to grow when she co-founded the Watts Repertory Theatre Company, where one of her understudies was Stanley Crouch from 1965 to 1967. Crouch learned to play drums so that he could accompany Cortez' poetry. Crouch, who notoriously disavows anyone connected to that era, still holds Cortez in high regard. He not only views her as the only interesting female poet of the Black Arts Movement, but he uncharacteristically praised her in a November 1995 interview with *The New Yorker*, in which Crouch reflected, "I'd never met anyone with that kind of aesthetic commitment, who'd drawn a line in the dirt and said, 'I am an artist.'"

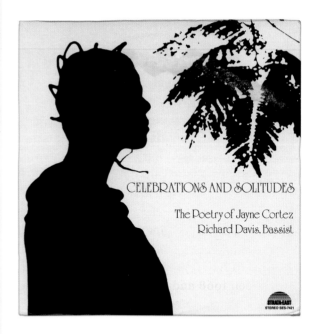

In the Spring 2001 issue of *African-American Review*, professor Tony Bolden called Cortez "The most profound manifestation of the tradition of African-American Resistance poetry." Bolden's description of Black Arts poetry is sublime. "Black Arts poets, who were attuned to the impact of Malcolm X and James Brown on black audiences,

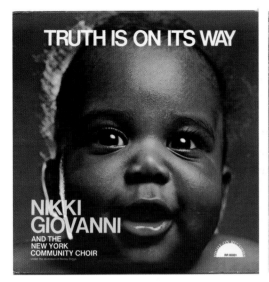

realized that sermon and song/shout could be utilized to create a popular people's poetry…[they could] blur the distinction between poetry and song by using the voice as an instrument."

Cortez' 1969 book *Pissstained Stairs and the Monkey Man's Wares* helped pinpoint music's relevance to the black community. The poem "How Long Has Trane Been Gone" is a blend of the blues, jazz and the ghetto. Cortez even incorporates the state of the music business: "There was a time when KGFJ played all black music from Bird to Johnny Ace on show after show — but what happened, I'll tell you what happened — They divided black music, doubled the money and left us split again is what happened."

Her 1970 collection *Festivals and Funerals* further reflected her sociopolitical imagination, setting the stage for her 1974 album, *Celebrations and Solitudes* on Strata-East Records. Recorded in July 1974, the album features nineteen poems written between 1968 and 1973 that cover the unification of Africa, Malcolm X, Watts, Harlem and points in between. *Celebration and Solitudes* has a distinctive sound, as Cortez' only accompaniment is a double bass played by Richard Davis, who's worked with Lou Donaldson, Joe Henderson, Andrew Hill and Roland Kirk. On *Celebrations and Solitudes,* Davis' jazz styling interacts exquisitely with Cortez' prose. He provides a mournful bowed bass on "Remembrance," supporting Cortez' solemn poetry about the 1973 death of Amilcar Cabral, murdered by the Portuguese while attempting to free Guinea from colonial rule. His percussive

plucking underlines "Lexington/96 Street Stop," while Cortez bristles in her description of a black man innocently drinking a soda on a subway platform being badgered by a "policemen with his fucking face of stink breath harassments."

NIKKI GIOVANNI: Over the past four decades, Nikki Giovanni has become famous through volumes of poetry, children's books and academic achievement. Despite her mainstream profile, she's retained some edge in her contemporary work — in the poem "All Eyez On You," a tribute to Tupac Shakur's album *All Eyez On Me*.

While in college, Giovanni was a member of SNCC. Meeting H. Rap Brown in May of 1967 at the Detroit Conference of Unity

OPPOSITE: Two silhouettes — one is human, one is part of nature — both public (*Celebrations*) and private (*Solitudes*). The outline of her hair is pivotal as part of the celebration of African-American culture. Cortez is moving artistically from intimidation to liberation through poems such as "Festivals and Funerals."

ABOVE: Only a couple of LPs in this book were ever re-released when they were still considered contemporary pieces of art (and not simply historic reissues). Of those, only Nikki Giovanni's *Truth Is On Its Way* received three distinctively different cover designs. The three different releases stand as a testament to Giovanni's popularity, as well as the marketing department's quest to expand her audience.

and Art propelled her into the Black Arts Movement. In 1968, she published two volumes of poetry, *Black Feeling, Black Talk* and *Black Judgment*. Her third book *Re: Creation* followed in 1970. Her writing contained a diverse mix of angry militancy and personal reflection. Poems like "The Great Pax Whitie" challenging the injustice of racism, "And the word was death to all niggers" sat alongside celebrations of family life expressed in "Nikki Rosa": "Everybody is together and you and your sister have happy birthdays." Her audience widened when she took her poems and successfully recorded them with the gospel New York Community Choir on her 1971 debut album, *Truth Is on Its Way*. Her public performances increased at this point, culminating with an appearance on *The Tonight Show* with Johnny Carson in June 1972. A second album, *Like a Ripple on a Pond*, followed in 1973. Also in '73, a book of conversations between her and iconic writer James Baldwin was published.

As the decade progressed, Giovanni toned down her militant rhetoric and her writing focused more on domestic life. This shift was reflected in her third record, when producer Arif Mardin (Aretha Franklin, Roberta Flack) was brought in to oversee her 1975 *The Way I Feel* album. Mardin's smooth production style did, however, make for an interesting contrast when she reached back to her 1970 poem "Revolutionary Dreams" and combined it with Mardin's choir of singers and a large band. She recited:

> *I used to dream militant dreams of taking over America, to show these white folks how it should be done, I used to dream radical dreams, of blowing everyone away with my perceptive powers of correct analysis…then I awoke and dug that if I dreamed natural dreams of being a natural woman…I would have a revolution.*

OPPOSITE: Lorraine Hansberry was "young, gifted and black" when cancer struck her down at the age of 34. Her seminal work, *A Raisin in the Sun*, was taken from the Langston Hughes poem "Harlem" — in which Hughes asks, "what happens to a dream deferred/ does it dry up/ like a raisin in the sun […]/ or does it explode?" Seen here holding a cigarette (a common pose for her) as she speaks out, she's asking in the same way that Hughes did — does the dream explode?

LORRAINE HANSBERRY: Hansberry was a playwright whose 1959 *A Raisin in the Sun* was the first drama written by a black woman to run on Broadway. It was based on true events from her childhood, when her family moved into a white neighborhood and was greeted by a racist mob — her father went to the Illinois Supreme Court and successfully won an anti-segregation lawsuit. *A Raisin in the Sun* takes its title from a Langston Hughes poem that questioned, "What happens to a dream deferred?/ Does it dry up /like a raisin in the sun?/ Or does it explode?" The play was turned into a popular 1961 movie starring Sidney Poitier.

Sadly, Hansberry's success was cut off in her prime when she died of cancer in early 1965 at the age of 34. Her legacy continued when other autobiographical writings were adapted into a play, *To Be Young, Gifted and Black* in 1969. The following year, it was published as a book. Speaking at a SNCC rally in June 1963, Hansberry recalled a confrontation with Attorney General Robert Kennedy in which she told him, "I am worried about the state of a civilization which produces that white cop standing on that Negro woman's neck in Birmingham."

Six months before her death, Hansberry appeared at a Town Hall forum in June 1964, with Amiri Baraka, Ossie Davis and Ruby Dee. She gave a lecture titled "The Black Revolution and the White Backlash," calling for a new militancy and a radically new relationship between blacks and whites in the struggle for freedom. In 1972, Caedmon Records compiled these and other speeches, TV and radio interviews in an album, *Lorraine Hansberry Speaks Out: Art and the Black Revolution*. Julius Lester's liner notes mention that Hansberry died nine months before [Langston Hughes'] "'deferred dream' exploded in the streets of Watts." He adds, "The genius of Lorraine Hansberry lies in her ability to meld her revolutionary commitment with her artistic skill and integrity."

Hansberry and Malcolm X's deaths were coincidently about a month apart. They also shared an acerbic tongue; Hansberry had declared in 1964, "The whole idea of debating whether or not Negroes should defend themselves is an insult. If anybody comes and does ill in your home or your community, obviously you try your best to kill him."

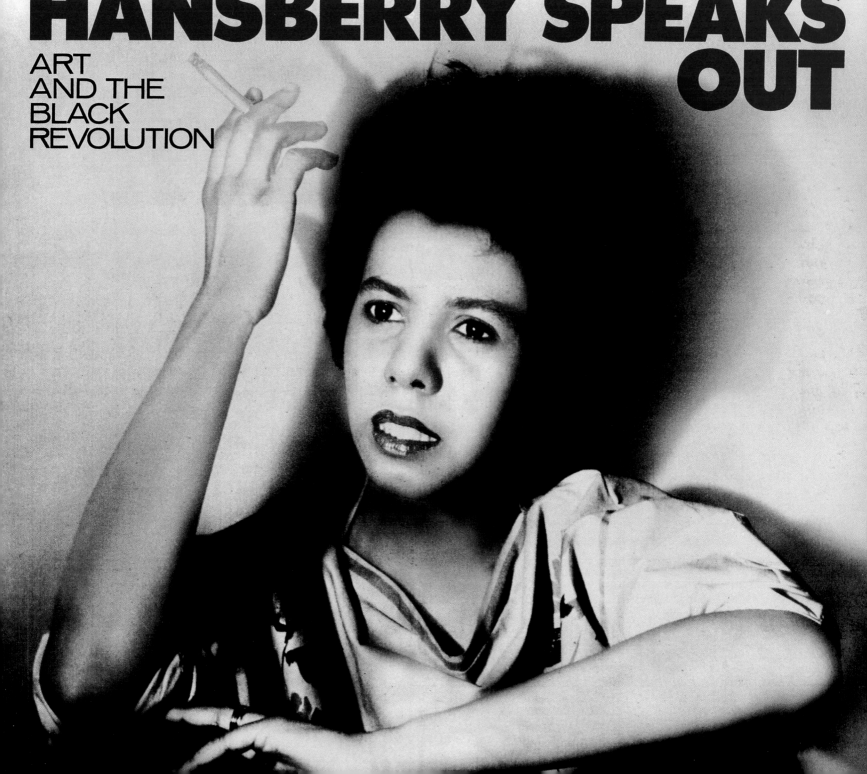

CAEDMON   TC 1352

LORRAINE HANSBERRY SPEAKS OUT

ART AND THE BLACK REVOLUTION

GENE MCDANIELS AND OTHER OUTLAWS
IN THE EYES OF AMERICA

The first words that Eugene "Gene" McDaniels sings on his 1970 album *Outlaw* are: "She's a nigger in jeans" — making it apparent that McDaniels (who'd rechristened himself as "the Left Rev. McD.") isn't in the same sphere as he was when he sang early '60s R&B hits like "A Hundred Pounds of Clay." McDaniels is something of a renaissance man: a singer of light-weight hits written by others — his 1961 single "Tower of Strength" by legendary lounge lizard Burt Bacharach hit #5 on the pop charts — while later in the decade, he wrote the soul-jazz protest anthem "Compared to What," which pianist/vocalist Les McCann and saxophonist Eddie Harris turned into a standard on their 1969 album *Swiss Movement*. Despite recording political albums like *Outlaw*, McDaniels could turn on a dime and pen the passionate late-night ode "(That's the time) I Feel Like Making Love" that gave Roberta Flack a #1 hit in 1974.

McDaniels is obviously a fighter and a lover, but it's only the former that I care to discuss. *Outlaw* was one of two political albums that McDaniels made for Atlantic Records; the other was *Headless Heroes of the Apocalypse* a year later in 1971. Legend has it that the White House was so offended by McDaniels' inflammatory recordings that either Spiro Agnew or Nixon's Chief of Staff personally called Atlantic, asking them to stop working with McDaniels. Atlantic was happy to stop recording him (the albums weren't selling anyway), although they had no problem allowing McDaniels to keep writing hit songs for their other artists like Roberta Flack. Also, as McDaniels pointed out to me, "they kept the [rights to the] masters" of his controversial albums.

The weirdest part of this conspiracy is that the last thing that McDaniels recorded for Atlantic was a 7-inch single, "Tell Me Mr. President," which was apparently directed at Nixon. Ironically,

McDaniels didn't even write the song! G. Lewis penned it, with string and horn arrangements supplied by Thom Bell, a founding father of the 1970s Philly soul sound via his production of The Delfonics, The Stylistics and The Spinners.

Recorded in March 1971, some six months after McDaniels had been in the studio finishing off *Headless Heroes Of The Apocalypse* in October 1970, "Tell Me Mr. President" recalls the folk-pop vibe of his *Outlaw* album (guitarist Hugh McCracken is back after sitting out on *Headless Heroes*) but the song is watered down by Thom Bell's cheesy strings and horns. Lyrically, it feels like a weak pastiche of the topics addressed on *Outlaw*. McDaniels tries to sing convincingly: "your silence could lead to our sorrow, men and woman have died you see, in the struggle to be free, brother; you and I could die tomorrow." It's similar to McDaniels' "Silent Majority" but missing the balls. No wonder, when I suggested it be added as a bonus track of the CD reissue of *Headless Heroes* that I produced in 2006, McDaniels vetoed it.

Recorded during February 1970, *Outlaw* featured diverse musicians. Mother Hen played piano (she'd recorded a solo album with The Byrds' guitarist Clarence White and Burrito Brother Sneaky Pete on pedal steel), session guitarist Hugh McCracken and Eric Weissberg (known for the *Deliverance* theme song as well as Dylan's *Blood On The Tracks*). Miles Davis alumni Ron Carter played bass.

Production was handled by Atlantic staff producer Joel Dorn, a household name amongst music buffs for recordings by Roland

OPPOSITE: The cover of *Outlaw* is America's worst nightmare come to life. There's the badass Reverend Lee holding a Bible. In a black "French resistance turtleneck" is Righteous Susan Jane wielding a machine gun; McDaniels' wife Ramona is a soul sister with cross-your-heart Viva Zapata! ammo belts. In the forefront is a human skull, just in case viewers didn't already get the message.

Kirk, Yusef Lateef, Herbie Mann and Roberta Flack. Musical Director was cult legend William S. Fischer, known for his string and horn arrangements for the likes of Eddie Harris, Roy Ayers and Jimmy Scott. Fischer recorded his own stoned soul LP, *Circles*, for Herbie Mann's Embryo label in 1971.

The title track "Outlaw" kicks things off with a vamp inspired by Bob Dylan's "She Belongs to Me." He turns lyrics such as "She's got everything she needs, she's an artist, she don't look back" into "She's an outlaw, she don't wear a bra." McDaniels channels Mick Jagger's sultry snarl and while the lyrics may not sound like much on paper, the song is a sex-driven rock 'n' roll nugget that holds its own against Stones songs of the era. McDaniels was so enamored with the Rolling Stones front man he wrote a song called "Jagger the Dagger" for his next album. "Welfare City" recalls songs that Lou Reed has written about Manhattan. I asked McDaniels if he was hip to Reed's New York song cycles, and he replied, "Yes, I've always been a distant fan of Lou Reed's. His music was never challenging for me, so I didn't get close to him. On the other hand, I did get close to Ornette Coleman, who did influence *Outlaw* in whatever subtle and non-subtle

ways because of how he expressed himself in the jazz medium. It somehow seemed universal to me."

I first became aware of "Silent Majority" on the 1970 Eddie Harris *Live at Newport* album, where McDaniels joins saxophonist Harris for a spontaneous run through of this vibrant rant.

ABOVE: The top photo (from the 1970 Newport Jazz Festival) shows Eddie Harris unveiling his unique "reed trumpet" — Harris was a saxophonist, not a trumpet player; but he could play trumpet by inserting a saxophone reed mouthpiece. Harris announced that day that his innovative idea would be a godsend for brass players, but sadly, they all ignored it.

As Gene told me, "Eddie Harris and I were a mutual admiration society. I thought he was great." McDanielss replied to Harris' 1960's popular instrumental "Freedom Jazz Dance" with "Freedom Death Dance" on *Headless Heroes Of The Apocalypse*. "Silent Majority" remains potent as a groundbreaking political "rap" and it was this song that McDaniels feels motivated Tricky Dick Nixon's White House to move in on him. As he mentioned to journalist Charles Waring of *Blues & Soul* magazine: "Our political system has code words and one is silent majority and that meant white people being quiet about the naughty actions of black people. So I wrote a song called 'Silent Majority' and it says 'Silent Majority is calling out loud to you and me from

Arlington Cemetery' and that pissed somebody off big time and I know that's the reason they contacted me."

On Feb. 9, 1970, the day that he recorded the version of "Silent Majority" released on *Outlaw*, McDaniels attempted his own version of "Compared To What." Because the song had been a popular hit already — besides fitting the lyrical, if not musical, theme of *Outlaw* — McDaniels tried recording it again the next day. As of yet, neither version has seen the light of day.

Despite being pigeonholed as a soul-jazz artist, McDaniels was capable of writing folk songs, as reflected in "Love Letter to America," a timeless ballad that could have been recorded by Bob Dylan or Joan Baez. In his interview with Charles Waring, McDaniels acknowledged, "Dylan was definitely an influence."

I can hear echoes of poet Allen Ginsberg. McDaniels sings "Hey America, I can see you now," while Ginsberg wrote in his *America* poem, "America … I'm addressing you." They both capture an America never reflected in a Norman Rockwell painting.

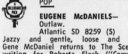

POP

EUGENE McDANIELS—
Outlaw.
Atlantic SD 8259 (S)
Jazzy and gentle, loose and liberated Gene McDaniel returns to The Scene after writing for Roberta Flack ("Compared to What"), adding his poetry and passion to the new directions in soul and jazz. Overwhelming in their simplicity and intensity, McDaniel's visions protest apathy towards the obvious in a clear, honest outcry on "Welfare City," "Silent Majority" and "Love Letters to America." A gripping comeback.

"Black Boy" is another ballad, taken from fiddler John Blair's pen with modified lyrics by McDaniels. It's a delicate acoustic song one could imagine performed at the Newport Folk Festival circa 1966. The climate that McDaniels constructs resembles an intersection between Fred Neil's protest song, "Tear Down the Walls" (amended by the Jefferson Airplane to "up against the wall, motherfucker") and the Black Power movement. But Gene told me, "I was not a Black Panther and I was not a Black Panther sympathizer, but I understood why they existed. So I did a couple of benefit concerts for them and I was pretty enamored of Angela Davis."

"Reverend Lee" is the most enigmatic song on the album, lyrically a possible reference to McDaniels himself (hence the name "the left rev mc d" on the album cover). McDaniels rarely discusses his songwriting, but he did acknowledge to me:

I was born the son of a minister, Reverend B.T. McDaniels. Born in Kansas, raised in Nebraska and experienced spirituality on a very deep level and the religious involvement of my parents. Reverend Lee kind of oozed out of my unconscious mind onto the paper about the temptations and torture of being a spiritual public servant.

Because it was the album's least controversial song, "Reverend Lee" was recorded by Roberta Flack, Natalie Cole and Herbie Mann. When I asked McDaniels if he was aware of any other cover versions from *Outlaw*, he replied,

I don't know of anyone, other than the people you mention, who recorded songs from Outlaw *or* Headless Heroes of the Apocalypse. *I must have really fucked people up, 'cause nobody would touch it with a ten-foot pole. I really either fucked up or I hit a nerve in the country, not really sure which. And I don't really care. I am told that I'm among the top ten sampled artists. At the least the rappers weren't afraid. Amongst the rest of the populace, I'm sort of persona non grata as far as these recordings are concerned. My witness protection name is Bill Clinton.*

The statement on the back of album, "Under conditions of national emergency like now, there are only two kinds of people — those who work for freedom, and those who do not … good guys versus the bad guys." That still says it for me, because that's where we are thirty years later. They're still trying to take over the country and they're much closer to doing it now than they were then.

With the narcissists running the show, we've got a heavy fight ahead of us to retain our freedoms. That's about all I've got to say.

THE WATTS PROPHETS ARE
RAPPIN' BLACK IN A WHITE WORLD

The Watts Prophets presented a more universal message than the Last Poets. While the Last Poets got caught up in their own infighting over changes in membership and the legal rights to their name, the Watts Prophets focused on crossing racial lines and reaching

a multi-ethnic audience. Despite their political agenda, or more to the point, as *part* of their political agenda, the Watts Prophets were about humanity, about suggesting a way to live. It's a common misconception that the Watts Prophets followed in the Last Poets' footsteps. In fact, the Watts Prophets had formed well before the release of the Last Poets' debut album.

Watts is a neighborhood of Los Angeles that became infamous for the riots of August 1965. Fueled by high unemployment, subpar local schools and inferior inner-city living conditions, the Watts Riots ignited when a policeman arrested an African-American man on suspicion of drunk driving and insisted on impounding his automobile along with two family members whose only crime consisted of riding in the car. The result was a six-day rage of fighting, looting and arson totaling over thirty deaths and one thousand injuries. Afterward, Watts was assured a spot on the map of the Black Power movement.

Despite the carnage, Watts wasn't hell on earth, but a hotbed of cultural and creative activity including the aforementioned Pan-Afrikan People's Arkestra (founded by Horace Tapscott in 1961), and the Watts Writers Workshop (which emerged after the '65 rioting). Numerous people passed through the Workshop, including future Miles Davis biographer Quincy Troupe, outspoken curmudgeon Stanley Crouch (both as students) and *Across 110th Street* movie actor Yaphet Kotto (as a teacher). The poetry performance group Watts Prophets also came out of the Workshop.

In 1967, three members of the Workshop, Amde Hamilton, Richard Dedeaux and Otis O'Solomon (then known as Otis Smith) began reciting, chanting, speaking and singing together as the Watts Prophets. Before the Prophets would record under their own name, Hamilton would perform on the 1969 album *The Black Voices: On The Street In Watts*. Besides Hamilton, the album included novelist and screenwriter Odie Hawkins (who later wrote several TV episodes of *Sanford and Son*) and Professors Emmery Lee Joseph Evans and Ed Bereal. With the majority of the tracks written by Hamilton, *Black Voices* is considered part of the Watts Prophets discography. Most of Hamilton's raps centered on streetwise black consciousness:

I'll stop calling you niggers when you start acting like black men. My fellow poets tell me not to write poems talking bad about

Photo courtesy of Amde Hamilton

ABOVE LEFT: Following the Watts Riots of 1965, the artist Robert Williams was commissioned by hot rod-icon Ed "Big Daddy" Roth's studio to design a T-shirt for the black militant organization "US" that appeared on this cover of *LIFE* Magazine. Williams would soon join Robert Crumb as a contributor to *Zap Comix* and later spearheaded the pop-psychedelic art movement on the West Coast (as codified by *JUXTAPOZ*, the art magazine he co-founded in 1996).

it's important to remember a few things. The Watts Prophets would begin their performance by announcing: "we're gonna rap to you." This was years before any popular vocalists were tossing around the word "rap." The Last Poets didn't call what they did "rapping," they called it poetry. It was only decades later, as the Last Poets legacy overshadowed the Watts Prophets, that the Last Poets were deemed the "godfathers of rap," and the Prophets, who'd introduced the phrase, got lost in the shuffle. Their 1971 album title says it all: *Rappin' Black in a White World*.

The song-poems on *Rappin'* segued seamlessly, as did the interplay between their four voices. McNeil's vocals add a degree of vulnerability and authoritative sensuality, providing another factor (a female member) that sets them apart from the Last Poets. Her voice sizzles as she intones, "honey, there's a difference between a black man and a nigger."

Lyrically, each Prophet shines. Richard DeDeux's "Dem Niggers Ain't Playing" is seminal.

Looks like they've developed the new black pride, it even show in the way they now stride, you better look around, y' all, can't you see what I'm saying? It sure looks to me like those niggers ain't playing. I think they're trying to get something started. I'm talking about SNCC and US and the Black Panther Party, is anyone listening to what I'm saying? Cause it sure looks to me like them niggers ain't playing!

black folk. But I ain't mad at whitey. I'm mad at you, you low down niggers… They're so hip, they can quote Farrakhan, Mao, Malcolm, Martin, LeRoi, and Eldridge — playing tough, but the niggers ain't really rough.

When the Watts Prophets released their own album *Rappin' Black in a White World* in 1971, the trio had become a quartet with the addition of Dee Dee McNeil, a singer and pianist who'd moved to Watts from Detroit. Motown acts The Supremes, Edwin Starr and David Ruffin have recorded songs she's written. Despite the Last Poets often being referred to as the "godfathers of rap,"

ABOVE: The heavily callused hands of a working person, this is not protest from the classroom, these are not "armchair radicals"; this is *On The Street In Watts* — exemplified by the classic Black Power fist.

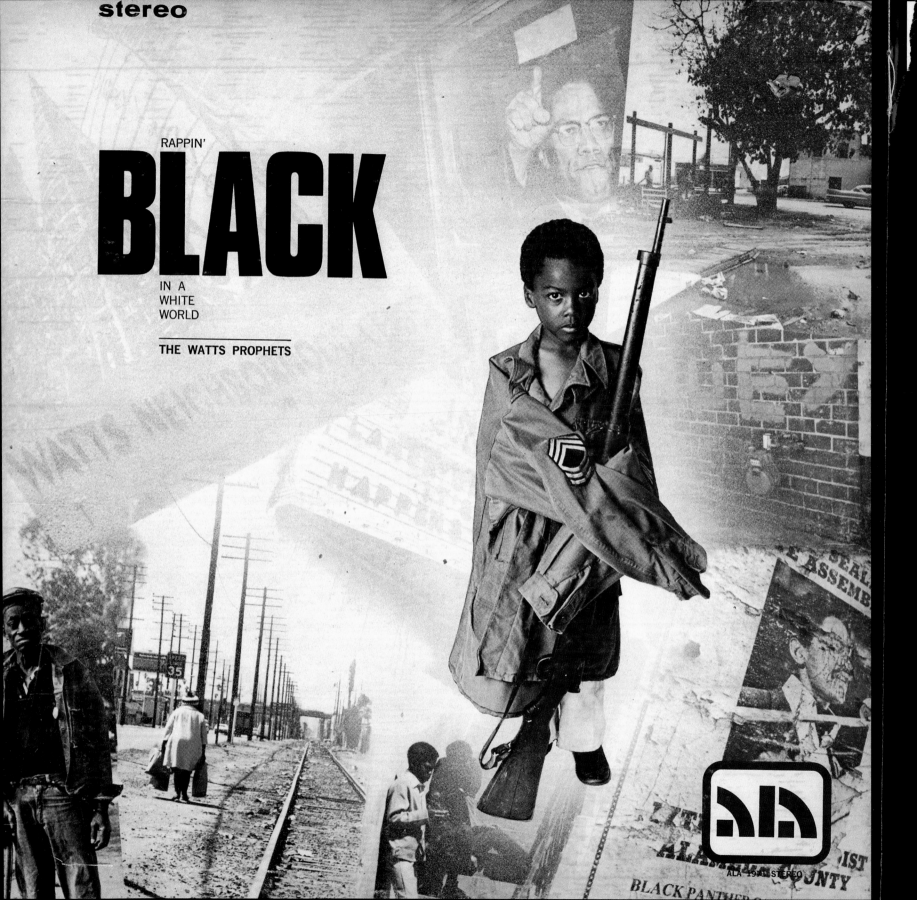

What the reader is missing from the printed page is the dynamics of the four voices in unison, how they call and respond to each other, weaving the words back and forth among them regardless of which member wrote the piece. Their voices are their instruments, creating magic, like the blend of Miles Davis' trumpet with John Coltrane and Cannonball Adderley's saxophones and Bill Evans' piano on *Kind of Blue*.

As the 1970s progressed, members of the Prophets were involved in several milestone events. Richard Dedeaux was the initial force behind the Wattstax concert. The Prophets were poised to release an album for Bob Marley's Tuff Gong label and while that didn't come to fruition, Ethiopian Orthodox priest Father Amde Hamilton spoke at Marley's funeral. Not surprisingly, it was the 1990s hip-hop boom that finally gave the godfathers of rap their due, as The Watts Prophets were sampled by Dr. Dre, Digable Planets and Too Short, among others.

The Prophets were also involved in a movie, *Victory Will Be My Moan*, which was broadcast on community television in Southern California in 1972, but has never been issued on video. The movie features Hamilton and O'Solomon, along with Ataullah Bashir and Nathanael Alle, in a prison setting, each man in his own cell, talking and rapping amongst themselves. The four actors wrote and staged their own performances, while the movie was directed by Allan Muir, best known for directing the rock group Traffic's 1972 Santa Monica concert film and a Cat Stevens 1971 Los Angeles TV performance. "Doin' It!" was the theme song for the movie, performed by pianist Gene Russell — founder of the Oakland-based Black Jazz Records, home of keyboardist Doug Carn.

KAIN AND THE BLUE GUERRILLA

As I described in the Black Forum section, *Black Spirits: Festival Of New Black Poets In America*, Gylan Kain was a founding member of the Last Poets, but had left the band (along with co-founder David Nelson) before the Poets' debut album was recorded. Kain and Nelson teamed up with Felipe Luciano to form The Original Last Poets, which recorded the *Right On!* album for the Juggernaut label in 1971. Also released on Juggernaut that year was a solo LP from Gylan Kain, released under the name Kain and titled *The Blue Guerrilla*.

Juggernaut was the brainchild of Henry "Juggy" Murray. Murray co-founded Sue Records in 1957 and brought us the earliest hit singles from Ike & Tina Turner, along with seminal recordings by jazz organist Jimmy McGriff. In 1968, Murray sold the Sue master tapes to United Artists, and by 1972 he was living in California, enjoying a successful solo career releasing singles for the burgeoning disco market. Information is slim on the bone, but Juggernaut fell in between these events in time, presumably in New York, where the various Poets were based.

The Blue Guerrilla is the most compelling album by any Last Poet, "original" or otherwise — lyrically polarizing and musically energizing. Kain easily shifts from the playful swing jazz of "Harlem Preacher," in which he describes a quaint 1925 bar scene, before exploding into the manic energy of "I Ain't Black." Kain recites the phrase "You black bastard" repeatedly, changing the tone of his voice from angry to happy to effeminate to a Jamaican accent and points in between. The result is humorous and provocative, as acoustic bass and drums punctuate each "You black bastard" with an aggressive staccato flourish of notes.

This continues for about two minutes before the song moves into a driving *Bitches Brew*-style groove propelled by electric piano. Kain continues to spit out "I ain't black" in increasingly deranged and demented form, until he begins screaming "you white motherfucker," countering quickly with "I ain't white." The music comes to a halt, followed by a series of a cappella "I ain't white" in diverse, expressive tones. The music starts back up, this time in a shuffling blues-rock vein as Kain vamps, "My mama knew I ain't white, my daddy knew I ain't white, I ain't white."

Then, when it seems as if it's all over, the band returns to the swinging jazz groove introduced on "Harlem Preacher," while Kain narrates with a detached sense of cool in a third party voice, "Oh, the people petrified by this shit, man, what the hell is happening here? The cat is walking in here just as bad as he please,

OPPOSITE: *Rappin' Black in a White World*, where Watts is a battleground with a young kid wearing an Army field jacket — referring to both the black youth compelled to serve in the Vietnam War and in the battles on the streets of Watts. The posters of Malcolm X and Bobby Seale reflect The Watts Prophets' alliance with diverse Black Power movements, be it Nationalism or revolutionary. The railroad tracks symbolize migration, bringing blacks from the South to the West and North.

KAIN
The Blue Guerrilla

JUGGERNAUT RECORDS
JUG ST/LP 8805

talking about 'he ain't white' and 'he ain't black,' that's all right man, the sun is still shining outside and everything's cool."

Kain is now back in that 1925 bar room with the "Harlem Preacher." These six minutes are a riveting mini-rap-opera — hands down the most innovative "rap" my ears have experienced. When I played it for music scribe Chris Estey, he described it as "black punk-jazz-skronk." With the exception of jazz, it predates those genres (let alone a mash-up of them) by nearly a decade. "Ain't It Fine" is another highlight, with a 1960s garage-rock riff played on a Farfisa organ. Imagine Kain jamming with The Seeds or the Chocolate Watchband. He keeps repeating "Ain't it fine" while happily describing a walk on a sandy beach. The lighthearted vocals, set against an ominous organ riff and reinforced by a pounding bass drum, are wonderfully perverse.

Producer Juggy Murray's liner notes aren't overreaching when he writes, "The Last Poets. You've heard the name. Gylan Kain is the brain-child behind this Third World movement. Kain is a genius, an innovator, the power behind the Last Poets." Murray makes clear that the Blue Guerrilla on the cover is Jesus Christ.

Another set of notes written by Last Poet Felipe Luciano suggests the same, adding, "Christ must have been a nigger!"

On the seven-minute churning epic "Look Out for the Blue Guerrilla," Kain pontificates about Rudyard Kipling before vividly describing seeing "Him [God aka the Blue Guerrilla] in the luminescent foothills of Missouri."

Kain is a consummate wordsmith who relies on others to provide the music. In some cases he simply borrows, such as his use of Sly Stone's "Sex Machine" as the basis for his own "Nubian II." Another tune credits the music to jazz pianist Duke Pearson. The most interesting songs feature music by a (pre-Chic) Nile Rodgers. During this time, young Nile Rodgers was a Black

Panther Party member and already playing music with Chic co-founder Bernard Edwards as The Boys — later changed to the Big Apple Band. Nile wouldn't cut wax under his own direction until 1977, when Chic released their first album. Kain is still active and now resides in Holland.

BAMA — THE VILLAGE POET
AND GHETTOS OF THE MIND

Not much is known about "Bama — The Village Poet" but his *Ghettos of the Mind* album was released by Chess Records in 1972, with reissues popping up on various labels since then. Apparently there was also a single on Chess the following year (which has yet to surface as a reissue), but with both sides titled "Dig It Interview," it would be safe to assume it's a promo disc of the artist speaking. Bama has a formidable backing band, including drummer Bernard Purdie, Richard Tee on keyboards and guitarist Cornell Dupree. Although they don't perform on the album, Jimmy Wisner and Billy Jackson set Bama's poems to music. Wisner was a jazz pianist who had a crossover hit in 1961 when he set Edvard Grieg's "Piano Concerto In A Minor" to a rock 'n' roll groove, titled it "Asia Minor" and released it under the pseudonym Kokomo. The album was produced and directed by "Those who believe blacks deserve something better."

OPPOSITE: Hands down the most enigmatic record cover on display in this book. A drawing depicting Jesus Christ as "The Blue Guerrilla," which Kain claimed to have seen "in the luminescent foothills of Missouri": whether "gorilla" (the animal) is deliberately misspelled as "guerrilla" (a radical freedom fighter) is worthy of debate. Rarely did LPs from this genre feature such surrealistic imagery: of note are the fetus, the axe and the Pan-like figure on the cross.

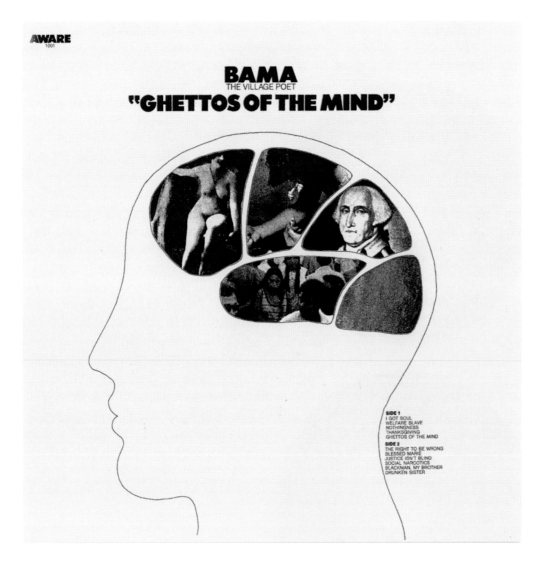

LEFT: What thoughts are lurking inside the *Ghettos of the Mind?*: a nude woman; someone shooting heroin; America's founding father George Washington; and a crowd scene. Bama, The Village Poet, has a lot of things on his mind, including "Social Narcotics."

RIGHT: Ranging in ages from 11 to 21, this group of youngsters exemplified a new era in the ghetto. Black Americans were now creating poetry, art and music in places like Watts, Detroit and Harlem as form of expression and self-confidence. The back cover of their debut declaimed, "We know who we are, and what we are, and we're free."

VOICES OF EAST HARLEM
AND RIGHT ON BE FREE

New York City's Voices of East Harlem comprised twenty urban youths assembled by Chuck and Anna Griffin, who had three children of their own in the choir. Around 1969, the choir caught the ear of New York Mayor John Lindsay, who led them to Jerry Brandt, who was running a club called The Electric Circus. Brandt then brought them to Elektra Records (not known for signing black artists, but for taking chances with the likes of the

MC5 and The Stooges as well as topical protest singers such as Tom Paxton and Phil Ochs). Soon after opening for Hendrix at the Fillmore East on Jan. 1, 1970 (the night he recorded his live *Band of Gypsys* album), the Voices recorded their debut LP *Right On Be Free* at Electric Ladyland studio. Hendrix' engineer Eddie Kramer recorded the proceedings, while Jerry Brandt produced. Chuck Griffin's "Right On Be Free" kicked off the album, with additional songs by various songwriters, including the group's music director Bernice Cole.

However, it was probably their soulfully grand version of Buffalo Springfield's "For What It's Worth" that helped the blossoming act get attention. The band opened for a slew of acts, including The Who and Sly and the Family Stone. They were invited to perform at the August 1970 Isle of Wight Festival in England, sharing the bill with the likes of Miles Davis, Joni Mitchell and The Doors. In March 1971 they journeyed to Ghana with Eddie Harris & Les McCann, the Staple Singers, Roberta Flack and Santana for the Soul To Soul festival and subsequent movie and soundtrack.

Upon returning, the Voices entered the studio with Donny Hathaway producing and playing keyboards. The result was a remarkable, upbeat gospel version of Bob Dylan's 1962 ballad "Oxford Town," which honored a pivotal event of the Civil Rights movement. Dylan's song is an account of James Meredith's attempt to become the first black student to enroll at the University of Mississippi in September 1962. When Meredith stepped on campus, many whites, including the state governor, vowed to keep the university segregated. Riots broke out, resulting in two deaths, including a French journalist found behind a campus building with a gunshot to the back. Dozens of others were wounded as a combination of U.S. Marshals, the Army and the National Guard secured the campus. Meredith continued on and graduated from the university with a political science degree.

Released as a single in 1971 on Elektra, "Oxford Town" sank without a trace. Their second Elektra album, provisionally titled *Nation Time*, was cancelled despite being halfway recorded with Hathaway. Five songs intended for that album appear as bonus tracks on the UK version of the *Right On Be Free* CD. Ranging in ages from 11 to 21, this group exemplified a new era in the ghettos of America. Black Americans were now creating poetry, art and music in places like Watts, Detroit and Harlem as a form of expression and self-confidence. The back cover of their debut asserted, "We know who we are, and what we are, and we're free." ◐

ABOVE: By 1970, kids were also caught up in the Black Power movement, as this picture sleeve attests. Not unlike the 1990s, when hip-hop artists (and their young fans) turned their baseball caps backwards, black youth in the early 1970s often wore large floppy caps turned sideways.

REV.C.L. FRANKLIN

The Meaning of Black Power

CHESS SERMON
STEREO CH76

BLACK POWER PREACHIN'

6

The Black Power movement also inspired "men of the cloth," such as the Rev. Jesse Jackson, who would emerge as a political figure, and Aretha Franklin's father C.L. Franklin, a popular preacher who recorded and released over fifty different albums, including an inspired sermon on Black Power. Tom Skinner was a member of the Harlem Lords gang before he blended the Bible and Black Nationalism in "crusades" at the Apollo Theatre.

THE REV. JESSE JACKSON: As discussed elsewhere, Jesse Jackson is featured prominently on Cannonball Adderley's *Country Preacher*. In 1965, Jackson participated in the legendary Selma to Montgomery march. He then returned to Chicago, where he was studying to become a minister at the Chicago Theological Seminary. However, he dropped out the following year to fully engage in the Civil Rights cause, when King Jr. made Jackson the head of the Southern Christian Leadership Conference (SCLC)'s Chicago-based Operation Breadbasket program. Known as a publicity hound ever since joining King Jr.'s team, it seemed that Jackson's main motivation during that era was to give blacks a sense of self-worth via his "I Am Somebody" mantra.

In April 1970, Jackson organized an album on Chess Records, *On the Case*, by The SCLC Operation Breadbasket Orchestra and Choir. Produced by Gene Barge (who played saxophone on the album), it featured saxophonist Ben Branch and guitarist Wayne Bennett accompanied by a big band and a choir of nearly two hundred vocalists. Alongside versions of "We Shall Overcome,"

OPPOSITE: The false dichotomy between the secular and the spiritual in the black church. Some would be startled by this image on the cover of an album from a preacher — but strength comes from not just the power of the Lord, but also the power of the man.

LEFT: It's not just a clenched fist, it's a fist holding "the rich heritage of Black People, [their] music." *On the Case* was a benefit album for Jesse Jackson's Operation Breadbasket program, so the images inside the fist include Jackson and poverty-stricken people of Chicago, along with images paying tribute to "gospel singing, spirituals, jazz, and the blues" — all genres indentified on the back cover by Ralph Abernathy as means of expressing the black struggle.

RIGHT: Jesse Jackson's facial expression says "The Country Preacher": naming it and claiming it! "I *Am* Somebody" — is punctuated by the gatefold sleeve that opens up to reveal his entire body in full flight of testifying.

"Lift Every Voice and Sing" and various gospel standards was Joe Zawinul's instrumental tribute to Jesse Jackson (by way of Cannonball Adderley), "Country Preacher."

When Jackson left Operation Breadbasket in December 1971 to start PUSH (People United to Save Humanity), a band called the Pace-Setters recorded a single on Kent Records, "Push On Jesse Jackson." Borrowing the repeating sixteenth-note high-hat pattern used on Isaac Hayes' "Theme from *Shaft*" (and other elements of the movie's funky theme tune), the song encourages the listener ("no matter if you're black or white") to get behind Jackson's efforts "with all your might" for freedom and justice.

Also released in 1970 was *I Am Somebody* by the Country Preacher, the Rev. Jesse Jackson. Besides Jackson's thirty-plus-minute "I Am Somebody" oration, the inside of the gatefold includes several pictures of Jackson hanging with other activists. While it's no surprise to see Jackson with King Jr. or Cleveland Mayor Carl Stokes, there are two unexpected images: a photograph of Black Panther Fred Hampton, the Rev. Ralph Abernathy and Jackson mingling, and another one of Jackson conversing with Amiri Baraka. It's unclear where Jackson stands on the Black Panthers' legacy in the 21st century, but at the July 1972 annual meeting of the NAACP in Detroit, he declared that the black community needed the energy of the Panthers, for which he received an enthusiastic response from the attendees.

TOM SKINNER: As a teenager, Tom Skinner became a gang member of the Harlem Lords, following the ideals of Black Nationalists he encountered on the streets of New York. Although Skinner eventually found God and dropped out of the gang, he didn't

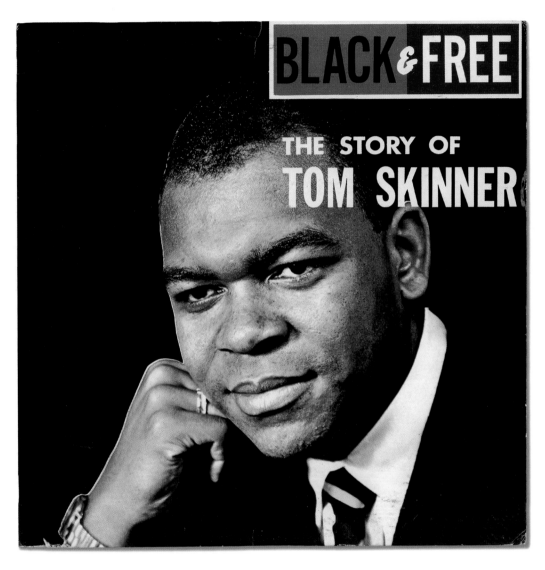

forget what the Black Nationalists had told him: "The Christian religion is nothing more than a white man's religion given to black people to keep them in their place. The same people who believe that Jesus saves will move out of the neighborhood when you move in."

Skinner became a minister known for his outspoken stance on race relations, penning the book *Black and Free* in the late 1960s. Skinner gained national exposure when he saw the need for black evangelicals to band together. However, many Christian radio stations banned his broadcasts as they couldn't handle his presentation of the Bible as a political text. To help get his

message across, Skinner released the album *Black & Free,* in which he "tells it like it is to black people," describing his life as a former gang member and his conversion to Christianity as a platform to deliver his message. Skinner gave sermons at the Apollo Theatre

ABOVE: *Black & Free* features the Rev. Tom Skinner's viscerally articulate first-hand accounts of competitive struggle and illumination through violent personal experience. The LP cover features his handsome, penetrating gaze, as much evidence of his experience overcoming the white man's religious chains as the scars on Sonny Liston's back are evidence of man's violence against his fellow man.

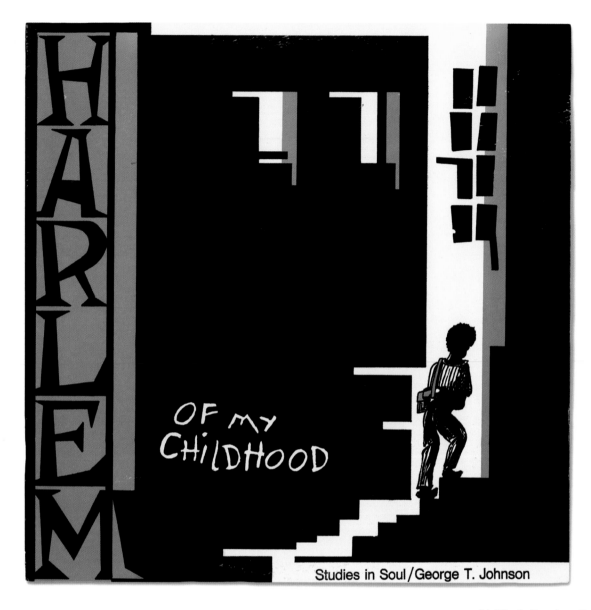

RIGHT: The cover is reminiscent of the great urban storytelling of Hubert Selby Jr. It captures the imagery of "the spirit of the black boy growing up in Harlem, who can find a back-handed pleasure in shining shoes, or the desperate confusion and understanding of a black mother who has given her sons to a world she never made." Orator George Johnson integrates religious testimony with an overt call to social justice. The child is carrying a book bag, eager for education.

in Harlem, and by the early 1970s had gained the support of Dick Gregory and Malcolm X's widow, Betty Shabazz.

GEORGE JOHNSON: Another curious album with religious overtones is *Harlem of my Childhood: Studies in Soul* by George Johnson, which was produced in 1968 by Blackside Inc. in Boston as a fundraising vehicle for the Unitarian Universalist East Bay Project, based in Oakland, Calif., where Johnson served as a minister and director of this social action organization. The album is a collection of sermons and meditations accompanied by guitar and trumpet. Topics include the joy of an Easter celebration on Adeline Street in Oakland, Johnson's youth in Harlem and a jazzy vamp on the gospel standard "What a Friend We Have in Jesus."

A track entitled "Moses Jackson" is of the most interest here, as the album notes explain:

Moses Jackson was written after the killing of eighteen year old Black Panther Party member, Bobby Hutton, by the Oakland, California, police on April 6, 1968, during an alleged shoot-out. I thought about Bobby and other members of the party who in their own way were taking care of business, who for many people in the Black Community are the real liberators, the real heroes of the freedom struggle. I thought of Bobby's family, of his mother and black mothers everywhere, who are the great heroines of our society. Moses Jackson more than any poem was something I had to write.

Despite being a man of the cloth, Johnson could still identify with the Black Panther Party. In February 1968, the National Conference of Black Unitarian Universalists took place in Chicago. During the conference, Johnson gave a report on developing congregational participation in Civil Rights activities in which he described "the Negro dilemma as a choice between integration and developing pride and power through Black unity."

THE REV. C.L. FRANKLIN: Best known as the father of the "Queen of Soul," Aretha Franklin, Clarence LaVaughn (C. L.) Franklin was a Baptist minister. Starting in the 1940s, he toured the country extensively and became known as the "Million Dollar Voice." He was one of the first to release his sermons on records, a practice he continued into the 1970s, resulting in seventy-five different albums.

Franklin was a personal friend of Martin Luther King Jr., who often attended Franklin's church when visiting Detroit. On June 23, 1963, Franklin organized and co-led with King Jr. a march to protest racial discrimination in Detroit. This event was recorded by Motown Records and released on their Gordy label as *The Great March To Freedom: Rev. Martin Luther King Speaks*. Franklin was also involved with the NAACP and served on the executive board of King Jr.'s Southern Christian Leadership Council. As a supporter of the Civil Rights movement, he was tactically not philosophically nonviolent. The emotional scars of growing up in Mississippi cut deep and he never forgot it.

In 1969, Franklin rented his New Bethel Baptist Church in Detroit to a black militant group known as the Republic of New Africa after they promised him they had no firearms. Franklin had no direct connection to the Republic of New Africa organization, and they claimed *Negroes with Guns* author Robert F. Williams as their president (then living in exile in China). The previous year, the RNA made their mark in Detroit calling for the establishment of an independent black nation in the Southern United States.

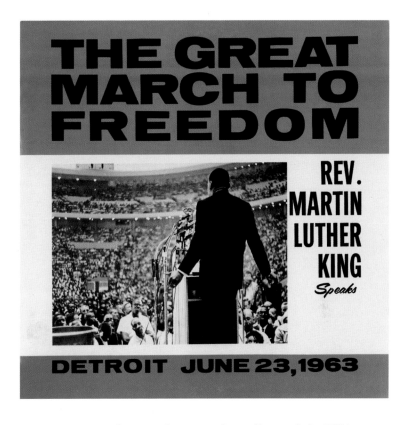

However, a shootout between the police and the RNA members occurred in Franklin's church, resulting in one policeman's death and another wounded. After the event, Franklin returned to his church and saw that many of the pews had incoming splinters and the shot-out broken glass had blown inside, while there was wasn't any evidence of bullets exiting the church. Obviously it was the police who were doing the bulk of the shooting. Distraught at this act of violence, he said, "We are in the throes of a revolution, a social revolution. Some people have lost their lives in this revolution, and we have lost a little glass. I think we got out cheap." ◉

ABOVE: As a warm-up to the historic march on Washington, D.C. in August 1963, King Jr. went to Detroit in June, co-led a march with the Rev. Franklin (Aretha's dad) and then spoke at Cobo Hall (pictured on the front cover), which music fans will remember as the site of several concerts by The Who, The Rolling Stones and Led Zeppelin throughout the '70s.

DIGNITY LP 102

"BURN BABY, BURN"

THIS IS AN EDUCATIONAL ALBUM AND IS NOT DESIGNED TO INCITE VIOLENCE

JOHNNY NASH

WE TELL IT LIKE IT IS
THE TRUE FACTS AS TOLD

NARRATED BY ATTORNEY DONALD WARDEN of the AFRO AMERICAN ASSOCIATION

THE UNCENSORED VERSION OF THE LOS ANGELES RIOT

- CHIEF PARKER
- "BLOOD BROTHERS"
- MAYOR YORTY
- DICK GREGORY
- "THE PREACHERS"

- JOHNNY NASH
- PAWN SHOPS
- SCHOOLS
- BURNING BUSINESS RECORDS
- THE ONLY REAL SOLUTION!!

NEGROES WITH GUNS AND RADIOS

Robert F. Williams' essays about self-defense inspired Huey Newton to arm the Panthers. When Williams was forced to flee the country, he began a radio broadcast from Cuba that combined discourse with contemporary African-American jazz and blues recordings. Donald Warden's social-political commentary was heard on the airwaves of the San Francisco Bay Area, while WWRL disc jockey Gary Byrd in New York City mixed soul music and consciousness-raising commentary, establishing him as one of the forerunners of rap.

ROBERT F. WILLIAMS: Long before The Black Panthers armed themselves, Robert F. Williams had a similar idea in the late 1950s, as the president of a North Carolina chapter of the NAACP. The NAACP has never been a militant organization, so when Williams organized armed resistance to the gun-toting Klansmen of the KKK, he was not only defying whites, but also the NAACP, King Jr. and others. As local and federal law enforcement began putting the squeeze on Williams, he fled to Cuba where, in 1962, he battled violent white supremacists and disagreed with pacifist Civil Rights organizations. Williams detailed his experiences in *Negroes With Guns*, a book that greatly influenced Huey Newton's self-defense strategies.

With the support of Fidel Castro, Williams broadcast his show "Radio Free Dixie" which beamed across the airwaves to the United States, so that blacks in the South could hear his political

OPPOSITE: With classic tabloid-style artwork (like a copy of the *National Enquirer*), this record provides a sensationalist account of the Watts Riots that seems to demean the reasons that ghetto residents were forced to stick up for themselves. The back cover is equally outrageous with narrator Donald Warden boasting that he himself is as "amazing" as the "earth-shaking events of Watts." In the course of three lengthy paragraphs, Warden details his accomplishments, including law student, radio DJ, philosopher and businessman.

messages, along with music like Max Roach's *Freedom Now Suite* and recordings of the SNCC Freedom Singers. Friends like Amiri Baraka would mail him jazz and blues albums, and Williams felt that the new jazz experiments of Max Roach, Ornette Coleman and others could stir up "a new psychological concept of propaganda, the type of music people could feel, that would motivate them." Williams hoped the new music would have the same effect that gospel songs had in the Southern churches, pushing people's emotions over the edge. Williams' broadcasts combined music with topical news regarding racial violence, marches, and protests happening in Georgia, Mississippi and other Southern states.

DONALD WARDEN: In 1962, Warden started the Afro-American Association, a cultural organization Newton and Seale had joined and rejected before forming the Black Panthers. According to Seale, Newton saw no reason to align himself with Warden's pro-capitalist brand of Black Nationalism.

By the mid-1960s Warden was studying at UC Berkeley law school and was a practicing attorney in the Bay Area. He was also a minister and a DJ, with a weekly radio broadcast under the banner of the Afro-American Association. On Sunday afternoon, Aug. 15, 1965, his radio show documented the rioting in Watts during the previous four days, with Warden narrating accounts given by Police Chief William Parker and Los Angeles Mayor Sam Yorty, Dick Gregory and various citizens and preachers of Watts.

According to the *Burn Baby, Burn* album notes, singer-songwriter Johnny Nash was signing autographs at Music City Records on Alcatraz Avenue in Berkeley when record store owner Ray Dobard whisked him over to the radio station so that Nash could give his opinions on the situation in Watts. Soon after, Dobard suggested to Warden that they release the radio transmission as an album on their self-produced label

Dignity Records. The album cover is a combination of sensationalist mini-headlines: "The uncensored version of the Los Angeles riots"; "We tell it like it is: the true facts as told"; "At last it can be told: the real story of the Los Angeles riots"; and biographical praise for the album's producers, Warden and Dobard. There's also the warning: "This is an educational album and is not designed to incite violence."

THE GARY BYRD EXPERIENCE: The "GBE" (The Gary Byrd Experience) premiered on WWRL-AM in 1969, eventually becoming the longest-running show on black radio in New York City. From the beginning, Byrd mixed music and consciousness-raising messages, establishing himself as one of the forerunners of rap. WWRL broadcast out of Queens at 1600 on the AM dial with just 5,000 watts, which meant that few people outside New York ever heard Byrd do his thing. But those who did acknowledge WWRL as "New York's Soul Powerhouse": where the Rev. Al Sharpton would hang out and occasionally preach on the air when he was in town; where the Los Angeles-based Charles Wright and The Watts 103rd Street Rhythm Band got airplay on the East Coast; and where listeners often heard rapping for the very first time.

Byrd certainly caught the ear of Stevie Wonder, who set Byrd's lyrics "Village Ghetto Land" and "Black Man" to music on *Songs In the Key of Life*. RCA Records also tuned into Byrd and released *Presenting The Gary Byrd Experience* in 1972. Fans of Afro-Cuban jazz will appreciate the arrangements by Chico O'Farrill, known for his collaborations with Gato Barbieri and Cal Tjader. Much later, he worked with David Bowie on *Black Tie White Noise*.

The back cover: "If people only knew the power of the people, we wouldn't be moving so slow. Gary Byrd's saucy Radio Land voice speaks the truth to the people, the gut funky electric guitar crackling out the beat under the voice. The heavy rhythms of drums, brass and female singers produce a great sound with a great message." And that's exactly what this album contains:

enamored with Byrd's lyrics, funk flute master Joe Thomas dug the music of "Every Brother Ain't a Brother" and recorded a lengthy instrumental version for his 1972 *Joe Thomas is the Ebony Godfather* on the Today label. The B-side "Are You Really Ready For Black Power?" castigates fake revolutionaries, admonishing those who are misusing the movement for their own ends.

Now listen, if you're really ready for Black Power then, of course, you already know, that true power is not in money because money is something that you can blow, that true power is a thing that lies in the heaviness of your mind, the key to Black Power is respecting your own kind. Are you really ready for Black Power? Have you decided to be a brother? Are you really ready for Black Power? Or are you just fooling one another? — Is the brother ready for Black Power when he pushes dope into young black hands?

And, as Byrd told James Maycock in October 2000:

At that time there was an ideological struggle about what Black Power meant. The idea I was attempting to do was to expose people who were, in effect, espousing values of the Black Power movement but, actually, were not true to those values, who were coming on, "right on, right on" but turning around and stabbing you in the back or turn right around and sell the community out. ◉

heavy grooves underpinning affirmative Black Power bulletins. Despite the over-the-top instrumentation, it's Byrd's distinctive spoken enunciation that steals the show — the grooviest PSA (Public Service Announcement) ever broadcast!

Byrd's 1972 LP was preceded by a 1970 single on Real Thing records: "Every Brother Ain't a Brother," backed with "Are You Really Ready for Black Power?". While Stevie Wonder was

ABOVE: The cover exemplifies that classic pimp daddy, black hipster vibe. Byrd was a popular radio disc jockey in the New York City area — he's working a mink hat and looking styling.

WATTSTAX:
A Festival of Brotherhood

8

After the success of Isaac Hayes' *Shaft* soundtrack, Memphis-based Stax Records started looking westward. They established Stax West in Los Angeles, helmed by jazz drummer Chico Hamilton's son, Forest. Forest Hamilton was a young concert promoter who'd first met Stax president Al Bell when he'd ventured to Memphis to book his artists. Bell and Hamilton connected, and Hamilton became a Stax employee, which led to the Wattstax Festival.

According to Rob Bowman's 1997 *Soulsville U.S.A. — The Story of Stax Records*, the seed for the August 1972 festival was planted in March that year, when recording artist John KaSandra, a funky philosopher who'd alternate between black consciousness monologues and down-home country-fried soul-singing with a message, went into the Stax West office and suggested they organize a black Woodstock.

To commemorate the Watts Riots of six years earlier and raise money for the community, a Watts Summer Festival had already been planned. As a result of KaSandra's suggestion, Hamilton put forth the idea that Stax should get involved in the Watts Summer Festival. The members of the Watts Prophets remember things

differently. Until now, Watts Prophets member Richard Dedeaux has been written out of the history of Wattstax. When we talked

OPPOSITE: After the death of King Jr., Jesse Jackson (and others) stepped up to take his place. Jackson focused on the younger and/or more militant blacks by aligning himself with jazz musicians like Cannonball Adderley, as well as including photos of himself with Amiri Baraka and Fred Hampton inside the gatefold sleeve of his *I Am Somebody* album. The record was released on a new sub-label of Stax named Respect (that was Stax' version of Motown's Black Forum label). In order to capture the attention of the white counterculture, this ad was run in *Rolling Stone* in April 1970. Whether it worked or not is up for debate.

in March 2010, Dedeaux spoke of his involvement. Hamilton and Bell were friendly with Dedeaux, and suggested that he write a screenplay based on real-life events surrounding a Muhammad Ali boxing match. The two Stax execs were considering producing a docudrama movie, which would recount several boxing fans being robbed of their jewelry and furs while attending an Ali fight. The movie was to be called *The Rip Off* but never saw production, as Dedeaux and the others couldn't agree on his writing fee. Nevertheless, Dedeaux spent time in Memphis working on the screenplay, where he got the impression that Stax was a bit lost emotionally and artistically in a post-Otis Redding world.

Redding had been Stax' flagship artist when his plane tragically crashed in December 1967 while on tour. Most of Redding's backing band, the Bar-Kays, had also perished, with the remaining members searching for a new direction and struggling to continue with replacement members. It had been more than four years since Redding's death when Wattstax started to get off the ground, and if the company was still feeling Redding's loss, it was nonetheless thriving in many respects, with blossoming hits by the Staple Singers and others.

It felt like Stax could use a boost, so Dedeaux began a dialogue with Forest Hamilton and Al Bell, suggesting that perhaps a couple of Stax acts could venture out to the Watts neighborhood and play a street fair. According to Dedeaux, the idea started very small: just a couple of Stax acts were to perform in front of the Mafundi Institute. The Mafundi Institute was similar to the Watts Writers Workshop, a creative arts center that supported poetry, theater and other artistic ventures. Dedeaux worked at the Mafundi as editor of their monthly newspaper. As more Stax artists agreed to play, it was decided to move the event off the street to a nearby park. As things swelled and the entire Stax roster agreed to play, they secured the Los Angeles Coliseum.

Whatever Stax intended by Dedeaux's involvement in their projects, one thing is for certain in regards to him and his fellow Watts Prophets: where was the Watts in Wattstax? Why weren't the voices of Watts performing at a music festival called Wattstax? That's a question the Watts Prophets would love to ask Al Bell. Dedeaux was brought in as one of the stage managers, helping to oversee and organize the bands that day, and he says you can see him in the film. The movie credits list a consultant credit for the Mafundi Institute, and according to Bowman's book, Stax contributed $3,000 to build a Mafundi Institute float for the Watts Festival Parade held the morning of the concert. John KaSandra, Melvin Van Peebles, actor Richard Roundtree and others emceed the festival. Van Peebles was also credited with Concert Artist Staging, but outside of the actual performers, the day belonged to the primary festival host: Jesse Jackson.

After the "Star-Spangled Banner," Jackson gave the invocation, which included his impassioned "I Am Somebody" litany. Encouraging the audience to give the Black Power Salute while he spoke, Jackson engaged the enormous stadium crowd in a stirring "I Am Somebody" call and response. Jackson and the assembled masses are one as he concludes with a nod to Amiri Baraka's 1970 poem "It's Nation Time." Jackson repeatedly asks "What time is it?" and nearly one hundred thousand people respond, "Nation Time!" The fervor rises as "Nation Time" resounds louder with each response. For one amazing afternoon the black community had a music festival with strong sociopolitical overtones, equally as important as the white hippie's Woodstock — Country Joe's "F-U-C-K" cheer had been replaced by Jesse Jackson's "I Am Somebody."

STAX RECORDS GETS RESPECT

I Am Somebody was the debut release on Respect Records (a subsidiary of Stax), whose slogan was "Tell it like it is." The Respect imprint also released *Drumbeat* by Jim Ingram. *Drumbeat* features sociopolitical narratives spoken and sung by Ingram, who accompanies himself on congas with Johnny Griffith of the (Motown) Funk Brothers playing keyboards. Ingram was a radically charged Detroit journalist and radio personality who appeared on WJLB AM 1400 and wrote for *Ebony*, the *Michigan Chronicle* and others. During the 1971 Attica State Prison riots, Ingram was the only black journalist allowed by the rebelling prisoners to enter the facility as a civilian observer. The back cover reads: "He decided to start writing after Detroit's 1967 rebellion when police and guardsmen broke his arm and burned his hand with cigarettes, although Jim was charged with no crime. And instead of responding with hatred for white people, Jim has responded with visionary love for his own people."

A segment of the album's title track (with Ingram announcing "It began in Africa") was later sampled by The Chemical Brothers for "It Began In Afrika," on the 2002 CD *Come With Us*. Norman Cook (Fatboy Slim) also used the song for the Urban All Stars track "It Began in Africa."

The final release on Respect would be a 1974 Jesse Jackson album titled *Pushing On: Holy Day/Memphis U.S.A.*, which was recorded at the Mason Temple in Memphis (where King Jr. had given his final sermon) on the anniversary of King's death.

THE *SWEET SWEETBACK'S BAADASSSSS SONG* SOUNDTRACK ALBUM: Melvin Van Peebles is a true renaissance man — a filmmaker, actor, novelist and composer — who expresses his political commentary and social satire through books, movies, plays and albums. In the early 1960s, Van Peebles moved to Paris, where he began writing plays in French employing the *sprechgesang* form of songwriting, in which lyrics are spoken over the music. He later utilized this style on his own albums.

The 1971 film *Sweet Sweetback's Baadasssss Song* was written, directed, produced, edited and scored by Van Peebles (fueled by a $50,000 loan from Bill Cosby). Van Peebles cast himself in the lead role and hired the (then) unknown band Earth, Wind & Fire to record the soundtrack. *Sweet Sweetback's Baadasssss Song* was the first film to show the black man kicking the white man's ass, and its antiauthoritarian message struck a chord with Huey Newton, who made it required viewing for all members of the Black Panther Party. The June 19, 1971 edition of the Black Panther Newspaper devoted the entire issue to the film, the first time that one subject was the focus of an entire issue of the Panther newspaper. The centerpiece was an essay written by Huey Newton, "He Won't Bleed Me: A Revolutionary Analysis of *Sweet Sweetback's Baadasssss Song*" in which Newton advocated, "the first truly revolutionary Black film made...presented to us by a Black man." Newton was enamored with the opening credits, in which the film presents a collective protagonist, "The Black Community," in the starring role. This substantiated Newton's belief that black community solidarity was a means to effectively challenge the white ruling class. The film ends with a title frame declaring: "This film is dedicated to all the brothers and sisters who had enough of the Man."

The film's soundtrack was released on Stax Records. The back cover added in the phrase "An Opera" underneath that it said, "featuring Brer Soul & Earth Wind & Fire." Brer Soul was a pseudonym for Van Peebles, who had released an album *Brer Soul* in 1968 on A&M Records. Earth, Wind & Fire, who would later become a household name, were just starting out. In fact, their own debut LP on Warner Brothers hadn't even been released when Van Peebles encountered them.

Recorded during October and November 1970, Van Peebles would suggest a tempo, a groove and a basic theme to Earth,

Wind & Fire while showing them the movie while they laid down a track in the studio. Although Van Peebles is credited with writing and composing the soundtrack, one would guess the robust, bubbling riff that drives the lengthy title song "Sweetback's Theme" is more Earth, Wind & Fire than Brer Soul.

Stax and Van Peebles marketed the album (released in April 1971) directly to the street, which inspired the film in the first place. Perhaps for the first time (although it's common now), the album was often sold in the lobby of the theatres screening the film. In some cities, Van Peebles would rent the theatre himself, show the movie, and let the theatre keep the money they made from selling popcorn and drinks while he collected the money from the ticket and album sales.

Besides inspiring Huey Newton and the Black Panther Party, *Sweet Sweetback's Baadasssss Song* unified black-owned communications companies across America as well as helped black

⚡ BRER SOUL ⚡

ABOVE: *Brer Soul* is a riff on the Brer Rabbit stories, African-American folk tales that focus on tricksters and shape-shifters. Van Peebles is a shape-shifter: the do-rag, folk roots, the masses. Brothers on the street saw it as a symbol of pride, whereas middle-class blacks saw it as shameful.

In 1968, A&M Records released Melvin Van Peebles' *Brer Soul*. Over the course of nearly fifty minutes, Van Peebles painfully rambles what might be considered poetry, but comes across as just a stoned soul stream-of-consciousness most of the time. On nine songs — and I use that term loosely — Van Peebles is accompanied by keyboardist Coleridge Perkinson, drummer Warren Smith, bassist Herb Bushler, guitarist Carl Lynch and three horn players: Al Gibbons on tenor sax and flute, Howard Johnson playing baritone sax and tuba and Nat Woodward on trumpet. Musically, however, the album is hot, with the players switching from rocking grooves to free-form jazz to beautiful melodic ambience — sometimes within seconds. Perhaps the album's most redeeming quality is the back cover, which is completely barren except for a small gritty photo of Van Peebles and the words "Author's comment: *Free Huey.*"

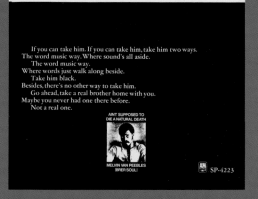

Take him black.

If you can take him. If you can take him, take him two ways.
The word music way. Where sound's all aside.
  The word music way.
Where words just walk along beside.
  Take him black.
Besides, there's no other way to take him.
  Go ahead, take a real brother home with you.
Maybe you never had one there before.
  Not a real one.

AIN'T SUPPOSED TO
DIE A NATURAL DEATH

MELVIN VAN PEEBLES
[BRER SOUL]   SP-4223

THEY BLED YOUR MAMA
THEY BLED YOUR PAPA
BUT HE WONT BLEED ME

USE YOUR BLACK ASS FROM SUN TO SUN
NIGGERS SCARED AND PRETEND THEY DON'T SEE
DEEP DOWN DIRTY DOG SCARED
JUST LIKE YOU SWEETBACK
JUST LIKE I USED TO BE
WORK YOUR BLACK BEHIND TO THE GUMS
AND YOU SUPPOSED TO THOMAS TELL HE DONE
YOU GOT TO THOMAS SWEETBACK

THEY BLED YOUR BROTHER
THEY BLED YOUR SISTER
YEAH BUT THEY WONT BLEED ME

PROGRESS SWEETBACK
THATS WHAT HE WANTS YOU TO BELIEVE
NO PROGRESS SWEETBACK
HE AINT STOPPED CLUBBING US FOR 400 YEARS
AND HE DONT INTEND TO FOR A MILLION
HE SURE TREAT US BAD SWEETBACK
WE CAN MAKE HIM DO US BETTER
CHICKEN AINT NOTHING BUT A BIRD
WHITE MAN AINT NOTHING BUT A TURD
NIGGER AINT SHIT

GET MY HAND ON A TRIGGER
YOU TALKIN REVOLUTION SWEETBACK
I WANTA GET OFF THESE KNEES
YOU TALKIN REVOLUTION SWEETBACK

YOU CAN'T MAKE IT ON WINGS
WHEELS OR STEEL SWEETBACK
WE GOT FEET
YOU CAN'T GET AWAY ON WINGS
WHEELS OR STEEL SWEETBACK
NIGGERS GOT FEET

HE BLED YOUR BROTHER
HE BLED YOUR SISTER
YOUR BROTHER AND YOUR SISTER TOO
HOW COME IT TOOK ME SO LONG TO SEE
HOW HE GET US TO USE EACH OTHER
NIGGERS SCARED
WE GOT TO GET IT TOGETHER IF HE KICKS A BROTHER
IT GOTTA BE LIKE HE KICKIN YOUR MOTHER
THEY HYPE YOU INTO SOPPING THE
MARROW OUT YOUR OWN BONES
JUSTICE IS BLIND
YEAH AND WHITE TOO
JUSTICE IS BLIND
THE WAY SHE ACTS SHE GOTTA BE
THE MAN IS JIVE
NOT TOO JIVE TO HAVE HIS GAME
UPTIGHT IN YOUR KINKY BEAN

STAND TALL SWEETBACK HE
AINT GONNA LET YOU
IM STANDING TALL ANYWAY
THE MAN KNOW EVERYTHING SWEETBACK
THE MAN KNOW EVERYTHING
THEN HE OUGHT TO KNOW IM
TIRED OF HIM FUCKIN WITH ME

USE YOUR FEET BABY
RUN MOTHERFUCKA
RUN SWEETBACK
HE WONT BLEED ME

IF YOU CANT BEAT EM JOIN EM
THATS WHAT THEY SAY
YOU TALKIN BOUT YESTERDAY
YOU CANT GO ON LIKE THAT SWEETBACK
NOT LONG AS YOUR FACE IS BLACK
CAH IM BLACK AND IM KEEPIN ON
KEEPIN ON THE SAME OLE WAY
THEY BOPPED YOUR MAMA
THEY BOPPED YOUR PAPA
WONT BOP ME
THEY BOPPED YOUR SISTER
THEY BOPPED YOUR BROTHER
THEY WONT BOP ME

(EVERYBODY)
THEY BURNED OUR MAMAS
THEY BEAT OUR PAPAS
THEY TRICKED OUR SISTERS
THEY CHAINED OUR BROTHERS
WONT BLEED ME
WONT BLEED ME

SWEET SWEETBACK'S BAADASSSSS SONG

---

politicians get elected. Stax realized that it needed regional marketing for their forthcoming film *Shaft*, so they sought consultants in Memphis, Los Angeles, Chicago and New York, weaving them into an umbrella organization they named Communiplex. Since *Shaft* wasn't ready, *Sweet Sweetback's* became the initial project. Later, *Shaft* and the *Wattstax* movie benefited from this consortium. Communiplex then funneled their profits into providing complimentary marketing for several Black congressmen's campaigns. ◉

RIGHT: The inside of this gatefold LP image captures the film's climatic ending, in which Sweetback ultimately escapes to Mexico, but vows to return and "collect dues." The surprising commercial success of the film was one way Van Peebles collected his artistic dues.

O'Bé RECORDS
STEREO

Kawaida

JAZZ, ARTIST COLLECTIVES AND BLACK CONSCIOUSNESS

9

While soul provided the soundtrack for the revolution on the streets, jazz expanded black consciousness. The Movement energized established artists such as Max Roach and Roland Kirk, while newcomers such as the Art Ensemble of Chicago and Eddie Gale made their reputations combining freestyle jazz and political statements. Horace Silver and Gary Bartz utilized Andy Bey to voice their sociopolitical

philosophy, while Miles Davis and Clifford Thornton let their instruments do the talking. Saxophonist Joe Henderson released three progressive jazz albums on the Milestone label with inspired titles: 1969's *Power to the People* (a Black Panther Party slogan), 1970's *If You're Not Part of the Solution, You're Part of the Problem* (a phrase attributed to Eldridge Cleaver) and *In Pursuit of Blackness* in 1971.

OPPOSITE: Rather than a clenched fist, the cover depicts an open hand, which reflects the idea that before there can be a political revolution there must be a cultural one. The African statue held in the palm reflects the "back to African roots" concept that Karenga's US organization espoused.

ARTISTS COLLECTIVES

Artistic collectives that raised black consciousness through music were springing up across America. In Watts, Horace Tapscott established the UGMAA (Union of God's Musicians and Artists Ascension). According to Tapscott, the mission of UGMAA was "[to play music] about depicting the lives of black people in their communities all over this country, where it has been turned around and people have been made to feel unworthy. We were trying to kill that kind of attitude about black folks through the arts."

Brooklyn was home to the Collective Black Artists (CBA), with membership including Reggie Workman, Donald Byrd and Stanley Cowell (founder of the Strata-East record label). Cowell spelled out that the CBA "are focusing on black artists because whites and blacks have different problems unique to their different cultures and life styles."

The most influential of these organizations was the Association for the Advancement of Creative Musicians (AACM). It originated on Chicago's South Side with a commitment to providing an outlet for music — be it a performance venue, a groundbreaking idea about composition or even the invention of new instruments. The AACM established a nine-point platform that addressed schooling for aspiring musicians, workshops for seasoned ones, finding gigs, stimulating spiritual growth through concerts, setting moral standards and perhaps most unusually, increasing respect between musicians and the business side — booking agents, managers and promoters. The AACM's impact was felt across the globe, bringing music to New York, Paris and beyond — it counted among its collective the members of the Art Ensemble, Henry Threadgill, Phil Cohran, Jodie Christian and Richard Abrams.

JAZZ GETS EMPOWERED
WITH CHARLES MINGUS AND MAX ROACH

Charles Mingus was notorious for being both outspoken and angry, but he channeled his fury brilliantly when he composed

"Fables of Faubus" in response to the 1957 Little Rock Nine incident in which Arkansas Governor Orval Faubus blockaded black students from a desegregated school by calling in the National Guard. Mingus' lyrics pulled no punches:

Oh, Lord, don't let 'em shoot us! Oh, Lord, don't let 'em stab us! Oh, Lord, don't let 'em tar and feather us! Oh, Lord, no more swastikas! Oh, Lord, no more Ku Klux Klan! Name me someone who's ridiculous. Governor Faubus! Why is he so sick and ridiculous? He won't permit integrated schools. Then he's a fool!

ABOVE: This historic album was recorded and released in 1960, the same year the lunch counter protests began in earnest. These three black students and the white "server" in this photo show the landmark defiance of young blacks and the bemusement of (some) white servers.

An instrumental version of "Fables of Faubus" debuted on the 1959 album *Mingus Ah Um* because Columbia Records blocked the recording of the inflammatory lyrics. The following year, Mingus recorded the song with lyrics on *Charles Mingus Presents Charles Mingus*, released on Candid Records.

Although Mingus could appreciate Black Power's philosophy of ass-kicking street tactics to attack the authoritarian ruling class, he was unequivocal about being attached to any organization, especially one promoting Black Nationalism. Though the Black Panthers weren't Nationalists, he rejected their advances as well. Panthers who frequented his performances often approached him at the Village Gate in N.Y.C., but he refused to hear them out.

When Mingus attended a Black Panther benefit in December 1971 (as a guest), he was apathetic towards the rhetoric, but felt the eyes of black women staring at him and his white wife. None of this should be seen as a judgment on the Panthers or Mingus. Similar to Hendrix and Miles Davis (both avoided aligning themselves with the Panthers), there wasn't enough space for dogmatic politics and mercurial creativity to share a room, even if there was admiration in both directions.

Also released on Candid in 1960, *We Insist! Max Roach's Freedom Now Suite* broke down barriers for all sociopolitical jazz albums to follow, addressing the movement's struggle

head on. Blending traditional jazz instruments with extreme vocalizations by Abbey Lincoln, *We Insist!* predates King Jr.'s march on Washington by three years and the height of the Black Power Movement by nearly a decade. It's still a provocative listen in the 21st century. Roach's song cycle chronicled the history of slavery, racism and the struggle for Civil Rights. The album featured tribal percussion echoing black America's cultural ties to Africa, signaling for a worldwide campaign for freedom. Lincoln's vocals cried out for change, her voice filled with anguish and contempt. The album cover photograph of blacks sitting at a whites-only lunch counter made a statement as well.

Roach composed the five-part protest suite in collaboration with singer-lyricist Oscar Brown Jr. Although Oscar Brown didn't perform on *We Insist!*, he recorded several solo albums. His *Sin and Soul* LP on Columbia featured Nat Adderley's instrumental "Work Song" with socially charged lyrics added by Brown — later covered by Nina Simone. Later, Brown released albums on Atlantic, including 1972's *Fresh* and 1974's *Movin' On*, which featured "Ghetto Scene" and "Gang Bang," speaking of

LEFT: *Members Don't Git Weary*: Members of the Civil Rights movement don't get weary and neither do the feet that keep them moving along in their march for freedom. The album title comes from an old Negro spiritual, while Max Roach (shown here in 1968) wears Nationalist African garb, showing the constant, centuries-long cross-fertilization between American and African cultures.

RIGHT: *Lift Every Voice and Sing*: The title track is considered the national anthem of Black America and has been recorded by dozens of artists through the years. The album incorporates the J.C. White gospel singers featured on the cover with songs dedicated to Malcolm X, Martin Luther King Jr., Medgar Evers and Marcus Garvey. Although one can't forget the past, one has to look forward, anticipating the time when victory is won.

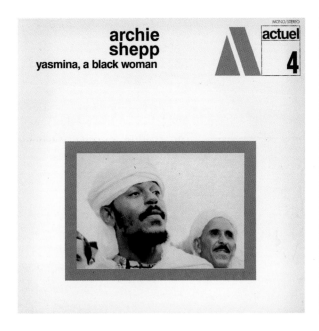

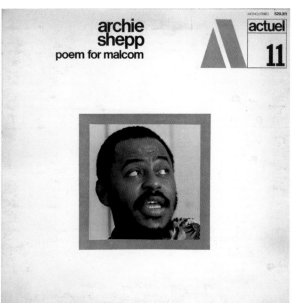

Supreme, but his contributions were left off of the original release, later appearing as bonus tracks on the 2002 expanded edition. That same year, Shepp released *Fire Music* for Impulse!, which included a spoken elegy called "Malcolm, Malcolm Semper Malcolm." The MC5 adapted "Hambone" from *Fire Music*, adding words by Rob Tyner, and retitled it "Ice Pick Slim." Tyner's lyrics were a nod to author Robert Beck,

harsh urban conditions, with an all-star backing band including Bernard Purdie, David "Fathead" Newman and Cornell Dupree.

In June 1968, Roach recorded *Members, Don't Git Weary* with alto saxophonist Gary Bartz and vocalist Andy Bey. His next release, 1971's *Lift Every Voice and Sing*, dedicated the song "Were You There When They Crucified My Lord" to Malcolm X, King Jr., Evers and many more, and "Motherless Child" to the godfather of the Black Power movement, Marcus Garvey.

ARCHIE SHEPP: Saxophonist Archie Shepp got his start playing with avant-garde pianist Cecil Taylor. He participated in the 1965 sessions for John Coltrane's seminal album *A Love*

aka Iceberg Slim, known for his street novels, including *Pimp* and *Trick Baby*. Shepp's album also inspired MC5 manager (and founder of the White Panther Party) John Sinclair to use *Fire Music* as the title for a 1966 collection of his own revolutionary poems.

In July 1969, the first Pan-African Festival of Culture took place in Algiers. Although it focused on African musicians, poets and theatrical troupes, Archie Shepp was invited to perform as well. Also in attendance was Black Panther Party Minister of Information Eldridge Cleaver, exiled in Algiers at the time. Cleaver's speech at the festival inspired Shepp musically and politically. The following month, Shepp went to Paris, where he recorded two albums for the French record label BYG Actuel.

In August 1969, Shepp recorded *Yasmina, A Black Woman* with cornet player Clifford Thornton (who had performed with him in Algiers) and members of the Art Ensemble of Chicago (who were living in Paris at that time). Just two days later, Shepp recorded another album, *Poem For Malcolm*. The title track was the polar opposite of Shepp's previous sad and reflective Malcolm X eulogy. Shepp's tone now switched to anger and fury, and instead of words, Shepp used maddening instrumental intensity to honor the slain black luminary.

Just as they impacted John Lennon, the September 1971 Attica State Prison riots infuriated Shepp. He brought thirty

LEFT: A month before recording this LP, Shepp had been in Algiers performing at a Pan African Festival. The clothing that Shepp wears in the cover photo reflects that experience and influence. That, coupled with the name *Yasmina*, is a reminder that Shepp's music pays tribute to both the West African and North African roots of jazz.

RIGHT: Recorded just two days after the *Yasmina* album, which celebrated his African continental roots, Shepp recorded the LP *Poem for Malcom* (the name is misspelled, probably because this cover was designed by a French graphic artist), paying tribute to his Afro-American roots via a salute to the iconic Malcolm X.

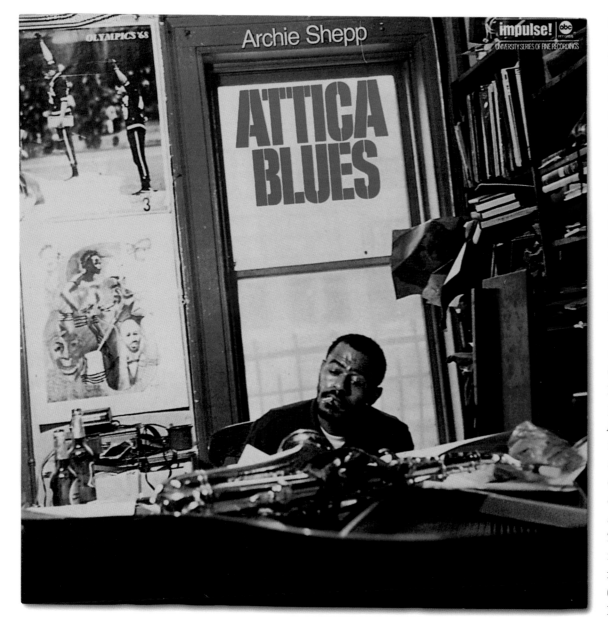

CLIFFORD THORNTON: Shepp's sideman Clifford Thornton recorded his debut solo album, *Freedom & Unity*, on July 22, 1967, the day after Coltrane's funeral, but the results weren't released until 1969 on Thornton's own label Third World Records. Shepp didn't appear on the recordings, which featured a thirteen-minute instrumental titled "Free Huey," but he did write liner notes which proclaimed, "One of the main themes of this album is to Free Huey!"

Besides BYG Actuel, another French label called (ironically enough) America Records released its share of politically charged African-American jazz. As 1969 turned into 1970, they released albums by the Art Ensemble of Chicago, Archie Shepp and others. Clifford Thornton's album on America Records, *The Panther And The Lash*, was recorded in Paris on Nov. 7, 1970 at La Maison de la Radio (the headquaters of the French National Public Radio Station).

musicians into the studio in January 1972, creating a conceptual masterwork entitled *Attica Blues* for Impulse! Records. Since George Jackson's murder had partially sparked the Attica uprising, Shepp paid homage with "Blues for Brother George Jackson." *Attica Blues* is a remarkable blend of big band swing, soul and avant-garde grooves with several vocalists. One of the tracks includes a narrative by attorney William Kunstler.

ABOVE: There are posters on the wall of W.E.B. Du Bois and the '68 Mexican Olympics with Tommie Smith and John Carlos. Shepp's facial expression reflects his despair at the death toll at Attica State Prison. He's at the piano, perhaps composing the songs contained within — surrounded by history (photographs) and culture (the books) as he looks forlorn — a sort of self-imposed solitary confinement while he contemplates the protest songs he's writing.

ABOVE: Although this black-and-white reproduction is hard to see, the full-color version of this cover reveals (among other things) an electric guitar being used as a flagpole for the Stars and Stripes (an "electric flag" à la Buddy Miles), a cornet, a nautilus shell (symbolizing trans-Atlantic journeys and a metaphor for artistic growth), a red rose (beauty) and a lion (royalty). Thornton was ultimately forced to go to Paris to record his musical statement(s) on Afro-Americanism, ironically enough for a record label called "America Records." A perfect image for spiritual evolution, because in order to grow, one needs to think outside the box.

RIGHT: *The Wire* magazine observed: "[Thornton] plays valve trombone, an enormously flexible instrument that allows him to meld with a variety of moods and produce music at once heart achingly simple and brain-twistingly complex." Because of the "new art" umbrella that this music falls under, it may be difficult to understand that it's rooted in Mingus and Ellington. Progressive free jazz of this era was based on what came before it — as illustrated in this traditional watercolor portrait of Thornton.

According to French journalist Philippe Carles, five days before recording *The Panther And The Lash*, Thornton performed at a Parisian benefit for the Black Panther Party, during which he proclaimed his support for imprisoned Panthers in the United States. When Thornton attempted to return to Paris from New York in February 1971, he was barred from entering by the French police and branded as an "undesirable." Now that Huey Newton had recently been acquitted of charges of murdering an Oakland cop, *The Panther And The Lash* celebrated with the opening track, "Huey Is Free." Over the course of the LP, Thornton switches between cornet, valve trombone and piano, accompanied by American and French musicians who, despite their "Free Jazz" pedigree, are more melodic and soulful than that term suggests. *The Panther And The Lash* is also the title of a 1967 volume of racially fueled political verse by poet Langston Hughes.

THE ART ENSEMBLE OF CHICAGO: The Art Ensemble of Chicago's motto is "Great Black Music: Ancient To The Future" and their formation grew out of the Association for the Advancement of Creative Musicians. Founded in May 1965, AACM's early members included Muhal Richard Abrams, Eddie Harris and Anthony Braxton. By 1969, the AACM were not just organizing avant-garde jazz gigs, they were enriching the Chicago ghettos by providing free music instruction and instruments to children. During this period of growth others came on board, including saxophonists Joseph Jarman and Roscoe Mitchell and bassist Malachi Flavors.

AACM co-founder Richard Abrams suggested fellow members expand their consciousness, encouraging Jarman to write poetry and Mitchell to paint. *DownBeat* profiled the AACM in their 1968 "yearbook" issue, asking Abrams, "Does the AACM have anything to do with Black Power?" Abrams replied, "Yes, it does in the sense that we intend to take over our own destinies, to be our own agents, and to play our own music."

In 1969, Mitchell, Jarman and Flavors traveled to Paris with a fellow AACM member, trumpeter Lester Bowie. Under the name The Art Ensemble of Chicago, they began recording albums, including *Reese and the Smooth Ones* on Aug. 12. *Reese and the Smooth Ones* was a spontaneous composition that blended horns, woodwinds, whistles, bells and percussion into a continuous, forty-minute ebb and flow. The liner notes declared, "Do not incite to riot, incite to revolt [and] revolution." The Art Ensemble members were no strangers to this type of rhetoric, having frequented the Detroit Artists Workshop, which also served as the living quarters of the MC5.

During the Art Ensemble's time in Paris, a French journalist, like many of his countrymen, had become enamored with the concept of Black Power and questioned Jarman: "What are your relationships to political organizations, for example, the Black Panthers?" Jarman said that the AACM had no desire to make linear connections with political groups, and associations

should be made on a personal level, not as a mandate of the organization. Jarman felt AACM members were responding to the social dilemmas addressed by the Panthers through art: "[Our] music is a response to these problems; that means when people hear it, they can experience a reaction to these problems. Thanks to the music, they can in turn become more active and more responsible."

For Parisians caught up in the intersection of African-American jazz and political activism, one man's opinion on this subject counted above all others: Amiri Baraka — whose writings on music were required reading. Baraka's name was dropped in intellectual circles as frequently as the American jazzmen themselves. For the devoted fan, "free jazz" symbolized Black Cultural Nationalism.

In Feb. 1970, at Studio Decca in Paris, the Art Ensemble recorded *Certain Blacks* with guest harmonica player Chicago Beau, who brought his radical freeform composition "Certain Blacks (Do What They Wanna)" to the proceedings. The piece begins with everyone reciting a cappella: "Certain Blacks, Certain Blacks — Do What They Wanna, Do What They Wanna; Certain Blacks, Certain Blacks — grow wild hair, grow wild hair, Certain Blacks, Certain Blacks — groove on love, groove on love; Certain Blacks, Certain Blacks — dig their freedom, dig their freedom."

ABOVE: The phrase *Reese and the Smooth Ones* is confusing since it's actually two separate song titles: "Reese" (composed by Roscoe Mitchell) and "Smooth Ones" (composed by Lester Bowie). When they arrived in Paris, it was as members of AACM (Association for the Advancement of Creative Musicians) and with this album, they become The Art Ensemble of Chicago — the four individual photos of each group member are melded together to present a distinctive group image.

The ensemble then explodes into a cacophonous jam that swings and flows with ugliness and beauty for over twenty minutes.

During this period, the Art Ensemble shared the bill with space rock pioneers Gong (led by Daevid Allen) at a Black Panther benefit. According to Art Ensemble percussionist Famoudou Don Moye, the event combined music and rhetoric. Black Panthers addressed the audience; however, musician Clifford Thornton was the most outspoken. Moye recalls that the provocative pathos that Thornton threw down was shocking even to the Panthers. The assemblage reportedly embraced him stirring up the shit, but as Thornton was exiting the stage, French authorities nabbed him. Thornton was forced to relocate to Switzerland.

MARZETTE WATTS AND SONNY SHARROCK: In the United States, the primary outlet for revolutionary jazz was ESP-Disk. ESP is remembered for putting free jazz mavericks Albert Ayler, Pharoah Sanders and like-minded souls on the map. A whole chapter could be written on ESP's avant-garde catalog, but for now I'll just give a shout-out to the December 1966 recordings of woodwind instrumentalist Marzette Watts. Released in 1968 as *Marzette Watts And Company*, the album

ABOVE: "Certain Blacks dig their freedom": Certain blacks found their freedom by recording in Paris, while certain black "free jazz" artists joined with Lincoln T. Beauchamp, a blues harp player from Chicago. Using half the cover to proclaim *Certain Blacks* was a bold artistic statement in itself, making sure that nobody glancing at the album missed their message. Another meaning of the word "certain" is self-assured and confident, expressed here with this bold block-faced type.

featured the lengthy, unrelenting track "Backdrop For Urban Revolution," which included Clifford Thornton on cornet and Sonny Sharrock on guitar.

Sonny Sharrock played on a diverse selection of albums, including Herbie Mann's *Memphis Underground*, Miles Davis' *A Tribute To Jack Johnson* and Pharoah Sanders' *Tauhid*. I have no idea what Sharrock's political philosophy was, but he certainly made a statement when he titled his 1969 Vortex/Atlantic Records album *Black Woman*. The album cover featured a photo of Sonny and wife Linda, glorious in their natural afro hairstyle. Sharrock's song "Portrait of Linda in Three Colors, all Black,"

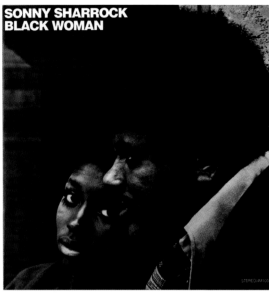

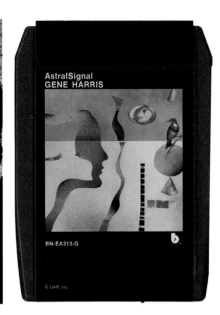

celebrated his beautiful black wife as she shrieked and wailed in the style of Plastic Ono Band-era Yoko Ono. For select listeners, *Black Woman* was beautiful.

LOU DONALDSON: In 1969, Lou Donaldson stepped up when he released a version of James Brown's "Say it Loud! I'm Black and I'm Proud." Donaldson's spoken intro kicks off a seven-minute vamp on Brown's masterwork: "Before you start, take aim! Hey y'all with your bad self — Say it Loud!" with a response of "I'm Black and I'm Proud" from his band. "Like you mean it," Donaldson adds. On the back cover, Jerry Boulding notes: "SAY IT LOUD is not the basic key to the feelings and meaning of this album, it's the second line of the title song that tells the whole story...I'M BLACK AND I'M PROUD. It's the musical culmination of a feeling of self assertion that has been a long time coming (on a major scale) and is most definitely here to stay."

On the 1971 album *Cosmos*, Donaldson upped the ante by recording Curtis Mayfield's provocative "If There Is A Hell Below, We're Going To Go." Donaldson left out the first part of Mayfield's proclamation, "Sisters, Niggers, Whiteys, Jews, Crackers," but did sing "there's a hell down below and we've all got to go" with a substantial jazz-funk groove. In 1974, when the capacity to shock had greatly diminished, Blue Note pianist Gene Harris let

loose with a version of Sly Stone's anthem "Don't Call Me Nigger, Whitey" on his album *Astral Signal*. At least Harris had the balls to keep the lyrics intact.

ABOVE LEFT: Marzette Watts: his hair and clothing against the backdrop of an abstract expressionist painting (de Kooning? Pollock?) is fairly eclectic for 1966, the year of this album. He moved to Paris in 1962 to study painting at the Sorbonne, and he had also been a member of SNCC at Alabama State College; both those experiences come together in a "Backdrop for Urban Revolution."

ABOVE CENTER: Featuring a photo of Sonny Sharrock and wife Linda in their natural afro hairstyle. The stark black-and-white image on the cover of *Black Woman* is in sharp contrast to the colorful photograph of two black women (also sporting afros) on Lou Donaldson's 1969 Blue Note LP, *Say It Loud!* And yet, both albums signaled a shift in how musicians presented their music and how their listeners wanted to see them. Folk-blues singer Odetta paved the way for artists by adopting a "black is beautiful" afro; she was doing it in 1959, nearly a decade before it was chic.

ABOVE RIGHT: Jazz and abstract art have always enjoyed a synthesis. Jackson Pollock called himself a jazz painter; while this particular painting is certainly not like Pollock — it's more of a Milton Glaser-styled work — it makes sense that a progressive jazz album would incorporate such a design. However, it's surprising that it was released on an 8-track tape cartridge!

Blue Note Records Embraces Black Consciousness

Eddie Gale and Horace Silver changed the sound of Blue Note with consciousness-raising / lyrical-jazz compositions. Andy Bey & Gary Bartz participated as well, while the expression of Black Nationalism culminated musically with several albums spearheaded by Mtume.

EDDIE GALE: While there are other politically conscious recordings in the Blue Note catalog, there's nothing quite like the two albums trumpeter Eddie Gale recorded in 1968 and 1969. Social messages aside, *Ghetto Music* and its sequel, *Black Rhythm Happening*, are delightfully unique by any comparison. *Ghetto Music* opens with an acoustic guitar and plaintive female vocal (performed by Gale's sister Joann Gale Stevens) before exploding into a choir of vocalists, tribal percussion and a swinging jazz rhythm, punctuated by Gale's trumpet. The ensemble quickly breaks down, returning to acoustic guitar and vocals for a moment before the group flares up again in a cross pattern of free jazz and a repeating vocal chorus. If British folksinger Shirley Collins, jazz guru Sun Ra and the Edwin Hawkins Singers converged at a stoned soul picnic, it might sound like Gale's song "The Rain."

While the image of Gale's group cloaked in hooded robes suggests militant Black Nationalism or a religious cult of badass mofos, Gale's concept of "ghetto" is not about kicking ass and taking names, but about close-knit community and inner peace.

As Gale explained to me in spring 2003, he felt empowered as a black artist from the ghetto. The sequel *Black Rhythm Happening* arrived in 1969. The title track was released as a single with its bouncy drum pattern, groovy bass line and slinky guitar. Gale's deep voice repeats "Black Rhythm Happening" and female voices respond in kind; a party atmosphere develops, not unlike the background chatter of "What's Going On." While Ed Williams' liner notes make comparisons to the Isley Brothers, Staple Singers, The Temptations and The Impressions, Gale's compositions are much more avant-garde than that. Like *Ghetto Music*, *Black Rhythm Happening* is a conceptual recording. The back cover reflects: "Black Rhythm is a dream called Harlem, Watts, Bedford-Stuyvesant, Newark, Hough, colored town, nigger town, AFRICA ... Black Rhythm is hip, angry, appeased, appalled, afraid, courageous ... Black Rhythm is affluent, arrogant, and art."

HORACE SILVER: Between 1970 and 1972, pianist Horace Silver released a trilogy of albums subtitled *The United States of Mind* on Blue Note. Vocalist Andy Bey and his sister Salome helped deliver Silver's universal message that "music knows no

ABOVE: Eddie Gale on trumpet with his sister Joann Gale Stevens on guitar and vocals. Photo courtesy of Eddie Gale.

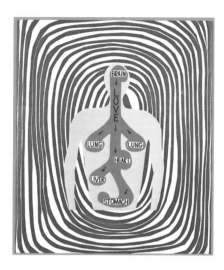

race, creed or color" and his hope that his songs will be absorbed by the listener to "bring a little more Health, Happiness, Love and Peace into your life." *Phase Two* of the trilogy, *Total Response*, was the most curious and compelling album with songs like "Acid, Pot or Pills," "What Kind of Animal Am I?" and "I'm Aware of the Animals Within Me." Within the spirited grooves were introspective lyrics: "Acid, pot or pills, which one will help me find all the answers to the questions, probing within my mind? Angry as a lion, gentle as a lamb, do I really know, just what I am? For the caterpillar changes into a butterfly, what kind of animal am I?"

GARY BARTZ AND ANDY BEY: On Nov. 19, 1970 and sporadically throughout January 1971, saxophonist Gary Bartz' group Ntu

TOP LEFT: Dressed like troubadours, the ominous hooded costumes of Eddie Gale and his band suggest a connection to folk ballads, the countryside and druid lore. An odd take for an album entitled *Ghetto Music*. However, the costuming of the band and their carrying of acoustic instruments an invitation to an alternate world of the ghetto, one where "inner peace" is their mantra.

BOTTOM LEFT: Horace Silver is contemplative, while his alternate state of consciousness looks over his shoulder. Perhaps the standing Silver is suggesting a route of "acid, pot or pills." Silver is having an out-of-body experience, searching for a "happy melody" to forget "aches and pains." The album cover and title suggest a journey from one reality to a higher sense of enlightenment.

ABOVE: This drawing done by Horace Silver's wife Barbara in the "folk art" tradition, diagrams the anatomy of the music — brain, lung, heart, liver, stomach — that constitute the total musical response. "Some will absorb the melody, some will absorb the words, some will absorb both.... bring[ing] a little more Health, Happiness, Love and Peace into your life."

Troop (with vocalist Andy Bey) recorded two albums' worth of material for Milestone Records inspired by Malcolm X and John Coltrane, which Bartz called "Harlem Bush Music." Since he didn't have the commercial pull of Miles Davis, Bartz couldn't release a double LP, so the results were spread across two separate albums: *Harlem Bush Music: Taifa* and *Harlem Bush Music: Uhuru*, both credited to Gary Bartz and Ntu Troop. As he did for Horace Silver on *The United States Of Mind* trilogy, Andy Bey provided soulful narration on numbers such as "Blue (A Folk Tale)": "I'm black and I'm blue. I'm not blue because I'm black; I'm blue because I'm me. Blue is black and black is blue — what color are you?"

On another composition, "Rise," Bey sings: "Another moonrise, another moon-set, Another spinning around. Our nation must rise, our nation will rise, Our nation's spinning around. Another revolution!"

Ntu Troop's music is more soul than bop, but when they need to make a point, they draw on free jazz, with sudden shifts in the

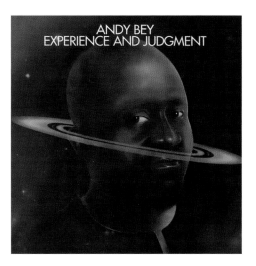

ABOVE: The cover imagery contrasts Bartz' traditional African garb against a Harlem setting, suggesting a progression from Africa's past to Afro-America's future as embodied by the face of an innocent child against a background of ancient hieroglyphics.

LEFT: The rings of Saturn surround Andy Bey's head, who has a saturnine expression on his face. Bey's album cover and the music within present a universe/universal message of celestial expression. This is the cerebral side of the Afro-Futurism, expressed in the sexually charged spacesuits worn by Labelle.

Black Forum label, Baraka released an illuminating album of poetry, singing and music with that title in 1972. In December 1970, inspired by Baraka's poem, tenor saxophonist Joe McPhee recorded an eighteen-minute performance, "Nation Time," at the Vassar College Urban Center for Black Studies, where McPhee was teaching a class: "Revolution In Sound." Before the free-swinging ensemble kicks in, McPhee shouts, "What time is it?" The audience replies, "Nation Time!" McPhee shouts this repeatedly, demanding the audience respond "Nation Time!" with more vigor each time; "oh, come on now, you can do better than that!" he pleads. The LP liner notes written by McPhee: "Baraka, a man firmly committed to the building of a black nation, suggests the time will come when a brother or sister is asked 'What time is it?' And the reply will be an overwhelming and resounding 'Nation Time!' I decided to use this call and response technique as means to involve the audience as an integral part of the performance."

Released on CRP Records in 1971, *Nation Time* by Joe McPhee promptly vanished. Thankfully, the album was reissued in 2001 on Atavistic's Unheard Music Series. Apparently, Baraka wasn't aware of the original release; decades later, when he heard the CD, he wasn't impressed. In a collection of essays published in 2009, Baraka disparaged the album, reminding us "The title of the CD and the first piece carry a phrase that this writer first introduced as a political statement animated by the Black Liberation Movement, most visible as projected by the 1972 Black Political Convention in Gary, Indiana and subsequently as the title of a Word-Music album."

rhythm and melodies. Their two *Harlem Bush Music* releases are among the most ambitious yet rewarding jazz albums discussed in this book. In 1974, Andy Bey recorded his own soul-searching album *Experience and Judgment* for Atlantic, in which "Celestial Blues" suggested meditation to fathom the essence of life. Black artists were now demanding existential freedom as part of their Civil Rights.

IT'S NATION TIME: In 1970, Amiri Baraka published a book of poetry: *It's Nation Time*. As discussed in the section on Motown's

HERBIE HANCOCK MEETS RON KARENGA: Before Herbie Hancock fully plugged into the groove with his monster funk epic "Chameleon," he led a somewhat freer outfit called The Herbie Hancock Sextet, which recorded the Warner Bros.' *Mwandishi* album on New Year's Eve, 1970 at Wally Heider's San Francisco studio. For classic rock fans, Heider's studio is legendary as the wellspring for Crosby, Stills, Nash & Young's *Déjà Vu*,

ABOVE: Joe McPhee is standing in front of a slave shack, but he looks adamant that it's *Nation Time*. The all-black image cements the bond between free jazz and Black Nationalism.

The Grateful Dead's *American Beauty* and Jefferson Airplane's *Volunteers*. As aforementioned, Hancock's *Mwandishi* contained an instrumental composition paying tribute to Angela Davis.

Recording a tribute to Angela Davis is merely a footnote in Hancock's career, but he was involved in another obscure-but-important recording tied to the Black Power movement. As detailed earlier, Karenga caught the ear of writer LeRoi Jones, who evolved into the supercharged activist, singer-songwriter, poet and outspoken renaissance man Amiri Baraka. Around the time of Baraka's conversion, James Forman joined US. Forman was the son of saxophonist Jimmy Heath and nephew of drummer Albert Heath and Modern Jazz Quartet bassist Percy Heath. Forman became known as James Mtume and played percussion on two of Miles Davis' most expansive and diverse 1970s albums, *Big Fun* and *Get Up With It*.

Mtume had been a member of US for two years when he crossed paths with Hancock in 1968, converting Hancock to some of Karenga's ways. Hancock took on the name Mwandishi (which is Swahili for "composer") and agreed to participate in an album paying tribute to US.

The US album was titled *Kawaida* and besides Hancock, it included Mtume along with his father Jimmy, his uncle Albert and trumpeter Don Cherry, all of whom adopted Swahili names for the project. Recorded in December 1969, the studio location was listed as "The Universe." Initially released on O'BE Records, the second pressing appeared on Trip Records. Trip was a division of Springboard International, which specialized in manufacturing cheap records to sell in supermarkets and discount stores. Not surprisingly, the Trip version dispensed with Baraka's sleeve notes, which outlined three criteria for Revolutionary Art: "First that is a collective, that it speaks from a whole people to a whole people...[Secondly] that it be functional. Yes, that it have a function, a real function for Black People...The third criterion for Revolutionary Art, paraphrasing Maulana, is that must be Committing. It must commit black people to the struggle for National Liberation. Drugs, for instance, are just chemical warfare against the Black Nation. And their volunteer use is just the slave cooperating with his master to keep the peace, (and keep a piece of our behind). Negroes who use drugs are just Toms."

Mtume composed the bulk of the material, including tributes to Baraka and Karenga, "Baraka" and "Maulana," as well as the title track "Kawaida," which reflected "US philosophy" by having each musician recite bits of Karenga's teachings, including Swahili phrases and their corresponding English-language meaning. The song "Baraka" begins with the chanting of a Swahili phrase that translates to "all praise to the Black man." The gentle backing of flute and percussion with occasional piano and bass gives the song a meditative, mystical charm. As volume and energy increase, a voice calls out Baraka's name. *Kawaida* combines several moods: modal with the meditative, cosmic with the tribal, resulting in a definitive expression of the African-American art of jazz.

MTUME AND BLACK NATIONALISM: In 1971, Mtume (no longer a member of US, but still expounding Karenga's philosophies) released a sequel to *Kawaida*. The Mtume Umoja Ensemble recorded *Alkebu-lan: Land of the Blacks* (subtitled *Live At The East*). It was recorded at the "Brooklyn Cultural Center of the Congress of African People" and released on the Strata-East label. The LP includes a large cast, including saxophonist Gary Bartz, drummers Leon "Ndugu" Chancler & Billy Hart, bassist Buster Williams, Black Arts poet Yusef Iman and vocalist

ABOVE: Mwandishi means "composer," a name given to him by Ron Karenga's US organization. While many US supporters changed their names (such as LeRoi Jones to Amiri Baraka), Herbie Hancock always kept his own name, while briefly using Mwandishi as his forename. Hancock is looking at himself in a mirror, taking on a new identity — but one that doesn't replace his old identity. He is recognizing his Africanness, but doesn't reject his Americanness.

Andy Bey. Although most participants weren't Karenga's disciples, they shared Mtume's desire to musically illustrate Black Nationalist culture.

Alkebu-lan opens with Mtume's spoken word "Invocation": 'The music retained in this album is the humble offering to the unity of the entire Black nation and all those who through Kawaida have tasted the nectar of its totality. The sounds which are about to saturate your being and sensitize your soul, is the continuing process of nationalist consciousness manifesting its message within the context of one of our strongest natural resources, Black music."

In 1974, Mtume's uncle, drummer Albert Heath, would continue the tradition of paying tribute to Karenga by releasing *Kwanza (The First)* on Muse Records, featuring Jimmy Heath on sax and Percy Heath on bass. A year later, these three would form their own group, The Heath Brothers. The weeklong Kwanzaa celebration held between Christmas and New Year's Day is the US organization's ongoing contribution to African-American culture, but the influence of Ron Karenga's Black Nationalist philosophy on jazz should not be overlooked.

THE SPOOK WHO SAT BY THE DOOR: As touched on earlier, Karenga would bestow the Swahili name Mwandishi on Herbie Hancock, designating him as the "composer." In 1973, Hancock wrote the soundtrack for *The Spook Who Sat by the Door*, based on Sam Greenlee's 1969 novel. The title refers to the early days of affirmative action, when the first black person employed would be seated near the office entrance, so everyone could attest that the company was racially mixed. The film is about a black man who quits the CIA after he's been underutilized, using his training to begin a war

ORIGINAL MOTION PICTURE SOUNDTRACK

the **spook** who sat by the **door**

CONDUCTED AND COMPOSED BY **herbie hancock**

©1973 UAR Inc. / All Rights Reserved

of liberation, kicking the honky National Guard's ass. As with *Sweet Sweetback's Baadasssss Song*, *The Spook Who Sat by the Door* isn't a generic Blaxploitation film, but a political statement that is deeply personal, told as an account of one man's reaction to oppression, making the film's message universal.

It was so universal that the film was removed from theaters. In a 2004 NPR segment, director Ivan Dixon said that when the film's distributor "United Artists screened the finished product and a saw a Panavision version of political Armageddon, they were stunned." The film was pulled and until it was re-released on DVD in 2004, it was nearly impossible to see. There has never been an official soundtrack release. However, underground LPs have been manufactured, with bootleggers recording the music from videotape by placing a microphone in front of their TV set.

The 1973 album *A Message from the Tribe* featured Wendell Harrison, Jeamel Lee and Phillip Ranelin on sax, vocals and trombone respectively. The album contained both an instrumental and a vocal version of Ranelin's composition "Angela's Dilemma." The septet provides a relaxed, progressive backing to Jeamel Lee's melodic vocals: "Angela is a sister with much pride, who has long seen too many greats die, imprisoned and far from the freedom, her power is still felt from within, she must be free."

A year later, Ranelin and The Tribe would record *The Time is Now!* Their second release replaced lyrical statements with a harder-edged instrumental direction. Compositions like the title track "The Time is Now!" and "Black Destiny" recall the free jazz of Archie Shepp, the electric keyboard punctuation of early '70s Miles Davis, and a soulful groove reminiscent of Hank Mobley. This time, Ranelin didn't use vocals, but in case listeners were unsure of The Tribe's message, the album jacket declared: "The time is NOW!! The time is now, for unity among the people! The time is now, for all men to be able to control their own destinies! The time is now, for oppression, racism, greed, hate and poverty to end! The time is now, for revolution!"

Dialogue and various noises from the movie blend into Hancock's funky compositions. In 2006, Hancock producer David Rubinson told me that the soundtrack's master tapes continue to languish in a vault, still waiting official release.

THE TRIBE: In Detroit, musicians Wendell Harrison, Phil Ranelin and others formed a band, record label, production company and publishing house — all brought together under the umbrella of musical, political and intellectual freedom. Their slogan was "A new dimension in cultural awareness." Known as The Tribe, they saw themselves as

> *an extension of the tribes in the villages of Africa, our mother country. In Africa everyone had a talent to display. There were no superstars: just people and collectively all the people of the village played a vital role in shaping that culture. We see all black communities within this country as villages and the tribes are the people residing within them. Pure music must reflect the environment that we live in if it is to be educational and beneficial to our culture. It must portray our way of life.*

LEFT: *Message from the Tribe*: a Venn diagram has been used as the template to show all possible and logical relationships between the three artists featured on the cover, to emphasize the fact that the Tribe is a "collective."

ABOVE: *The Time is Now*: despite strong African images and figures, the album cover blends both a "sand clock" and a conventional Western clock — reflecting both his African and American roots. The "hour glass" doubles as a conga drum.

RAHSAAN ROLAND KIRK
AND THE JAZZ PEOPLE'S MOVEMENT

Multi-instrumentalist Rahsaan Roland Kirk was more than just a blind musical prodigy. He was a renaissance man who could play three saxophones simultaneously. He crafted several

ABOVE: Roland Kirk and company onstage in full regalia, performing a John Coltrane tribute that encompasses one side of this album. On the flip, the title track composed by Kirk makes the statement "we are all driven by an invisible whip, some run, some have fun, some are hip, some tip, some dip, but we all must answer to the invisible whip." *Volunteered* is another way of saying, "forced into against your will." From the looks of things, Kirk and his band have at least won their artistic freedom.

OPPOSITE: On this Roland Kirk LP, "Blackness" has been spelled as "Blacknuss" — the us incorporates "us" (as black people) as well as the people in the U.S. (United States). Just as the black keys of the piano are highlighted without sacrificing the white keys, Kirk embraces his blackness-blacknuss without rejecting his humanness. There's no better way to express this than this "all black" cover art.

instruments himself (attached to his body while he performed), and was both a creative composer and interpreter of others' compositions. Like Coltrane, he was a blistering soloist, able to blow without pause using the technique of circular breathing — in through his nose, simultaneously blowing out through his mouth, using air stored in his cheeks to produce a continuous sound from his instrument.

Released in October 1969, *Volunteered Slavery* showcased an inspired title track, "Volunteered slavery has got me on the run… Volunteered slavery is something we all know…" There's an instrumental version of Burt Bacharach's "I Say A Little Prayer" that begins with Kirk intoning, "they shot him down, they shot him down to the ground, but we're gonna say a little prayer for him anyway." "One Ton" is a fiery instrumental that Kirk introduces by saying, "At this time, we'd like to play a composition called 'One Ton' and it's not gonna get any lighter, 'One Ton.'"

Recorded in the fall of 1971, *Blacknuss* was primarily cover songs including a medley of "What's Going On" and "Mercy Mercy Me," while the self-penned title track, "Blacknuss" expressed racial pride via a fusion of "black," "in" and "us." Kirk pronounces, as conga drums roll underneath: "Now we gathered here on the universe at this time, this particular time, to listen to the 36 black notes of the piano. There's 36 black notes and 52 white notes. We don't mean to eliminate nothing, but we're gonna just hear the black notes at this time, if you don't mind. Blacknuss."

Kirk spells out "B-L-A-C-K-N-U-S-S." As African percussion, piano and drums fall into a groove, Cissy Houston accompanies Kirk's chant of "Blacknuss" while instruments intensify and gather speed, switching tempos and melodies throughout. If "Blacknuss" and Eddie Gale's "Black Rhythm Happening" are played back to back, there are two thematically similar (and utterly essential) messages of black pride.

Inspired by student protestors who occupied buildings at New York's Columbia University in April 1968, Kirk began considering his own subversive action in the name of black classical music (i.e. jazz). Initially, Kirk wanted to send jazz bands out on the back of a truck, "delivering jazz to every corner of the city like fresh baked bread." Kirk and a pal named Mark Davis formed a gang of insurgents they branded "Jazz and People's Movement," with endorsements from the likes of Lee Morgan, Elvin Jones and Archie Shepp.

RAHSAAN ROLAND KIRK · BLACKNUSS

STEREO
SD 1601
ATLANTIC

One of the main gripes of the "Jazz and People's Movement" was that jazz — a completely original art form that is uniquely American — was largely ignored by the American media and rarely broadcast on television or radio. In collaboration with Shepp and others, Kirk drew up a manifesto. During the summer of 1969, Kirk stopped performing to focus on his new mission, culture-bombing by protesting *The Merv Griffin Show*, sneaking onto *The Tonight Show Starring Johnny Carson* and creating a ruckus and following suit on *The Dick Cavett Show*. According to Kruth, there was talk of the jazz renegades merging with Jesse Jackson's Operation Breadbasket. Had this occurred, it would've been an amazing combination of artistic consciousness and community fundraising. Given Kirk's transcendent music and larger-than-life persona, it's no surprise he was on a friendly basis with Bobby Seale and Huey Newton.

COMPARED TO WHAT:
EUGENE McDANIELS, LES McCANN AND EDDIE HARRIS

While Atlantic executives may have regretted releasing Eugene McDaniels' albums, which drew heat from the White House, they didn't mind when a McDaniels protest song put serious money in their pockets. Although it's often thought to be inspired by the 1968 assassination of King Jr., "Compared to What" had

been written by McDaniels years before, appearing on the 1966 Limelight record *Les McCann Plays The Hits*. But it was the colossal 1969 version on Les McCann & Eddie Harris' *Swiss Movement* that took the world by storm.

The lengthy jazz-boogie workout featuring McCann on piano and vocals with Harris on tenor sax, Benny Bailey on trumpet and McCann's rhythm section of drummer Donald Dean and bassist Leroy Vinnegar is a monster. At the June 1969 Montreux Jazz Festival, this ensemble ripped through "Compared to What," which was captured for posterity by Atlantic Records. In the decades since the song was recorded, McDaniels' lyrics are still apropos: "The President, he's got his war — folks don't know just what it's for, nobody gives us rhyme or reason — have one doubt, they call it treason, We're chicken-feathers, all without one nut."

Other lyrics attack poverty, religion, material possessions and anti-abortion laws in succinct, witty stanzas. Although "Compared to What" has been recorded by many artists, the only other definitive version is on Roberta Flack's 1969 debut *First Take*. While McCann's version smokes, Flack's simmers as she delivers a wonderfully seductive vocal performance punctuated by a Stax-like horn section. In 1971, McCann and Harris tried to duplicate the success of *Swiss Movement* with the studio album *Second Movement*. McCann still refers to it as "Second Bowel Movement," because the duo couldn't recapture the magic of their live effort. However, the album contains one inspired song, "Carry on Brother," a gospel number written by Harris and sung by McCann, calling for communication and integration over segregation.

Separately, Harris and McCann continued releasing albums with instrumental or lyrical declarations. Even before recording "Compared To What," Harris had given his sax-driven grooves socially charged titles like 1965's "Freedom Jazz Dance" and 1967's "Listen Here." Harris' 1969 *Free Speech* contained the instrumental "Bold and Black," while the title track to *I Need Some Money* from 1975 album features Harris demanding cash to combat the rising cost of rent, groceries and clothes. Easily Harris' most captivating lyrical composition, "I Need Some Money" is like an imaginary Sly Stone theme song for the TV sitcom *Good Times*. Coincidentally, the title track to McCann's 1975 *Hustle to Survive* treads similar ground, as he pleads to stay alive in difficult times.

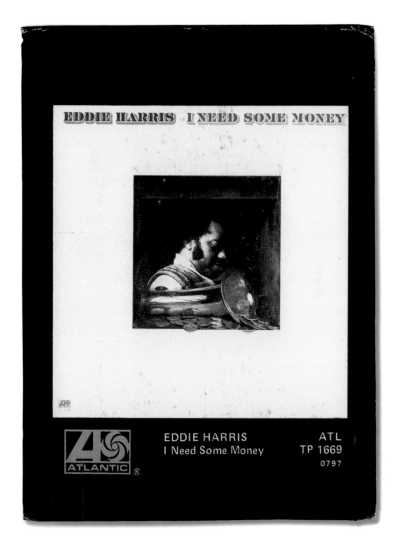

OPPOSITE: *Swiss Movement*: jazz moves into the mainstream. The cynical lyrics of social protest appealed to white hipsters "keeping it real" ("Compared To What"); the phrase "keeping it real" still stands today. The title *Swiss Movement* plays on words in several ways: the traditionally accurate timekeeping of a well-made Swiss watch (the album was recorded in Montreux); movement (also the groove of the musicians and their music); and finally a nod to the social protest movement. The photo of Les McCann in particular captures an artist in the full flight of performance, aka "movement."

ABOVE: The popularity of some jazz artists increased by the mid-'70s, as they crossed funk with jazz and political themes. That meant that jazz recordings were becoming available on 8-track tape along with popular rock bands. It also allowed "the message" to be played on street corners on portable tape machines.

DONNY HATHAWAY: After years as a utility man for The Impressions and Staple Singers, (singer, pianist and songwriter) Donny Hathaway recorded his debut *Everything is Everything* for Atlantic in September 1969. On the first day of his sessions, Hathaway cut "The Ghetto," a sprawling soul anthem illustrating life in the inner city. In June 1973, Hathaway released *Extension Of A Man*, which included "Someday We'll All Be Free." Written by Hathaway with Edward Howard, numerous versions of this lament have been recorded, most notably by Aretha Franklin as the closing theme of Spike Lee's film *Malcolm X. Extension Of A Man* also featured a sequel to "The Ghetto" entitled "The Slums," and in the album notes, Hathaway wrote: "It is of the same idiom as The Ghetto — being happy, lively, and reflecting the joys of a people in a suppressed area. I recruited the entire Atlantic gang to rap some of that 'good ole alley talk' that has made the Ghetto a haven (as well as a hell) shared by all included in the immediate area just around the corner from the suburbs!"

Sadly, in 1979, the struggle became too much for Hathaway and he jumped off of the fifteenth floor of a Manhattan hotel, but not before expanding "The Ghetto" (co-written with Leroy Huston, who cites King Jr.'s and Bobby Kennedy's assassinations and a student uprising on the campus of Howard University as inspiring the composition) into an energized twelve-minute testimonial on the 1972 LP *Donny Hathaway Live*.

CANNONBALL ADDERLEY: The Cannonball Adderley Quintet's 1966 recording "Mercy, Mercy, Mercy!" was a hit single for the saxophonist and his band. The song quickly became a standard, with dozens of versions released in the ensuing years. On the *Mercy, Mercy, Mercy!* live album, Adderley introduces the song

RIGHT: Donny Hathaway and a group of kids are playing a game: "ring around the Rosie, a pocketful of posies" — two different expressions of a circle — the circle of life and a children's game. The standout track from this album was "The Ghetto" — and this photo proved that though there might be graffiti and trash on the street in The Ghetto, it was still possible to smile.

with a monologue: "You know, sometimes we're not prepared for adversity. When it happens sometimes we're caught short. We don't know exactly how to handle it when it comes up. Sometimes we don't know just what to do when adversity takes over. But I have advice for all of us... And it sounds like what you're supposed to say when you have that kind of problem. It's called 'Mercy, Mercy, Mercy!'"

In that monologue, Adderley mentions keyboardist Joe Zawinul wrote the song. Zawinul wasn't black, but an Austrian-born immigrant who'd continue to capture the African-American spirit with several songs on Adderley's *Country Preacher* as well the title track he wrote for Miles Davis' *In A Silent Way*.

Country Preacher was recorded live at Operation Breadbasket in Chicago in October 1969. Led by the Rev. Jesse Jackson, Operation Breadbasket was the economic arm of Martin Luther King Jr.'s organization. The ballad "Country Preacher" was written by Zawinul as a tribute to Jackson (who often referred to himself as such). Still, it was the energizing, funky opening track, "Walk Tall," preceded by Jesse Jackson's bold introduction, which made the biggest impression:

We're getting ready to have a live session. [...] We're get-ting ready to do a little walking and when you have real change, everybody's thing begins to change, teacher begins to teach a new lesson, preacher begins to preach a new sermon, and the musician also tries to capture the new thing, so we might have melody and have rhythm, as we do our thing. We say every Saturday, the most important thing of all, is that no matter how dreary the situation is and how difficult it may be, that the storm really doesn't matter until the storm begins to get you down. So our advice to you, mes-sage that the Cannonball Adderley Quintet brings to us, is that it's rough and tough in this ghetto, a lot of funny stuff going down, but you got to Walk Tall, Walk Tall, Walk Tall!

After Jackson's intro, the band grooves with Cannonball's sax and brother Nat Adderley's cornet providing a punctuating and repeating riff on par with the best Stax/Volt horn parts. Yet another highlight on *Country Preacher* is the Adderley Brothers composition "Oh Babe." Over a bluesy gospel motif, Nat Adderley improvises the lyrics: "please Mr. Nixon, babe, don't cut that welfare off me lord."

MILES DAVIS AND JOHN COLTRANE: In early 1970, Miles Davis recorded *A Tribute to Jack Johnson* as the soundtrack to a film about early 20th century heavyweight boxing champion Jack Johnson. Comprising two tracks of twenty-five minutes each, the LP included contributions from Herbie Hancock and Sonny Sharrock. Side One is titled "Right Off" and borrows a riff from Sly and the Family Stone's "Sing a Simple Song," while much of Side Two's "Yesternow" adapts the bass line of James Brown's "Say it Loud (I'm Black and I'm Proud)." At the end of "Yesternow," actor Brock Peters (who appeared in the 1959 film version of *Porgy and Bess*) shouts "I'm Jack Johnson, heavyweight champion of the world! I'm black! They never let me forget it. I'm black all right, I'll never let them forget it."

Davis would continue to mirror the social transformation of the times via the cover art of 1972's *On The Corner* and in song titles like "Mr. Freedom X." In Davis' 1989 autobiography, he discusses John Coltrane and Black Power:

[Coltrane] was expressing through music what H. Rap Brown and Stokely Carmichael and the Black Panthers and Huey Newton were saying with their words, what the Last Poets and Amiri Baraka were saying in poetry. He was their torchbearer in jazz, now ahead of me. He played what they felt inside and were expressing through riots — "burn, baby, burn" — that were taking place everywhere in this country during the 1960s. It was all about revolution for a lot of young black people — afro hairdos, dashikis, black power, fists raised in the air. Coltrane was their symbol, their pride — their beautiful, black, revolutionary pride. I had been it a few years back, now he was it, and that was cool with me.

Because of his notorious outspokenness, I had assumed that Davis supported the Black Panther Party, either by playing benefits or making financial contributions. When I asked Chief of Staff David Hilliard about Davis in 2007, he said that Davis never did come around, unlike Redd Foxx, Marlon Brando and Candice Bergen, all of whom helped finance the Party's activities. John Coltrane didn't see himself as a social-political activist, only as an artist. In the years since his death, some scholars, most notably Frank Kofsky, have tried to pigeonhole

Album cover text:

Columbia Stereo
KC 30455
ORIGINAL SOUNDTRACK RECORDING

Miles Davis

A TRIBUTE TO

Jack Johnson

Director: WILLIAM CAYTON
Producer: JIM JACOBS
Jack Johnson's Voice: BROCK PETERS
Script: ALAN BODIAN
Cameraman: LAWRENCE GARINGER
Editor: JOHN DANDRE
Musical Director: TEO MACERO

"JACK JOHNSON"
The rise of Jack Johnson to world heavyweight supremacy in 1908 was a signal for white envy to erupt. Can you get to that? And of course being born Black in America … we all know how that goes. The day before Johnson defended the title against Jim Flynn (1912) he received a note: "Lie down tomorrow or we string you up–Ku Klux Klan." Dig that!

Johnson portrayed freedom–it rang just as loud as the bell proclaiming him Champion. He was a fast-living man, he liked women–lots of them and most of them white. He had flashy cars because that was his thing. That's right, the big ones and the fast ones. He smoked cigars, drank only the best champagne and prized a 7 ft. bass fiddle on which he'd proudly thump jazz. His flamboyance was more than obvious. And no doubt mighty Whitey felt "No Black man should have all this." But he did and he'd flaunt it. There wasn't a "smile-smile chuggin' along" implication in his broad grin that seemed to always be on his ebony face–in other words he was putting them on! What was a reality to Johnson was a living-color nightmare for the anti-Johnson Americans who couldn't get ready for his "truly sophisticated attitude." And the more they hated him, the more money he made, the more women he got and the more wine he drank. "Hate is the opposite of Love and both gain momentum." He won all his fights, when he wanted and how he wanted–including "The Great White Hope," Jim Jeffries on July 4, 1910. On July 5th they got it on with a riot–that's right, fire, at least ten dead, and the later (1911) Congressional law barring fight films from interstate commerce.

After his high society white wife committed suicide in a cafe he owned in Chicago, Johnson married another white woman–it was no coincidence. But one could question the frame-up he faced. I mean, Jack Johnson being convicted of violating the "White Slavery Act" and being sentenced to a year and a day imprisonment. But exiled to Paris with joy–and as usual "Very Grand." It had to be Europe and they say he had a pet leopard he'd walk while drinking champagne with crowds following.

Dig this–The fight he lost (1915) in Havana was rumored to be thrown–Jack Johnson died like he lived–in a fast car (1946–age 68).

The music on this album speaks for itself! But dig the guitar and the bass–They are "Far in"–and so is the producer Teo Macero. He did it again!

–Miles Davis

ABOVE: Miles Davis is in a coiled position, ready to strike back like a boxer, except his weapon is a trumpet and he's going to punch everyone in the face with a piercing high note. Wearing a tank-top shirt, he's emphasizing his boxer-like muscled biceps and triceps, in tribute to heavyweight champion Jack Johnson.

In any case, Coltrane was drawn towards events of the era. In 1964 he played a series of benefits for King Jr. and recorded songs inspired by the movement including "Up 'Gainst the Wall" (Sept. 1962) and "Reverend King" (Feb. 966). In 1995, Coltrane's producer Bob Thiele said,

I knew Coltrane during the intense period in the 1960s when the long overdue Civil Rights insurgency had produced militant movements in all the arts. A black musician with massive popularity and worldwide critical attention, John had become a profound cultural icon for his people. [But], John Coltrane was never one of those 'haters,' anti-establishment people such as Amiri Baraka or the Black Panthers, for example. Everyone really read more into his music than they should have. They assumed too much. Coltrane was playing music and that was it. I never heard him say two words about social or economic problems. He gained freedom from all of that through his music.

PHAROAH SANDERS AND LEON THOMAS: In June 1965, tenor saxophonist Pharoah Sanders played on Coltrane's *Ascension* and in November they recorded *Meditations*. His given name was Ferrell Sanders, but legend has it that Sun Ra named him Pharoah when they played together in the early '60s. Other accounts give Amiri Baraka credit, claiming that when introduced to Sanders, Baraka thought that he said "Pharoah" rather than Ferrell, naming him as such in a *DownBeat* magazine review.

After Coltrane, Sanders, along with Archie Shepp and Albert Ayler, comprised a holy trinity of mind-blowing, intense "sheets of sound" saxophonists. More than the others, Sanders was capable of producing music of deep warmth coupled with lots of air and space — reflected in pieces like "The Creator Has a Master Plan" with Leon Thomas on vocals. "The Creator" was recorded twice in 1969, with an epic thirty-two-minute version laid to tape in February for Sanders' *Karma* LP on Impulse! Records. Sanders and Leon Thomas recorded a more succinct version in

Coltrane as a Black Nationalist. In Kofsky's writings about Coltrane (his book was published in 1970 as *Black Nationalism and the Revolution in Music* and updated in the 1990s as *John Coltrane and the Jazz Revolution of the 1960's*), he interprets the music with a political agenda that Coltrane never professed. Even when Kofsky speaks to musicians who knew Coltrane, he disagrees with their position that Coltrane doesn't fit into Kofsky's thesis.

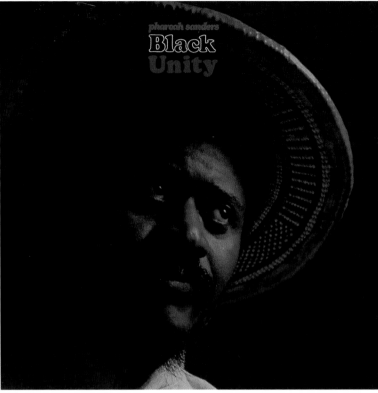

November for Thomas' *Spirits Known and Unknown* on the Flying Dutchman label. *Spirits* also contained an expressive eulogy, "Malcolm's Gone," in which Thomas declared, "I know he's gone, but he's not forgotten, I know he died — just to set me free." The album included an anti-war protest, "Damn Nam (Ain't Goin to Vietnam)." Over a playful cocktail jazz melody, Thomas sings "You can call me crazy, but I ain't going to Vietnam…how can a man get a thrill? If he's got to drop some napalm and never see the guy he's gotta kill?"

In November 1971, Sanders (without Thomas) recorded *Black Unity* for Impulse! A continuous, thirty-seven-minute, free-flowing statement, it was the sole composition on the album. Featuring two bassists, three drummers, two saxophones, a trumpet and piano, *Black Unity* stands alongside the Art Ensemble's *Certain Blacks* as a defining moment in jazz influenced by traditional African culture. Sanders' wife Thembi wrote the liner notes: "…The message is 'Black Unity Now'….Black Music is the life style of black people as expressed in sound rather than words. This album gives you a cross section of the ups and downs of our life. Listen well, and enjoy the music, you will get some insight into your life and a feeling of belonging — Black Unity!"

Like Eddie Gale's albums, Pharoah Sanders' music wasn't militant, but spiritual, not one of exclusivity, but one of inclusion. As Gale is fond of saying: "inner peace, my friend, inner peace!" ◉

LEFT: Rhythm, percussion and drums with Leon Thomas dressed in a Pan-African outfit, reflecting his social-political stance: two concentric circles, his name and album title surrounds the circular tambourine.

RIGHT: Pharoah Sanders — *Black Unity*: His name and the album title are in red, black and green (the colors of Black Nationalism). On the cover he's wearing his trademark hat for that era, suggesting a Pan-Asian unity — despite the title *Black Unity*, this is a cross-cultural experience (Egypt in his name, Asian and/or South American in his hat and Native American sounds on the LP itself).

LPS 1002 STEREO
TWINIGHT
is it because
i'm Black
Syl Johnson

GRITS 'N' GROCERIES:
Miscellaneous Recordings

10

The following recordings did not necessarily spring from a particular organization or ideology, but are worth noting as individual expressions of Black Power. Many of them were privately pressed and/or regionally released, adding a unique perspective to the rich musical response of the movement.

IS IT BECAUSE I'M BLACK?: In 1967, soul-blues singer Syl Johnson came on the scene with the Twinight Records single "Come On Sock It to Me." A successful hit, Johnson continued with more "come on, let's party" singles. But by 1970, he jumped off that train and joined the likes of James Brown and Marvin Gaye with a shift towards political messages. Johnson's 1970 Twinight LP presented the question "Is It Because I'm Black?" as the opening title track. Over a mid-tempo groove, Johnson pleads: "something is holding me back — is it because I'm black?" Other standouts include "I'm Talkin' 'Bout Freedom" and "Concrete Reservation," which compared Black America's urban life and many Native Americans' domiciles: "here in the ghetto, it's just a bad situation, call it what you want, it's just a concrete reservation."

"POWER STRUGGLE": The influence of the movement turned up in some unlikely locations, such as Austin, Tex., known for its abundance of folk & country singer-songwriters. James Polk and the Brothers were an organ-led, horn-fueled Austin combo that cut a fat R&B groove with their single "Power Struggle." Over a James Brown-styled backing, a sister asks "What about the power struggle? You got the power?" Regionally released, it's doubtful that anyone north of the Panhandle ever heard it. But keyboard wiz James Polk made it out of Texas when he joined

OPPOSITE: Reminiscent of *West Side Story*, the graffiti of the ghetto provides the inspiration for this album cover. The album contains a song, "Concrete Reservation," that compares the landscape of the inner city to life on an Indian Reservation: "here in the ghetto, it's just a bad situation, call it what you want, it's just a concrete reservation."

Ray Charles in the late '70s, spending eight years touring with Brother Ray's orchestra.

"PROJECT SONG": Another Austin band feeling the heat was the strangely named Techniques IV and their 1973 single "Project Song." Delivered by a male vocal group à la The Temptations (one singer sounds just like Eddie Kendricks), the "Project Song" would have fit nicely on The Temps' 1969 Norman Whitfield-produced *Puzzle People*. Their message of empowerment reflects the ideals of the Black Panther Party: "People got to organize, get to know each other… I'm gonna work through you, you, you, we're gonna put this place together."

"MARY DON'T TAKE ME ON NO BAD TRIP": Although best known for composing the Etta James standard "I'd Rather Go Blind," Ellington "Fugi" Jordan's career peaked as a vocalist when Eddie Kendricks suggested Fugi join Black Merda (pronounced "Black Murder"). Inspired by British bands like Cream and The Who, Black Merda began in the mid-1960s and is considered America's first all-black rock group. The Detroit-area band also served as the backing band for The Temptations and Edwin Starr. The meeting of Fugi and Black Merda resulted in "Mary Don't Take Me on No Bad Trip," a wacked-out, psychedelic funk single released by Chess Records' subsidiary Cadet in 1968. A complete LP was recorded at the time, but remained unreleased until 2005. In 1970, Fugi cut the "Revelations" 45 which

continued his funky black-people-on-acid sound. The song's apocalyptic tone envisions The End if African-Americans can't work out their differences. Fugi pleads with his listeners to stop infighting and focus their energies into battling the system.

"ONE LESS BROTHER": "One Less Brother" by Village Sounds is an early '70s soul tune that warns if a black person tries to gain knowledge and empower themselves, the white power structure will rub them out. Sounding remarkably like Curtis Mayfield (yet still worth checking out in its own right), their opening call out of "Brothers! Sisters!" is reminiscent of Mayfield's "If There's a Hell Below, We're All Going to Go."

"PEACE OF MIND" AND "TELL IT LIKE IT IS": S.O.U.L. (Sounds of Unity and Love) was a Cleveland band with an Earth, Wind & Fire vibe. While their 1971 debut *What Is It* included cover songs like The Temptations' "Message from a Black Man" and James Brown's "Say it Loud!," their second album *Can You Feel It?* saw the band expressing themselves with the original songs "Peace of Mind" and "Tell It Like It Is" (not to be confused with the 1966 Aaron Neville standard), which centered on the significance of piecing together a fractured community: "Going to have to stick together, going to have to sacrifice, going to have to pay the price." Other lines in "Tell It Like It Is" addressed the escalation of black-on-black violence: "brothers killing brothers, killing sisters too."

"BLACKS TRYING TO MAKE IT": Very little is known about Murray McKay and his 1972 single "Blacks Trying to Make It." Released on the Message label, the song was produced and written by Milwaukee natives Will Crittendon and Robert Taylor. As turntablist Dante Carfagna told me in April 2010, "Message was distributed by Mercury Records, who were gathering a lot of talent from Chicago and Milwaukee during this period." When I asked if Message had released other social-political recordings, Dante replied, "This is the only record on this particular Message label that I know of."

"Blacks Trying to Make It" is horn-driven soul replete with female gospel backing vocals and McKay describing a situation in which "they just can't take it, whenever they see blacks trying to make it." Ironically, McKay is not speaking to racist whites; he's calling out down-and-out blacks who resent seeing their neighbors rise out of the ghetto. McKay pleads for black unity: "Come on y'all, let's face it, you know we all gotta make it — if we all don't make it — we're all gonna be wasted." Whites are also folded into the equation, "anything to bust up me and you — yeah, oh yeah, you know they hate it, whenever they see black folks trying to make it." Furthering the directive, the B-side was called "Don't Let the Pusher Push You." If the Message label only released this one record, they still lived up to their name with this forgotten masterpiece.

"INVITATION TO BLACK POWER": Another rare 45 is "Invitation to Black Power" by Shahid Quintet, released on S and M Records. The composition is spread over both sides of the 7-inch (Parts 1 and 2). Composers Richard and Earl Shabazz waste no time getting down to business. Over a mournful bop saxophone riff, a dialogue between the two men kicks in.

Say brother Richard.
What, man?
Look at that black brother looking so mean.
Look like he's carrying a can of gasoline.
Listen brother let me pull your coat, that's no way to have
    a black revolt.
See that brother across the street, selling those "Mohammed
    Speaks," go talk to him, let him run it down, don't try to
    burn up half the town.
[a voice begins imitating a police siren]
Uh-oh, here comes the man and you're standing here with
    that can in your hand.
Drop it brother like I asked you to and let the brother run it
    down to you.
Sticks and stones and kerosene, coke bottles filled with
    gasoline, bricks and bats and bicycle chains, with tools
    like these, what could you possibly hope to gain?

All 45 rpm labels above, courtesy of the collection of Noel Waggener.

LONG HOT SUMMER READING

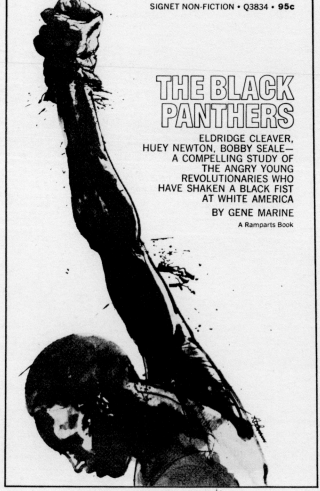

SIGNET NON-FICTION • Q3834 • **95c**

THE BLACK PANTHERS

ELDRIDGE CLEAVER,
HUEY NEWTON, BOBBY SEALE—
A COMPELLING STUDY OF
THE ANGRY YOUNG
REVOLUTIONARIES WHO
HAVE SHAKEN A BLACK FIST
AT WHITE AMERICA

BY GENE MARINE

A Ramparts Book

95¢

CONFRONTATION ON CAMPUS
The Columbia Pattern for the New Protest
The anatomy of one campus—and an entire
generation—in revolt   By Joanne Grant
author of Black Protest

95¢

FROM THE AFRICAN GENESIS TO
THE AGE OF BLACK POWER,
AN "EXCELLENT, CANDID, IMPRESSIVE
HISTORY OF NEGRO PROTEST"

BY ROBERT GOLDSTON

THE NEGRO REVOLUTION

95¢

A SIGNET NON-FICTION • T3891 • 75¢

GUERRILLA HERO OF A GENERATION IN REVOLT
CHE THE MAKING OF A LEGEND
BY MARTIN EBON

75¢

Available now wherever
paperbacks are sold

NAL
TIMES MIRROR
Publishers of Signet, Signet Classic
and Mentor Books

Burning and looting and cries of Black
  Power! Black Power! All types of cries,
  soul brother will holler!
Brother, try and think like a wise man, how
  much Black Power can you hold in a can?

As the song continues, they address King
Jr.'s assassination, calling for a divine plan
for black men to unite and "get some land to
call our own, that we can live on, long after
whitey is gone." Then the Shabazz Brothers
praise (nonviolent) Black Nationalism via
the message of Mohammed. Although they
reference the 1967 "long hot summer" of
Detroit rioting, DJ Daniel Shiman speculates
that it was probably recorded in 1968 or '69
in Chicago. The mention of King Jr.'s death
certainly marks it as post-April '68. Shiman
also points out that their style is "more a
throwback to earlier beat-poetry with cool
jazz collaborations than the screeching
saxophones and intellectual aspirations of
contemporaries like Archie Shepp or Amiri
Baraka."

"DETROIT IS HAPPENING": Black
Muslims weren't the only ones to musically
speak out against Detroit's Summer of '67
riots; Motown stepped up as well. In early
1968, the Federal Department of Housing and
Urban Development (HUD) gave $60,000 to
the Detroit Youth Opportunity Program. The
money was earmarked for jobs, education
and recreation to keep the summer of '68
cool for Detroit area youth. Motown produced
two theme songs in support of the social
economic program. The first, "Detroit Is
Happening," was a variation of The Supremes'
"The Happening," with words of encouragement spoken by local celebrity Willie Horton
of the Detroit Tigers. Jack Combs and Jimmy

Side One

SOMETHING TO REMEMBER HER BY
(A. Rankin / C. Colbert / R. Evans) Star Point 7(BMI)
☐ Vocal by Johnnie Taylor.
  (Stax Record Company)
☐ Arranged and conducted by
  Richard Evans & Charles Colbert
☐ Johnny Taylor recorded at Sumit Sound Studios (Dallas)—
  Engineer: Bob Sullivan
☐ Recorded at P&S Sound Studio—Engineer: Paul Serrano
☐ Remix Engineer: Paul Serrano

Johnnie Taylor   Denise Kain   Gylan Kain
                      LEOPOLDO FLEMING   Curtis Colbert

Side Two

IT'S FREE
(Gylan & Denise Kain) Star Point 7 (BMI)
☐ Vocal by Bishops of the Holy
  Rollers Fallout Shelter, with
  Curtis Colbert & James McCloden
☐ Recorded at Minot Sound Studios—
  Engineer: Richard Adler
☐ Remix at D&B Sound Studios—Engineer: Curt Frisk

☐ Art Direction: Communicon, Inc.   ☐ Cover illustration: Michael Orange   © 1974 Communicon, Inc.—All rights reserved

Produced by COMMUNICON, INC., for the CITIZENS ALLIANCE for VD AWARENESS, 222 West Adams St., Chicago 60606
312 / 236-1135

VD CONFIDENTIAL 842-0222	Englewood Neighborhood Health Center 641 W. 63rd St. 874-5955	Uptown Neighborhood Health Center 845 W. Wilson 744-7410
Chicago		
n Health Center ntral Pa	Cook County Department of Public Health 1425 S. Racine CH 3-5832	Municipal Social Hygiene Clinic 27 E. 26th St., 842-0222

Not for Sale

Clark wrote the second release, "I Care About Detroit," specifically for the occasion. The song was erformed by Smokey Robinson and The Miracles, but it's too bad they didn't ask Robinson to write it, as the music is flat and the lyrics are cornball: "I'm proud to call this city my hometown, it's been good to you and me, let's learn to work and live in harmony, as I care about Detroit." It sounds more like a greeting card from the Chamber of Commerce than a deflection to chill out pissed-off urban rioters.

Songwriter Jimmy Clark specialized in insipid message songs. Two years earlier he penned "Play it Cool, Stay in School," a one-sided promotional single by Brenda Holloway, released on the Tamla label in cooperation with the Detroit Women's Ad Club. Record collectors should note that the 1968 singles weren't released on Motown, but on logo-free labels; "This special record by permission and cooperation of Motown Record Corporation and Stein & Van Stock, Inc."

"IT'S FREE": While little is known about Gylan Kain's 1971 *Blue Guerrilla* album, an even more oblique part of his discography is the song "It's Free." Recorded in 1974, "It's Free" was used as a promotional single for the Citizens Alliance for VD Awareness in Chicago. This PSA regarding the dangers of venereal disease was composed by Gylan & Denise Kain and released under the odd moniker Bishops of the Holy Rollers Fallout Shelter. On "It's Free," Denise and three men — Gylan Kain, Curtis Colbert and James McCloden — candidly describe a woman wondering "what's this sore?" and a man puzzled as to why his Johnson feels strange while zipping up his pants and asking why his drawers have brownish stains — but he has no cash to go to the doctor. But "it's free, it's free — free shots to cure VD." They say it's a slow destruction and you may not even know it's happening: syphilis and gonorrhea — breeding grounds for bacteria and fungus, "moist and wet with heat." The lyrics get more descriptive, but I'll spare further transcription.

ABOVE: This stereotypical image of a 1970s pimp is used to let people know that if they want a venereal disease, he's not charging for that: "It's Free!" Notice that during this era, the bigger the hat, the badder the wearer was.

John Giorno

Giorno
Poetry
Systems
records

THE DIAL-A-POEM POETS

At this point, with the war and the repression and everything, we thought

this was a good way for the Movement to reach people

This provocative Public Service Announcement evokes Kain's previous outfit, the Last Poets, with goading affirmations punctuated by tribal drumming. The percussive wallop is supplied by Leopoldo Fleming, who also appears on Melvin Van Peebles' *What The...You Mean I Can't Sing?* and Camille Yarborough's seminal *Iron Pot Cooker.* Stax recording artist Johnny Taylor is on the flip side with the lushly produced "Something to Remember Her By" — detailing how his woman has left him, but gave him *something* to remember her by, and that he has to see a doctor to have it taken care of.

DIAL-A-POEM: Performance artist John Giorno founded Giorno Poetry Systems in 1965. The concept was to expose poetry to new audiences by innovative means, such as "Dial-A-Poem," in which contemporary poets could be heard via a telephone message. In the early '70s, this expanded into compilation albums with spoken word, tape loops and music from the likes of Allen Ginsberg, William S. Burroughs, Patti Smith, Laurie Anderson and Jim Carroll. 1972's *The Dial-A-Poem Poets* sandwiched Bobby Seale's and Kathleen Cleaver's speeches given at Bill Graham's Fillmore East on May 20, 1968 between counterculture iconoclasts.

The next LP in the Poetry System series, 1974's *The Dial-A-Poem Poets: Disconnected,* was a double album augmented by an April 1970 Amiri Baraka reading at Buffalo State College entitled "Our Nation Is Like Ourselves." The albums that Giorno curated capture an era that no longer exists: a time when "the counterculture" encompassed multi-genre forms nationwide, from the visual art of Andy Warhol's Factory to the bohemian poetry of Greenwich Village and North Beach, to the innovative music of the Fillmores East and West. Just two days after Bobby Seale and Kathleen Cleaver's appearance at the Fillmore East was a concert by The Doors. On May 25, 1967, Huey Newton, Amiri Baraka and Stokely Carmichael were speakers at a Black Panther benefit at the Fillmore in San Francisco — followed the next night by Janis Joplin. ◉

THE DIAL—A—POEM POETS

Giorno Poetry Systems records

DISCONNECTED

OPPOSITE: "At this point, with the war and the repression and everything, we thought this was a good way for the Movement to reach people." The scramble of urban passersby in an everyday street scene is on the cover of this anthology (which includes Bobby Seale and Kathleen Cleaver speaking at the Fillmore East), wherein John Giorno curates a city of sound, compiling diversely voiced poetic expressions of life and contemporary revolutionary thought together.

ABOVE: On this uncanny 1974 album cover, spoken word artist and underground literary maven John Giorno "mind fucks" the average mid-'70s soft rock music consumer, juxtaposing a foamy splash in the subconscious with an oddly languid pose beneath a presumably *Disconnected* phone. Most surprisingly, Amiri Baraka is waiting for the listener inside!

CONCLUSION:

A Dream Deferred

Recently, while I was presenting a lecture about the music featured in this book, an audience member asked, "What happens to a dream deferred?" I replied, "That's a question I don't feel entitled to answer." As I write the final pages of this book, I toss it back to readers, to make their own connections and hopefully derive inspiration from the ideologies and music I've presented. In a landscape of hypertext narrative and postmodern cultural critique, I feel interpretations are better left as a free form, ongoing debate.

The only historical revisionism I've done is to present Black Power with the respect it deserves. I challenge those who view the activists and artists of the movement as a blemish on 20th century American history to reconsider them as patriots.

In lieu of a conclusion, I prefer to share a shocking album I stumbled upon as I was wrapping this book up, *The Fourth Reich: The CommuNazis Exposed By Their Own Words, Revolution Today In The U.S.A.* At first glance, I was amused by the contrast of Bobby Seale, Huey Newton, Eldridge Cleaver, Abbie Hoffman, Jerry Rubin and William Kunstler on the front cover, with Hitler, Lenin, Fidel Castro

and Chairman Mao on the back. What the hell was this all about? The commentary was intriguing: "This recording is a condensation

OPPOSITE: *The Fourth Reich*: This mostly black-and-white, post-Sgt. Pepper's "Right On!"-style LP front cover collage combines controversial spokespeople beneath its screaming title. Seeming like another youth culture-scramble-toward-oblivion graphic, it places various headshots of Bobby Seale, Huey Newton, Eldridge Cleaver and other well-known political personalities bobbing around in a tumultuous visual image implying inimical social chaos.

of highlights from actual speeches made at the Black Panther Party's National Revolutionary Conference for a United Front Against (so-called) Fascism, Oakland Auditorium, July 18-20, 1969."

My interest was piqued, as I saw that besides Bobby Seale, there was dialogue by Charles Garry, William Kunstler, historian Herbert Aptheker (known for his research on 19th-century-African-American slave revolts) and members of the SDS. Then came the (right-wing) punch line: "The similarity of words and actions of today's 'storm troopers' with those of the Nazis of the 1930's is brought out. In effect, this recording is a Declaration of War today against our Free Enterprise System by the New and Old Left Revolutionaries as never heard before in one recording — their manifesto for violent takeover of the U.S.A."

The record begins with the voice of Adolf Hitler and "Sieg Heil!" cheering from the Nuremberg Rallies. Commentator Sidney Fields (a producer of anti-communist propaganda films) speaks, "Those are the voices of the Third Reich of Nazi Germany." Then it cuts to Bobby Seale: "We're going to fight Capitalism with some basic Socialistic programs." Seale's voice is intertwined with "Sieg Heil!" cheers — blatant and ridiculous manipulation on the part of General Records, who produced this right-wing propaganda.

Sidney Fields continues "These are the voices of the Fourth Reich; 'CommuNazis' at the Black Panther Party's National Revolutionary Conference." He concludes with, "Listen to today's Storm Troopers!"

Everyone's speeches have been edited and taken out of context. Black Panther Carol Thomas speaks, "We need Socialism in practice! We need an understanding of Marxist-Leninist principles so that we may put our knowledge into revolutionary practice." The slanted commentary between the Panthers' dialogues continues to drive home the relationship between Chairman Mao's *Little Red Book* and the conference participants. Communist manifestos *were* required reading for Panther members, but Huey Newton was *not* Joseph Stalin.

Other Panthers sampled include Don Cox and Kenny Horston, who founded a Black Caucus amongst the autoworkers at the General Motors Plant in Fremont, Calif. In the April 20, 1969 issue of the Panthers' newspaper, Chief of Staff David Hilliard credits Horston with traveling to Detroit and forming a coalition between the Fremont employees and blacks working in the Motor City. There's also a snippet from Minister of Education Ray "Masai" Hewitt, who declares, "The best defense is a good offense, that's why we dropped that 'for self defense' — a long time ago. There's no need for it in the name for the Black Panther Party."

For those listening to *The Fourth Reich: The CommuNazis Exposed* for the "right" reasons, one cannot help but feel inspired by the number of female Panthers represented: Carol Thomas, Roberta Alexander, Carol Henry and Ora Williams. Other women include UCLA sociology professor Marlene Dixon and editor of *Capitalism Stinks* magazine Susan Ker. The sense of female empowerment, especially within the Black Panther Party, overrides the right-wing propaganda intended by the album's producer.

My interest in presenting this material springs from a passionate connection to the iconoclasts who I was privileged to befriend. The glimpses of the past that they shared coupled with the music I uncovered along my journey inspired me to write this narrative. My favorite moments include: eating Jamaican food with the Watts Prophets (while the restaurant owner engaged us in a conversation about the Bob Marley song playing in the background, unaware that Amde Hamilton had spoken at Marley's funeral); driving around Oakland with David Hilliard while he pointed out momentous locations in Panther lore — Huey's teenage home, the Party's original headquarters, the street where Bobby Hutton was shot down; long-distance phone calls with Elaine Brown about politics and philosophy — interspersed with singing our favorite Motown songs to each other; listening to Bobby Seale recount a gun-running trip to battle white supremacists in North Carolina, over dinner in a Mexican restaurant (while he confused the waiter by asking for some "French Dressing" for his salad).

I didn't record these conversations nor write them down. They were personal insights into people whom I admire, inspiration for a book that I didn't realize I *needed* to write until I sat down and the first thirty thousand words flowed out without stopping. Even if the luminaries I hung out with disagree with my assessment, I hope they'll appreciate the love and intentions behind it.

— Pat Thomas, November 2011

STAY IN THE STREETS

FREE THE PANTHERS

ACKNOWLEDGMENTS

This book took me five years to put together, a journey that involved so many helpful people along with the way, some generously shared valuable insights, while others gave me just a scrap of info that I needed. However, each person was important to the final result:

Chris Estey, Professor Chico Herbison at Evergreen State College, Mitch Myers, Kristy Valenti, and Katherine Wolf all made significant contributions to the text.

Without the friendship of Elaine Brown and David Hilliard I would never have felt the urge to write this book, I'm in awe of both of them. Along the way, I was also inspired by conversations with; Bobby Seale, Ericka Huggins, Fredrika Newton, Amde Hamilton & Richard Dedeaux of the Watts Prophets, Billy X Jennings, Gene McDaniels, Les McCann, Barbara Dane, Miller London, and Eddie Gale. It is important to remember that these individuals each have their own perspective, ideologies, and political beliefs—obviously all fighting for the same goal of respect and freedom, but in no way should they all be lumped together. This diverse set of activists, musicians, and poets, don't necessarily speak *for* or *to* each other.

Kathy Wolf revived the original manuscript, suggested text edits, added images, and brought the 'work in progress' to Eric Reynolds at Fantagraphics who shared it with Gary Groth, who provided a completion bond. Without these three people, there would be no book. Throughout the process, Rickey Vincent and I had countless telephone calls discussing the subject(s) contained within. Sonia Clerc provided support during the initial stages of research and writing. Noel Waggener shared plenty of obscure 7 inch singles and a handful of record sleeves that I didn't have.

Additional support provided by;

Peter Bagge, Joel Bernstein, Dean Blackwood, Paul Bradshaw, Professors Robert Brem and Mustafa Popal at the College of Alameda, Dante Carfagna, Jacquelene Cohen, Jacob Covey, Michael Cuscuna, Mary Ellen Doyle, Bob Dylan,

Professor Andrew Flory at Carleton College, Tim Hayes, Ian Hetzner,

Charles L. Hughes at the University of Wisconsin-Madison, Professors Barbara Joans and Larry London at Merritt College, Graham Nash, Yoko Ono, Alec Palao, Tim Plowman, Thomas Porter, Ann Powers, Derk Richardson, Dave Segal,

Joel Selvin, Michael Simmons, Michael Shrieve, Mark Stevens, Denise Sullivan,

Matt Sullivan at Light in the Attic Records, Gerald Thomas aka "Dad," Tommy Tompkins, Richie Unterberger, Robert Wade, Chris Weber at Bumbershoot,

Dave Weller, Mason Williams at Rhino, Professor Tiffany Willoughby-Herard at San Francisco State University, Steve Wynn, Jim Yoshii, Andy Zax and readers like you!

A 'soundtrack' is available to this book on CD and double vinyl LP from:

Light in the Attic Records | www.lightintheattic.net
Listen, Whitey! The Sounds of Black Power 1967-1974 | LITA # 081